YOU ARE MINE

YOU ARE MINE

SISTER ANASTASIA

St Vladimir's Seminary Press
Yonkers, NY
2024

Publisher's Cataloging-in-Publication
(Provided by Cassidy Cataloguing Services, Inc.).

Names: Anastasia, Sister, 1991- author.
Title: You are mine / Sister Anastasia.
Description: Yonkers, NY : St Vladimir's Seminary Press, 2024. | Includes bibliographical references.
Identifiers: ISBN: 978-0-88141-756-2 (hardback) | 978-0-88141-757-9 (ebook) | LCCN: 2023952282
Subjects: LCSH: Spiritual biography. | Spirituality. | Spiritual life--Christianity. | Witness bearing (Christianity) | Self-actualization (Psychology) | New Age movement. | Witchcraft-- Psychological aspects. | Guides (Spiritualism) | Spiritualism. | Occultism. | Mysticism. | Demonology. | Neopaganism. | Spiritual formation. | Spiritual healing. | LCGFT: Autobiographies. | Self-help publications. | BISAC: BODY, MIND & SPIRIT / General. | SELF-HELP / Personal Growth / General. | SELF-HELP / Spiritual. | BODY, MIND & SPIRIT / Witchcraft. | HEALTH & FITNESS / Yoga. | RELIGION / Christianity / Orthodox. | RELIGION / Christian Living / Spiritual Warfare. | TRAVEL / Special Interest / Religious, Classification: LCC: BL73.W38 W38 2024 | DDC: 204/.092--dc23

Copyright © 2024
Sister Anastasia

ISBN: 978-0-88141-756-2 (hardback)
ISBN: 978-0-88141-757-9 (electronic)

The views of the authors of St Vladimir's Seminary Press books
do not necessarily reflect those of the Seminary.

All Rights Reserved

PRINTED IN THE UNITED STATES OF AMERICA

Though it may be startling, the cover image was inspired by Scripture: *Christ is the Lamb slain from the foundation of the world* (Rev 13.8). *You Are Mine* traces the transformation of an individual soul, but the narrative is not merely a biography of one woman's life. Rather, it is an account of a cosmic mystery that all are invited to enter. It is a journey like the Apocalypse itself: the revelation of a mystery that is hidden everywhere and fills all things, which is now opened to each of us. One question remains: will we enter and be transformed?

For the seekers

The publication of this book was made possible in part by generous donations from Liz Coelho and Dr Don Tamulonis.

TABLE OF CONTENTS

Foreword	xi
Preface	xiii
Acknowledgements	xv

PART ONE	1
The Spirit	1
Genesis	2
The Sleep of Death	7
Kundalini	10
Orthodoxy	13
Mother Nature	17
The Forest	19
Your Thoughts Determine My Life	25
Eat Hard	28
Tribes	30
Mexico	34
Continual Thirst	37
Noble Truth	39
Samsara	42
Living Theology	46
Womb Healing	49
Feast	53
Water	57
Purification	60
Opening	63
Goddess Complex	66
The Heart	69
He Revealed Himself to Me	72
Vision	75
Light	79
Heresy	82
The Jesus Way	86
Completion	90

PART TWO	93	PART THREE	179
I Belong to Jesus Now	93	The Test	179
Cleansing	96	The Prince of Peace	183
Spirits	99	Garden	185
The Jesus Prayer	104	The Prodigal Daughter	190
The Narrow Gate	110	Repentance: The Joy Filled Life	192
Exodus	113		
Pilgrimage	115	Carve Your Culture on My Heart	194
Temple	119		
Warfare	121	Honor Your Father and Mother	197
Worship	123		
The Unseen	126	Rest	202
Wilderness	131	Silence	204
Fast	134	Alone	208
Holy Week	136	Mission	213
Resurrection	138	Mental Chastity	215
Magic	142	Energy Harvesting	219
Air	147	Free	222
Lord of Heavenly Armies	151	Solitude	224
The Force	154	Fire	227
Witchcraft	159	Molech	231
The Body	161	Possession	234
Cosmology of the Cross	163	The Holy Spirit	237
Gender Trouble	167	The Logos	238
Give Blood, Receive Spirit	175		

FOREWORD

I am pleased to have been asked to write a foreword to *You Are Mine*, something I have not done before. I met Sister Anastasia when I visited one of the women's monasteries of my diocese. She was visiting her sister, who is one of the nuns of that monastery. We had spoken several times, but I had no idea of where she had come from spiritually and of her journey to Christ until I read what you are about to read. In some ways it is the story of her generation, but it is also the uniquely personal account of one woman's struggle to find healing, peace, and love.

In a question-and-answer session with a group of Orthodox young people in Europe, Klaus Kenneth said that Christianity is the one religion in the world where God seeks us, rather than the other way round. His words rang true and came to mind again and again as I read Sister Anastasia's spiritual journey.

There is, I believe, in every human heart a void. And, like the missing piece of a jigsaw puzzle, the picture of one's life is incomplete without it. Christ is the only one who can fit that empty space and make a person whole. And, like the person assembling the jigsaw puzzle, one very often must search for the missing piece.

Sister Anastasia's memoir is the account of a young woman's search for that missing piece and for deep healing. Like many of her generation, she initially rejected the Evangelical Christianity of her parents. She became a child of the New Age, hungry for spiritual experiences that would satiate her thirst for what was fundamentally missing in her life, trying various spiritual traditions.

"I had met many healers, yogis, lamas, and gurus, all of whom had immense wisdom regarding living in harmony with nature, and the sacrifices required for spiritual development. They were often incredibly humble, loving, and generous." But it was her encounter with a humble Orthodox monk in a little kitchen in a suburb of London where she experienced something she never had before—holiness. She did not know it then, but her life would never be the same.

One is reminded of the Parable of the Prodigal Son who gathered all he had and journeyed into a far country where he squandered his inheritance. Sister Anastasia tells us in detail about her wandering through several spiritual far countries, spiritual practices, joining herself to citizens of those countries (yogis, healers, lamas, and shamans), full of the pride of youth, only to find herself in spiritual want and still hungry. Then there is that all important moment where she, like the prodigal, comes to herself, realizing how deeply she is loved, and has been always loved, by Christ. She then takes that road back to her Father's house. Sister Anastasia permits us to accompany her on her journey back to the Father. She shares her struggles and temptations with us along the way as well as the joy of the embrace that awaited her upon her return.

+Benjamin
Archbishop of San Francisco and the West

PREFACE

When I sat down to write about what had happened to me, I had no idea that it would turn into a book. And not only that, but that the book would be published. However, what I have come to learn during the four years that I have spent under the spiritual protection of a living elder is that miracles are not only real, but—potentially—frequent occurrences in the life of the Christian.

Father Theophan, the spiritual father under whose wing I have had the blessing of being placed, has integrated and now embodies Scripture to such a degree that the illumined silence of the early Fathers of the desert, the bright stillness of soul that comes about as a result of the consumption of the living word, is manifest in him. As a result, his words have a prophetic power.

At the urging of my mother—a gifted poet and writer, who had for many years patiently, and at times desperately, prayed for the lifting of "the veil" that inhibited her daughter from perceiving the truth that Christ, both fully divine and fully human, alone is God—I had agreed to write about my encounter with Jesus and the experience of His divine grace beginning to pour into my life.

When I told Father Theophan that I was going to write my testimony (I had pictured a couple of pages), he responded with excitement, telling me that he was "so touched" by the idea, and that it would, by God's grace, be printed, "as a voice for the generation." Printed? My horizons widened.

I believed his words and began to sincerely pray that the memoir that the testimony then turned into would help people who, like me, had been deceived by the complex power and subtle operations of the kingdom of darkness in its confounding variety of manifestations.

Although I was aware that the story belonged to Christ in a very specific way, the actual reality of its being published "in real life" was almost inconceivable. Like everything in Christ, it was defined by paradox. Between its conception and birth, I knew, *in my bones*, that this story would be published. But, at the same time, I couldn't, across those years, really believe that it actually would. And, not only that, but that it would be published by as intimidatingly reputable a publishing house as Saint Vladimir's Seminary Press.

This is not a scholarly book. Rather, it is an account. The process of writing a memoir meant navigating completely foreign land. There are only a few footnotes, and I have simplified where possible, omitting parenthetical discussions of the use of certain terms. Spirit-world practices are free flowing, intuitive, and actively anti-intellectual. "You think too much" was the "illness" I was most frequently diagnosed with on entering the subculture of alternative spirituality—a mixture of paganism, traditional witchcraft, and New Age syncretism. As such, I have written, more or less, as we spoke. We were friendly, open-hearted hippies. It was not an academic symposium. Mostly we were singing round the fire.

What follows is a retelling of what took place.[1] It is written from my heart. I hope that it speaks to yours.

---

[1] Names and locations have been changed, and some characters have been combined, both for privacy and clarity.

ACKNOWLEDGEMENTS

Everything I write here is insufficient. Nevertheless, I want to express my deepest gratitude to all the people who have made the creation and publication of this book possible. First, I would like to thank my parents—two wild, free spirits in disguise—for all the sacrifices that they have made, both individually and as a couple, in order to make the wonderful life that I have lived possible, and for teaching me the most important thing that a human being can learn: how to love. Thank you for your radical decision to risk your identities in the world and to abandon it, with all its riches, in order to dedicate your lives to Christ, and to bring your children up for the kingdom. May your sacrifice be blessed, eternally.

Without Father Theophan's decision to take me on as a spiritual child and to dedicate himself, without reservation, to my transformation, not only would this book not exist, but I would not exist. It is as a result of him offering up his entire life to serve Jesus, that I am now free. I owe you everything and have given you nothing. You have given me everything and have asked for nothing. Thank you for being a vessel for the true love of Christ. Second-in-command, I thank my spiritual mother, Mother Syncletica, for throwing her arms open to me and pulling me into her prayers, her monastery, and her heart. You have fought—and won—the battles that I am fighting and that I am due to fight. Your example gives me the strength to proceed, and to do so with joy. Thank you for the blood shed.

It was through the humble, reverent, and tender-hearted example of the monastics who welcomed me into the kingdom, that I was convinced of the gospel truth that Christ alone is God and the sole means through which love abounds in the cosmos. Thank you to all my mothers and sisters, Mother Evgenia, Mother Raphaela, Mother Valentina, Mother Lydia, Mother Ivana, Mother Thais, Sister (now Mother) Damaris, Sister (now Mother) Eleni, Sister Michaela, Sister Nectaria, Sister Sophia, Sister Methodia, Sister Tatiana, and Sister Simona. A particularly special thanks to Sister (now Mother) Cherubima, for your many prayers and for your prophetic role in this story. For your shining, ascetic witness, thank you also, Father Georgios, Father Peter, Father Mark, Father Kyriakos, Father Sergius, Father Romanos, Father Ephraim, Brother David, Brother Bartholomew, Brother Sava, Mother Apollonia, Mother Beatrice, Mother Joachima, and Mother Macrina. Sister Veroniki, and all those in your monastery: thank you for all that you have given and continue to give.

Holiness, however, is not something required only of monastics but is rather something that is commanded of all Christians. It is through the example of the devoted laity I have had the blessing of meeting, that living proof of this commandment's pragmatism exists. Thank you, Father Damascene and Khouria Anna, for taking me in as a(nother) kingdom daughter. Your generosity—and authentic joy—knows no bounds, and your dedication to me, my family, and this book is a gift that can never be repaid. I would like to thank Elizabeth, for publication guidance and for offering me a space to retreat; Paisia, for a river of generosity in practical advice and for your friendship; Omni Angelina, for accompanying me in this process and for giving me a beautiful home to live in; and my sister and brothers in Christ, Aleja and Dn Tesfay and Daniel, for your sincere love and continued support. I am grateful also to my siblings, for your curiosity, encouragement, and enthusiasm.

Importantly, I would like to thank those who dedicated their prayers to the book's completion and publication. It would not have happened without you. Further, I would like to thank all those who supported this

ACKNOWLEDGEMENTS

ministry financially. Without your generosity, the past four years would not have been possible. Thank you, Watchmen of the Nations, the River Trust, Nick and Ginny, Craig and Em, Edward and Antonia, Father Damascene and Khouria Anna, Gilly, Davina, Michie, Ben, Cherie, Aleja, my parents, and those who donated anonymously. My deepest, deepest thanks.

Finally, I would like to thank Saint Vladimir's Seminary Press for agreeing to publish this book. Thank you, Dr Ionuț-Alexandru Tudorie, for initiating the process, and Very Rev. Fr Chad Hadfield, for your keen support of it, once in motion. Sarah Werner, despite many obstacles, the fire inside you that was lit by the testimony was not stamped out. I am so grateful for your willingness to take such a huge risk and for all that you have done to bring the project to completion. Thank you also, Fr Bogdan Bucur, for your insightful comments and for your vision for the dissemination of this story. Finally, thank you to my incredible reviewers. Your inspired feedback and enthusiastic responses gave me the clarity—and energy—required to shape the book into its final form.

PART ONE

The Spirit

The Church cannot live on principles of faith to be studied. Faith in Christ is not a theory. It is a power that changes lives.
—Matthew the Poor

I knew that I had felt something very special in that room. In the years leading up to my first meeting with Father Theophan, I had met many healers, *yogis, lamas,* and *gurus,* all of whom had immense wisdom regarding living in harmony with nature and the sacrifices required for spiritual development. They were often incredibly humble, loving, and generous. But meeting this ascetic Orthodox monk in a little kitchen in a suburb of South London, I encountered something that I never had before—holiness. It was a purity that was so special, so specific. I now know, though I didn't at the time, that this is because it had heaven as its source. My mother told me that when I came out of the room, I was crying and all I could say was, "He's so beautiful, he's so beautiful, I trust him with my life!" This is what differentiated it from everything else I had experienced. It was the *beauty* of Christ's light, the beauty of Christ's *life* inside this monk that touched me. It wasn't intellectual. It was emotional, spiritual, energetic, magnetic . . . It was mystical. I also thought that if following the Bible and being Christian makes you like *that*, then this is the best "method of enlightenment" I have ever come across.

This intimate, living connection to the *person* of God and the holiness that resulted from it was what I had been searching for, though I didn't know it. I was studying the *Lam Rim* (a very long text outlining the basis of Buddhist philosophy) full-time with a revered Buddhist lineage holder who was entitled "His Holiness," and I had spent thousands and thousands of pounds traveling across the world to attend different healing rites, ceremonies, and fasts and to train in different pagan traditions. But the relationship with my Creator that I was unconsciously seeking eluded me. When Father Theophan prayed for me at the end of the meeting, he spoke to God as if God were right there in the room with us. With familiarity, with intimacy. And with reverence. I felt a divine presence fill the room as his hand rested on my head and then anointed my forehead with holy oil. Something inside me relaxed and opened. It felt innocent and sweet and had nothing to do with strength or force or *power* (buzzwords from my pagan world). This was new. A seed of certainty—that I was known and loved by God—was planted in my heart.

Genesis

The object of our search is the fire of grace which enters into the heart.
—St Theophan the Recluse

The search for healing that led me to this encounter began when I entered my first addiction-recovery meeting, at twenty, eight years earlier. I had been bulimic since I was twelve, and after a year of attempting to be seen by a therapist on the national health service, I decided to try the Twelve Step route. Recovery only really began the following year, and it was a year after that, at twenty-two, that I started getting sober after years of out-of-control drinking. Realizing that it was impossible to heal an eating disorder while cycling through drug and alcohol binges, blackouts, and comedowns, I tried to heal both addictions: food and alcohol (and the drugs that went with it). Halfway through my masters in English literature and critical theory, I reluctantly accepted that the way that I related to people was also not healthy, so I began to look into codependency, wondering if this was the underlying root of my eating disorder and excessive drinking.

During this period, I began to practice meditation as part of my recovery. In theory I was an atheist at this point—encouraged by my academic environment. Despite my aversion to the Evangelical Christianity that I was brought up in, the Bible somehow ended up being central to both my M.A. and Ph.D. projects. Although I struggled with the God-focused literature of OA,[1] its rigor and discipline rescued me from the chaos of addiction and brought me to a more stable state. Newly sober and introduced to mindfulness, my spirituality opened up, and I started reading self-help books, practicing yoga, and attending Tibetan Buddhist meditation meetings. The irony, cynicism, and wild party-girl identity, my fortress against my repressed sensitivity, began to die, and I became more comfortable in my skin. I still wore heels and hot pants—I had always been a *femme*[2] feminist—but free from drug- and alcohol-induced anxiety, I felt confident enough to stop wearing makeup and to let my body hair grow wild and free.

The spirituality espoused by New Age gurus gave me the answer I had been looking for in terms of a vision of God that was nondual, did not involve the Father, and aligned (though in an unorthodox way) with

---

[1] OA stands for "Overeaters Anonymous," which is one of the branches of the Twelve Step addiction recovery program. Even the name of the program generated a considerable amount of shame. Although, of course, false, the veneer of dangerous glamor that alcohol and drugs carried was unequivocally absent when it came to the question of binge eating donuts.

[2] Although definitions may vary, a *femme* is a queer person presenting in a stereotypically feminine manner.

the Derridean deconstruction theory with which I was enamored. After ending my toxic relationship with my OA sponsor, I took part in my first *ayahuasca* ceremony.[3] A close friend had entered the world of plant healing a year before, but I had waited because of my program commitment. From that moment on, the world of spirit contact and worshiping Mother Nature opened up, and I joyfully plunged into the mysterious, intense, and supposedly gender-balanced realm of ancient, elemental spirituality, a reborn animist. My heart exploded open.

Throughout the next six years, I existed primarily in this alternative subculture, in service to Mother Earth, the spiritual mother I had been desperately seeking in the ever-available false love of food. I fell in love with nature and began learning from different ancestral traditions, going on pilgrimages, and attending—and then organizing—ceremonies, rituals, and retreats. My entire life was consumed by devotion to these plant spirits. In Christianity, paganism, witchcraft, sorcery, divination, astrology, and spiritism would be the terms used to describe these practices, but we called it "the medicine world."

The emphasis was on ceremonies organized around each country's "master plant"—powerful plant spirits that were renowned for their miraculous healing properties and ability to transform the soul through visions, purging, and the unlocking of one's psychic powers. Each spirit had its own attendant sect (though we didn't use this word). Anyone who attends one of these ceremonies will tell you it is a life-changing event. Some would receive the healing needed and then continue on with their path. Others, such as myself (and most of the people I knew), would leave the mainstream world to follow the spirits, becoming "medicine workers."

Interwoven with this was a meditation practice that began on my ketamine-fueled travels around India at eighteen. It had developed into

---

[3] *Ayahuasca* is an Amazonian entheogen. Like *peyote* and *yopo* (two other plants that I used in a ritual context), it is a psychoactive substance that induces alterations in perception, mood, consciousness, cognition, or behavior for the purposes of engendering healing, divination, and spiritual experience in a ritual context.

PART ONE

an important part of my recovery, and I became a devotee of the tantric goddesses of yoga. This led to receiving an initiation to become a psychic channel for a 5,000-year-old Hindu lineage that then supported the "womb work" I practiced: alternative therapies that focused on aligning the chakras;[4] removing entities or impurities; and integrating trauma with a focus on fertility, female empowerment, and cultivating self-love. It was with this as the basis that I then began to study Tibetan Buddhism in more depth (partly as a result of beginning a relationship with an adherent). I invited him into the ecstatic world of *kundalini*, the divine feminine and Mother Earth, and he, in exchange, enticed me with the promise of achieving eternal liberation from suffering through the *dharma*,[5] the knowledge of the nature of reality. We were dedicated seekers, and we dove as deep as we could dive and flew as high as we could fly to find it.

I, however, had reservations about Tibetan Buddhism. It is philosophical and very scholarly, whereas the plant world and my kundalini practice were all about intuitive experience. Having quit my Ph.D. a year or so previously to focus on applied practice, encouraged by the anti-intellectual, anti-theoretical teachings of the kundalini lineage I was part of, I was resistant to getting boxed back into the world of text. But,

---

[4] The *chakras* (from the Sanskrit "wheel") are believed to be energy points that correspond to nerve centers in the body. The degree to which they are opened and aligned is said to determine one's spiritual, emotional, and mental equilibrium. Eastern philosophies have various teachings around the *chakras*.

[5] The *dharma* is the Buddhist doctrine of the universal truth of reality and its conception of cosmic law and order, as taught by Buddha and encapsulated in the Four Noble Truths: the truth of suffering's existence, the truth of suffering's origin, the truth of suffering's cessation, and the truth of the path to its cessation. Within Hinduism, kundalini is understood to be a form of divine, feminine energy that is conceptualized as a coiled serpent that sits at the base of the spine, awaiting awakening. Kundalini awakening is a phenomenon that is both desired and feared, as a result of the fact that in extreme cases, it can result in intense upheaval, mental illness, physical ailments, or in some cases, paralysis. My kundalini awakening took place while I was being initiated into the lineage, and it was an enjoyable experience.

ignoring these instincts I continued on. Maybe Tibetan Buddhism had the truth I was seeking. Maybe *this* would heal me once and for all. We studied the *Lam Rim*, which takes about three and a half years to complete. Tibetan Buddhists are very thorough. The process involved taking refuge as a Buddhist and taking the *Bodhisattva* vow—devotion to Buddha and a promise to remain in *Samsara* (suffering-fueled re-birth) till all sentient beings were liberated.

Concurrent with these studies, I was running a nature-focused womb-healing retreat for women, organizing initiations and rituals, going on pilgrimages, completing a four-year spiritual fast, traveling to the Amazon to study curative plants, and beginning my yoga teacher training. All while setting up my independent massage business. It was into this frenetic context that an email from my mother appeared, asking if my boyfriend Nick and I would like to meet Father Theophan. This Orthodox monk had been a mentor to my parents for twenty years, and he was in London for a night. He was the spiritual father of my little sister, and it was under his eldership that she had converted to Orthodoxy and become a nun.

Initially I was very skeptical of this mysterious man. Not only, but in part, because he had told my sister that my beloved ayahuasca came from the devil. But observing her journey into Christ through the asceticism of the Desert Fathers, about whom I had read a book as part of my Ph.D. research, I was open to meeting him. As I saw it, Christians were on their way to the spiritual truth I had accessed, but they just hadn't gotten the full "download" yet. I knew, however, that he had been praying for me for many years, and I was grateful for that. There followed the meeting that dramatically changed the direction of my life and brought me into contact with the thing that I had been manically running around seeking. It was the thing that I yearned for above all else but that seemed to constantly evade me. The thing that was promised but which never manifested: peace. And the source of this peace was Jesus Christ.

The Sleep of Death

Little lamb, arise.
—Mark 5.41[6]

Following my meeting with Father Theophan, I had a vision. The next morning I was woken at five-thirty by an urgent sense that I needed to go upstairs to the room that I used for my channeling work: "Go to the *mandala*, go to the mandala."[7] The instruction came twice. Normally waking any time before seven was a cause of intense stress and anxiety, as my inability to get back to sleep triggered memories of my insomniac past. But this time I got up immediately. I sat and activated the mandala with the appropriate invocations to the spirits that governed the tradition I was initiated into.[8]

As I began to direct the energy with my mind, opening myself up to the healing flow and allowing it to move up through my chakras one by one, I felt and saw Jesus' presence before me, and He took over the

---

[6] Translated from the Aramaic. All other translations are from the NKJV unless noted.

[7] Channeling is an occult technique, in which the facilitators open themselves up as a vessel to be inhabited by a spirit, which they then "channel" for the purposes of divination, clairvoyance, worship, inspired speech, spell-casting, necromancy, or healing. My focus was solely healing and worship. I was asked to contact the dead on people's behalf, but I didn't want to get involved with that aspect of the spirit world. Unlike a lot of those in my community, I preferred not to encounter spirits outside the context of a healing ceremony. However, I would perform ancestral healings (sorcery) in which I would use the channel to purify, or in some cases, break apart, the attachments between patients and those in their lineage. Within the medicine world, channeling was also something that was discussed in a lighthearted manner. One would "channel" recipes, a forgotten phone number, or directions to the nearest parking space.

[8] A *mandala* is a configuration of geometric symbols. Mandalas are used across different traditions in order to establish a sacred space, aid meditation/channeling/trance, initiate practitioners, and focus one's attention in spiritual practice.

process. I stopped moving the energy and sat backward in the chair as His love began to wash over me, flooding my heart with its power. I began to sob uncontrollably. His love poured onto me, filling every part: you are loved, you are Mine, you are loved, you are Mine. I could see Him before me, and He could see me. I was His daughter. Jesus loved me and He was allowing me to feel it. I don't know how long I was sitting there. I felt like I was pinned to the chair by a torrent of love coming out of Him. I couldn't move. All I could do was receive this love into my heart and cry. It was so blissful that it hurt. Then the vision changed.

I was lying on a bed, with Jesus sitting beside me, His hands hovering over my body. His mouth was moving, but I couldn't hear what He was saying. The vision was blurred, as if I was underwater. I could feel other people in the room and hear muffled sounds of the activity and His words above me. I could sense that He was trying to bring me "up" from the surface under which I seemed to be stuck. After a while He stopped and got up, but I remained under the surface, looking up at Him as He stood. At that moment it clicked—it was the story of the young girl whom Jesus had raised from the dead: *Then He took the child by the hand, and said to her, "Talitha, cumi," which is translated, "Little girl, I say to you, arise"* (Mk 5.41). She was the biblical character whom my parents had named me after. I was the little girl, and He was raising me from the dead. Then the vision stopped, and I left the mandala.

After this healing experience with Jesus, I started to include Him in my channeling work. There were a few occasions when I would feel His presence amidst the psychic energy. It was always very peaceful and, importantly, had the strength to cut the power of whichever dark spirit was being exorcized from the client. Within the context of my mind at the time, this felt great, as if I had discovered an incredibly powerful healing "ally" to help me in my work. Jesus was to my mind, another spirit guide.[9]

---

[9] A spirit guide is a spiritual entity that guides the magical practitioners in their work, worship, and life path. Within the New Age, these spirit guides were always understood to be benevolent forces. However, within witchcraft, a healer could be guided by dark

PART ONE

I began to have daydreams imagining myself at the nature retreat I ran, crucifix in hand, channeling the power of Jesus and Mary Magdalene.

Exorcism was only one aspect of the channeling work I did. However, the practice's ability to expose and then force impurities out of the client through the application of a concentrated shaft of energy that I would direct toward different sections of the client's body through psychic control, was one of the main things that gave it its power. After a healing of this kind—"exorcism" was not a word that was used in our world—there was a discernible physiological lightness, as well as a potent sense of emotional and spiritual release.

Following these experiences, a second vision took place. I was sitting inside the psychic field,[10] meditating with my eyes closed, when I saw Jesus in front of me. He was above me, and I was looking up at Him. He had His arms outstretched, and birds were flying around Him. Above Him beautiful clouds were rolling, and the wind was blowing through His hair. I remember being struck by how . . . human He looked. How natural. Completely different from the multi-armed, -eyed, -headed, sword-swinging gods and goddesses I was used to seeing when meditating in the channel. He looked like a man. He *was* a man. He was familiar. Homely even. Cozy. Not words I was used to associating with the fierce deities I worshiped. He was smiling and appeared totally at peace. But then His eyebrows would knit together slightly. He was standing looking over the whole of creation. He was aware of me but didn't look directly down at me.

Then I understood. He wanted to continue to raise me from the dead. I felt that He was saying, let Me take you higher. And more importantly,

---

forces, specific to the lineage being practiced, on the understanding that the dark forces would help bring about the desired outcome of whatever process was taking place. Within the New Age, this darkness was understood to be incidental.

[10] Most broadly, "psychic field" is a term used within the New Age to describe the spiritual realm. However, it is most frequently used in the context of either spiritual healing or ritual, to categorize a certain area of the spiritual realm that is being acted on, or in, in some way, by the practitioner. Successful purification of another would require awareness—and control—of what is taking place in the immediate psychic field.

this (the spiritual world I inhabited) is beneath Me. But it was said without haughtiness, without pride—it was just a simple statement of facts. After this I stopped inviting Him to support me during the healing sessions with the spirits.[11] It felt disrespectful in some way. However, I continued to feel connected to Him in a way I never had before.

Kundalini

No one has ascended into heaven by means of ease.
—St Isaac of Nineveh

I had been introduced to this esoteric channeling practice by Maya, the same friend who had invited me into ayahuasca worship. Maya wasn't a channel herself, but she was planning to be initiated. It was the summer break of the first year of my Ph.D., and I had moved back into my parents' house in the countryside after a short period of living in a "medicine house" in London.[12] Toward the end of the summer that followed, an invitation arrived in my inbox from the host of the next initiation. It was to be held in London. Indecision plagued my life, and I went round and round, trying to decide if I should attend. It was a five-day process, with kundalini activation, teaching, meditation, healing, and practical training. Following

---

[11] One of the main spirits I channeled was an enlightened guru who was, as far as I understood, completely free from darkness. Kundalini is focused on the light. We saw ourselves as the guardians and healers of the spiritual realm, who worked only with, and for, the light. The lineage was yogic and thus governed by belief in the law of karma. As such, we were taught that any action that was negative in intention would return to us with horrendous consequences. Furthermore, if one were to do something of this kind, the living gurus, aware of what all the practitioners were doing, would shut down their psychic powers and their connection with this particular branch of the Hindu matrix.

[12] A medicine house is a communal setup (though often one of the members would be the owner of the house and receive rent), in which adherents lived and worshiped together.

the initiation, I would be equipped to perform the healings myself, channeling the energy of the spirits.[13]

After several excruciating weeks of flipping between yes and no, I decided I wouldn't go and asked a close friend in London to instead put me down for the residential five-day waitressing job she was signed up for. That solved it. The decision had been made. I would work and save, rather than spend money on the training. I couldn't afford it, and I needed to focus on the different plants and my Ph.D. anyway—I was already overloaded. A whole other lineage was just going to be too much. However, the text I sent to the friend telling her that I would "do it" had been interpreted by her as meaning I would do the *training*. I wasn't on the list for the job. Initially frustrated, I began to relax and then became joyful, suddenly aware of the divine hand involved in the mix-up. I was to attend the training. I was to be initiated. I took it as an unmistakable sign from above.

Sitting in a circle in a beautiful house in west London, we took turns introducing ourselves, bowing our heads in prayer after speaking. Sachin, the guru, was clothed in white and sat in silent meditation as we entered the room. Cressida, the host of the event, was lighting candles and welcoming the trainees as she censed the room. She attended to the guru, who was in a state of hyper-focus, his face expressionless and his gaze penetrating. However, when he spoke, he was polite and gentle and would occasionally smile and laugh. The setting was similar to other yogic events but had a particularly luminous quality to it. It was the prettiest room I had ever been in. The purity of the atmosphere had a strong effect on me, however, and I felt very raw and exposed on entering the circle.

---

[13] I use the term loosely here, in order to make the process as easy to understand as possible. Technically it was not a selection of "Hindu spirits" so much as the spiritual output of multiple spirits, gods, goddesses, and beings, which had been synthesized into a cohesive force through the praxis of different, enlightened Hindu gurus and the paranormal, supernatural, and magical powers and abilities they had attained through rigorous yogic practice.

Usually, I would subtly compensate for any latent insecurity with exaggerated confidence, and perhaps a little haughtiness. However, I was eager to heal as deeply as possible, so I didn't do anything to cover up how I was feeling. As was the case with every ritual space I entered, I was drawn to the person leading, and yearned to be noticed by him. Though he was only in his early twenties, Sachin had been handpicked by elders in the lineage and entrusted with spreading the information around the world, initiating different channels who would then extend its healing power across the globe.

After I had been initiated, my life dramatically changed direction. With a deeper awareness of how the spirit world operates and the role I had within it as a channel, I immediately quit my Ph.D., ignoring the distressed supplications of my supervisors, and moved to London to set up my practice.[14] The spiritual worldview that underpinned my practices emphasized the organic and the automatic. If one relaxed and let go of all preconceived notions of how to bring about good ends, goodness would spontaneously manifest, in any given arena. Let go, relax, and do not struggle. I had no money, no job, and no plan. However, I did have a huge bag of crystals and a fervent desire to help people to heal.

As well as starting to carry out cleansings for others, I would also practice self-healing with the channel, in order to remove blockages within me, and I would intermittently receive sessions from Sachin. I had fallen in love with him during the initiation, but our relationship only ever remained on a professional level. Meeting him had profoundly affected me, however.

---

[14] The title of the Ph.D. I had started was "Mother Nature, Father Text: Sexual Trauma and the Bible." Focusing on the book of Genesis the project assessed the exclusion of the feminine in the Trinity and subsequently Christianity as a whole. Everyone had mothers and fathers—how could the entire godhead be masculine? This was what my research was questioning through examining biblically influenced modernist texts about rape, incest, and its subsequent trauma in relation to the feminine. My life at the time was all about the womb, and my work had always focused on women: first in a queer feminist academic context, then in a therapeutic spiritual context, and then in this Ph.D. (which was about how restoring gender balance to spirituality could heal trauma)—which drew both together.

He was, as far as I could see, the perfect example of what a man should be—ascetic, reflective, sensitive, kind, and spiritually determined—and so I decided I would not enter into a relationship until I was either with him, or with someone as good as him.

Sometimes the healing sessions would be in-person, and I would lie on a bed in front of him while he meditated. As soon as the process started, I would feel the energy around me palpably increase and begin to engulf my body, and I would sometimes drift off to sleep. Coming to afterward, I would feel deeply relaxed but also as if I had been "emptied," and it would take me a while to come back to the room. However, sometimes I would remain alert, and during those times, I could feel the energy of the grid moving across the surface of my body, penetrating into different areas.

While this was taking place I would travel in the astral plane, encountering different spirits and beings, some loving, some threatening, and see images connected to my healing process, such as the three main gurus of the lineage showering me with affection and pouring liquid gold into my womb. This practice completely opened up my psychic abilities and intensified and supported my work with the plant spirits, which continued on unabated. It took a couple of months to get moving, but, once I integrated massage and womb work into what I was offering with the channeling, the business started to build up, and I began to get on my feet and climb, very slowly, from beneath the poverty line.

Orthodoxy

Until you have suffered much in your heart, you cannot learn humility.
—Elder Thaddeus of Vitovnica

Following my meeting with Father Theophan and the visions of Christ that ensued, I went to visit an Orthodox monastery at the invitation of one of its nuns, Sister Veroniki. She was a close friend of the family, who had wanted Nick and me to come and visit for a while. The moment, however, never seemed to arrive, so I decided to go alone in advance of the seasonal, nature-immersion retreat that I ran. My younger sister—now Sister Cherubima—had spent some time at the monastery before moving to America to become a nun, and my elder sister and my mother (a devout Christian) had visited as well, though in a less intensive capacity. Despite their relationship with Father Theophan, neither of my parents was Orthodox, but they supported my sister's journey, and my mother, whose yearning for the transformative depths of the desert gave her insight into monastic practice, felt an affinity with it.

My upcoming retreat involved a group of women coming together as a sisterhood, to heal and celebrate with the elements. Although I never considered myself someone who *worshiped* nature, it was the axis around which my spirituality rotated and was in this regard the object of my devotion. It was my "god." Occasionally I would use the word God, but this was interchangeable with Source, Spirit, the Force, Mother Nature, the Mother, the Divine, the Goddess, the Universe, the Sacred, the Womb, or simply, Creator. One thing was clear—acknowledgement of femininity (or at least gender neutrality) within this naming was crucial. My urge to help women heal from the wounds of gender violence and my resultant focus on the wild and divine feminine, which was what the retreat was an invitation to connect with, meant that I focused intensively on the restoration of the feminine. This was partly political, a rebalancing of the oppressive force of patriarchy that I, at the time, held Christianity to be primarily responsible for.

While at the monastery, I learned a Hebrew song that Sister Cherubima had sent me from America, and following the visit, I began to sing it in the ceremonies I attended. I could sense that some of the attendants were not particularly enthusiastic about the fact that it referred to the God of the Bible, but I continued to sing it anyway, hoping that the presiding elders didn't mind. It was clear to me that the Orthodox had a very deep understanding of spiritual reality. Before I left the monastery, Sister

PART ONE

Veroniki had given me a large standing gold crucifix inlaid with mother of pearl and a large, very finely detailed, wax crucifix, as a gift at the end of my stay. These objects then also entered my ceremonial context, becoming part of the tool kit I used in my healing sessions: the gold cross would stand in the center of my altar, and I would hold the wax cross in my hand while I was either sitting in meditation, channeling, or womb pulsing (a Tantric Buddhist physical/spiritual practice).[15] I could feel that my heart was opening more and more to Jesus. My commitment to my other practices, however, remained unchanged.

"Shamanism" was not a term the indigenous healers or western adherents whom I gravitated toward used. Roberto, one of the people I assisted, was very critical of the guru devotion situation that had gained pace in the medicine world, snorting with derision at anything that smacked of, in his words, *"chamanismo* express" spirituality.[16] This was an attitude upheld by most of the people I spent time with. Don Mateo, a medicine man I followed, advised me to get some eagle feathers in order that I could clean myself after my healing sessions but concluded with, "Don't use them to

---

[15] Tibetan womb pulsing is a tantric practice in which the practitioner straddles the pelvic bowl of the person receiving, and pulses the body up and down for an extended period of time. Generally, it's practiced between women, but as I was interested in exploring "the male womb" (anatomically, the pelvic bowl area; spiritually, the point at which the male connection to divine femininity could be accessed) and its connection to the inherited trauma that comes through the female ancestral line, I—before Nick—also pulsed men. Depending on how much blockage there is in the person's womb space, the effect of this physical pressure ranges from pleasant neutrality to excruciating suffering. The person would often receive messages and visions while being pulsed and might either laugh, cry, or scream in agony. Not a lot of people in the UK pulsed, and as my abilities built up according to the different empowerments I received, the strength of the practice and its positive effects, such as pregnancy in women struggling with infertility, increased.

[16] *Chamanismo*-express shamans were those who took on positions of power without adequate training, preparation, or knowledge. It was understood that years of spiritual sacrifice were required to ascend in the spiritual realm.

play the shaman though; they're just for you."[17] Despite his line of work, Roberto was always dressed in hiking boots and a North Face jacket and tried to minimize the fanfare around the whole process as much as possible. He was a self-styled medicine myth buster.

During my first retreat with him and his team, he had pulled us all aside before we entered the *Temazcal* (a ceremonial Mexican sweat lodge), to explain elements of how the weekend was going to work. Tracing his finger across the ground in front of him, he picked up some soil and rubbed it between his thumb and forefinger, encouraging us to remember that, "There is no guru-master here. We are all dust." I was attracted to this humble and grounded approach and became close to him and his group. However, "shamanism" has come to be used as a catch-all term for all forms of elemental healing practices that involve transformation through manipulating energy and communicating with different animal, mineral, or vegetable spirits. As well as spirits of lower rank, such as different non-psychoactive plant spirits and animal spirits, there were also higher, more powerful spirits, some of which were considered and named as masters. The three main plant spirits I served were peyote (a cactus), ayahuasca or *yage* (a tea brewed from vines and leaves), and yopo (a snuff made from the ground seeds of a tree).[18] All three have a powerful purgative effect (ayahuasca and yopo more so), whether through vomiting, shivering, sweating, or crying, and all induce strong visions.

---

[17] Eagle feathers, because of their rarity and perceived spiritual power, are used in many elemental traditions in order to cleanse, purify, and heal illnesses, and to assert authority in the unseen realm.

[18] Also, cacao. Cacao is a plant medicine in its own right, famed for its heart-opening properties and venerated as a sacred substance. It is used in various ceremonial contexts in Central and South America. *Cacao* ceremonies were commonplace within the medicine world, as *cacao* is both relatively inexpensive and easily accessible.

PART ONE

Mother Nature

The earth was without form and void, and darkness was over the face of the deep. And the Spirit of God was hovering over the face of the waters.
—Genesis 1.2

The darkness of the different plant spirits was not hidden. The fact that they had a shadow was something we respected and celebrated. Earth worship always involves appreciation of the dark because the divine feminine is double in nature. She is both life *and* death. The first time I drank ayahuasca, I had very little idea of what it was going to be like. I hadn't done any research but had simply told Maya, who had invited me, that I wanted to participate. Realizing that I qualified for an interest-free overdraft of £2000, I booked flights immediately and went out to meet her and her community in Brazil. Fernanda, the Brazilian shaman who would be teaching us, had been married to an Ecuadorian medicine man and had learned the craft at his side. She arrived at the location set up for the ritual with two helpers, one male and one female. The women were dressed in floor-length printed dresses and were carrying carved wooden pipes, which would later be used in the ceremony. They were all covered in beaded jewelry from the jungle and were holding feathers. Although the work Fernanda did could be tracked directly back to the jungle, the more western side of the medicine world sometimes combined influences.[19]

I looked on coolly but was secretly desperate to become part of their gang. Fernanda was greeting everyone in Portuguese and showering them

---

[19] I, and those I gravitated toward, were purists who looked down on this "New Agey" approach to medicine and were keen to maintain the traditions as strictly as possible. However, sometimes the indigenous leaders would laughingly tell me to relax and stop thinking in such a "white" way. People would often tell me that I took things too seriously.

with love. I wanted that love. Before the ceremony began, she explained how the process would work and opened up the floor for people to share their purpose for attending the ritual and anything else that they had on their mind. One of the helpers translated for the English speakers. When it got to my turn, I introduced myself and shared my healing intentions. Uncomfortable with the vulnerability I was feeling, I slid my eyes across the attendants gathered and added that I was "a little skeptical about it all." Fernanda nodded her head in silence, gazing ahead, and then said in a thick and rasping Brazilian accent, "The medicine will knock that out of you, sister, don't you worry." Eeek.

After drinking the medicine, I lay down and nervously waited for the encounter to begin. Fernanda started chanting and as she sang, I began to feel the room come alive with the sounds of the forest. The quivering, rattling, buzzing sounds of thousands of different insects, reptiles, and birds. I felt the room suspended within a black expanse, with miles and miles of the spirit world extending outward from where we lay. My hands, legs, and face began to vibrate, and the visions started. The most beautiful jungle night expanded around me as palm branches unfurled out into the electrified atmosphere. Everything vibrated in unity with the songs being chanted, dissolving any sense of boundaries between the physical and the spiritual. Everything was one. A glinting creature began to move down one of the branches toward me. I wanted to reach out and connect with her, to be consumed by her. It was "Mother Ayahuasca" (the name affectionately given to the spirit). She was coming to heal my pain. The medicine began to speak to my soul, telling me I had to look into my feminine ancestry. "You have to look, Tali," she said, "*this* is the source." I fell in love immediately.

PART ONE

The Forest

Do not know your own will, know only God's will.
—St John of Kronstadt

Following this introduction with Fernanda and traveling to the jungle with her to learn from her *maestros* (spiritual teachers), I started to explore different traditions. I became very close with a group of brothers who ran a medicine community in Costa Rica and started to study with them. I found nourishment in the joy of their family life and the power of their particular brew. In the ceremonies that followed, my experience with the medicine began to open up and take me into deeper places of communion and understanding. I was a completely open vessel, ready to be filled with the knowledge of the forest, and because of my sensitivity, I began to absorb *a lot* of information. I went to stay with them for several months to drink medicine and do internal work, and during that period worked through many issues. One ceremony in particular marked a turning point in terms of my healing.

I had been preparing internally for the ritual and had an intuitive sense that something huge was about to take place. After I drank the medicine, it then started to come on more strongly than usual. I went to the bathroom but was aware that I was about to throw up. This was a very quick turnaround. Walking out to one of the porches (the ranch was situated on the side of a hill), I began purging. It was the most satisfying purge in the world. Normally purging immediately meant losing out on the visionary power of the brew, as it would be leaving your system, but I could feel that tonight, something extra special was happening.

I stood outside under the stars, bathed in the beauty that shone down from above. Everything vibrated with the force of the forest. The trees swelled and swayed in ecstasy, melting into the night air, as waves of pink, orange, and purple energy cascaded around me. Fluttering spirits and geometric symbols spun and sparkled in the frenzied atmosphere. The force of the medicine inside me began to intensify and, my heart beating faster and faster, I walked toward the fire. As I walked, beams of light erupted out of the earth around me, soaring into the air and exploding into the pink and orange sky. Everyone was going through an internal process, but I was unaware of what anyone else was doing. I couldn't see anything around me because the visions were so thick. I began to sit by the fire. The fire was white. Its center aglow with heat, I sat at its opening, wanting to climb inside and melt in the flames.

The force of the medicine continued to rise inside me, until I got to the point of feeling that I was about to explode. A healing then started to take place and I began to bellow, crying out as the medicine dragged the darkness of my past and everything that had happened from within me. It was an energetic purge. Juan-Pablo, the oldest of the three brothers, stood by the fire, trying to help me stabilize within the intensity. "*Harmonize* yourself with the moon, *hermanita* (little sister). Mother Nature is calling you home, but you must *harmonize* with her." After this process of expulsion came to completion, joy surged up inside me, and I began to sing, completely released from the exorcism, each word sending waves of delight down through my body. Singing with the medicine was a spiritually ecstatic experience. Your entire voice would open up and roll out, suffused with the power of the spirit inside you. It was blissful. Juan-Pablo was playing the harmonica and began to tone along with the song that I was singing. Anderson, the middle brother, then joined, and they began playing guitars until we were all singing together in Spanish, worshiping the medicine.

The medicine continued to pour love down onto my soul—my entire body, heart, and mind felt suffused with the cosmic love of God. It swelled within me and rippled out into the atmosphere around me. Everyone in the ceremony having now joined, we continued to sing into the dawn joyful jungle songs of thanksgiving and praise. After a while, the ceremony began to gradually quiet down, and people peeled off, falling asleep in the hammocks situated around the outside of the *maloca* (a ceremonial hut).[20] I lay alone by the fire, looking up at the fading stars in stillness. I felt so light. It had been many hours since I had drunk any medicine, so the force was now soft. No more visions. The fireplace was situated on one of the porches, and beneath it was a large drop that then rolled down into the river. It was surrounded by trees. I turned my head and looked out across the garden to see the ayahuasca spirit resting in the branches of the largest tree. She was completely white, manifesting as a vast, translucent cloud. I stared at the spirit as she hovered, watching over me. My heart was filled with gratitude for the special gift I was receiving.

It is not possible to adequately explain how powerful the process of purification through medicine is. These plant spirits are described as hallucinogenic, but they are something much, much more. During a ceremony I later organized for Fernanda (with whom I had become close) and her indigenous *maestra* from the jungle, the physical force of the spirit—as she descended into the *cabana* (a shaded wooden structure) from above—was so strong that most of the attendees were pinned to the floor, completely unable to move. The shamans sat behind an altar laid out with the medicine and other healing tools. Lua, the other assistant, and I sat on either side of them. The medicine had been administered, and everyone had returned to his or her place. The candles were blown out. They began to chant the beautiful songs of the tradition and I joined in. As we chanted, the energy in the room began to build, and people began to moan, some crying. The energy behind the altar was very strong, and the force in the room began to rise as the chanting got louder. People continued to groan and sob as a result of the energy that was building, with some crying out. If they continued, or asked for help, Lua or I would attend to them, but at the beginning, we held back, so that the medicine could minister to them directly.

As we continued to chant, the ephemeral form of the ayahuasca began to slowly unfurl into the cabana from above, her undulating presence

---

[20] A *maloca* is a religious longhouse used in the Amazon.

rippling outward to cover all the attendees. I looked at her in awe. However, all the others seemed as if they were about to disintegrate. Fernanda, who was sitting next to me, stopped chanting and muttered that we'd have to give them a break soon. "They cannot handle this much longer!" she exclaimed, looking behind her for a special bottle of ointment to purify her hands. We both laughed as I passed her the bottle. I tugged her shawl back up around her shoulders and gently teased out the long rope of thick, golden hair that had become trapped under the delicate fabric. I rearranged her hair and kissed her shoulder, before making sure that she had everything that she needed. She looked at me, "Oh, you are so sweet, my *querida* Talita!" (that is, "dear Talitha"—none of my Latin associates pronounced the "h"). There was nowhere in the world I liked being more than in the middle of a ceremony, chanting, healing, and serving the spirits.

Unlike the other master plants around which tourism industries had developed fairly large—if still relatively underground—yopo use was less widespread in the medicine world. I was introduced to the medicine by Marcia, who, along with Rodrigo, her husband, lead the Mexican community I became part of. Like the majority of Mexicans, they were baptized Roman Catholic. Thirsty for genuine experiences of healing and holiness, they, like many, began to explore other means of accessing the truth. Marcia had spent many years studying Yopo under tribal tutelage and would share the medicine in small circles with those who needed healing. She was a devout Tibetan Buddhist, and her medicine practice was built upon the spiritual foundation of the dharma.

I became very close with both Marcia and Rodrigo, spending long periods at their house in and around ceremonies. They were—and are—two of the most self-sacrificial people I know, self-funding their work, supporting tribes, and making their home (and resources) available for all those who would pass through it. Some stayed for months on end. They gave me a lot. Unlike other medicine prayers, the Yopo ceremonies were quiet because—as the elders described it—too much noise made the medicine "shake." Rather than celebration and exclamation, the focus was on internal reflection, which Marcia liked, as it meant more opportunities for purification and transformation.

The Yopo, once ground into a fine powder, was then snorted by the person receiving it, through a special pipe. Before receiving the powder, a bitter root would be chewed and swallowed, in order to prepare the internal environment for the reception of the medicine: it was taught that it was possible to "travel" with just the root, but that it required a certain level of mastery and inward contemplation to do so. After receiving the medicine, you would return to your place and sit, with your head resting between your legs, to wait on the spirit. Marcia explained the process as a "glimpse into the illuminated mind." Once the consciousness of the plant began to activate and expand, there was nothing that could be done to reverse the process. You had to endure it till the end. Some people were wary of this plant spirit, arguing that its capacity to make people go mad was evidence of intrinsic darkness. Believing that at root, all was held within the unbroken whole of divine love, my view on this perspective was—if there is madness within you, it should probably come out sooner rather than later. The truth will out.

One night a small group of us went to the medicine lodge Rodrigo and Marcia used for rituals, in order to experience the force of this spirit. After I had taken the medicine, I went to my place and waited in silence. The Yopo began to manifest its mysterious power. Although all the medicines express themselves with varying degrees of physical intensity, with Yopo, there is a sense of internal and external pressure that is different from anything else. I breathed deeply. The pressure started to build throughout my head as strong light began shining within a mind that felt like it was being cleaved open. Completely uniform geometric patterns—unlike anything in the visions of ayahuasca and peyote, both of which are earthy spirits—began to lower down across a background of blinding white and began to flash, preparing me for what was about to come. I could feel that I was about to be lifted up.

Although I wanted the process to be over, I also wanted to go to where the spirit wanted to take me. To the stars. I kept very still. While this was happening, my entire body was being squeezed by an immense sense of pressure, both from the outside in and the inside out. I observed the rising intensity, noting that this was the point at which people probably began to panic, as a result of realizing that the process is much stronger than anticipated but that it is not going to end until the spirit says it can end. There's nothing you can do. You have to just endure it. The sensation of all gravity falling away was then compounded as the plant lifted my spirit upward into the cosmos. It is a totally astral experience. The world drops far beneath you.

But I knew I couldn't panic. I continued to breathe deeply, maintaining my focus. It will pass. *Todo cambia* ("Everything changes"). Virulently forceful purging then began, shaking my entire body. After the purging had come to completion, the visions ended and the nature of the process began to change. I sat up and looked at the open doorway. "Grandfather *Yopo*" then entered the room.[21] I knew immediately that it was him. Everything else was normal, but he was visible.[22] He walked silently through the room and stood before me. His body was structured according to human form but was completely diaphanous in quality, his brown featherlight outline sparkling in the darkness. His head was bordered by a huge, pale crown, which vibrated, suspended in the space around him. Looking around the room, I could see that no one else had seen him enter.

Marcia was busy behind the altar, while Rodrigo helped Nick, who was next to me. The spirit reached out his hand and beckoned for me to come

---

[21] Although the feminine and masculine principles were acknowledged within the indigenous traditions, the process of naming the spirits in this regulated way came, as far as I am aware, as a result of the influence and intermixing of the traditions within Latin cultures.

[22] This is what distinguishes entheogens from hallucinogenic substances. Although there will be periods where they show you images that are devoid of actuality, they also open you up to the psychic realm, allowing you to see spirits that have observable existence, even if only on a very subtle level.

with him and I stood up, following him out of the cabana into the starlit night. After a while of the spirit guiding me through more intensive purging outside, he disappeared, and I returned to join everyone. The room was pitch black. Rodrigo was chanting. As he finished, Marcia began to explain what the medicine was doing, and how we needed to respond. She was as polite and graceful in ceremony as she was outside of it. She then began to say a powerful prayer about the importance of sexual purity, tearfully concluding that, "When you engage with porn, you connect yourself to very dark spiritual energy. You must *not* engage with this darkness. My beloved brothers and sisters, *do not* watch porn." The first round of visions having more or less finished, she then began to prepare more medicine, and we all sat in our places in silence, waiting to travel again.

Your Thoughts Determine My Life

A person who is entrapped in the vicious cycle of chaotic thoughts, in the atmosphere of Hades, or has only so much as touched it, feels the torments of hell.
—Elder Thaddeus of Vitovnica

I had been tormented by my thoughts all my life. For as long as I could remember, I would be overcome by relentless sequences of negative thoughts that would frequently leave me in a state of ungrounded, paranoid paralysis. These intrusive, high-speed, obsessive thoughts, which were generated by, and generated, intense anxiety, had several manifestations. There were those concerned with life circumstances and my bodily functions, which provided the raw material for my long-term insomnia and the panic attacks I frequently experienced. There were those activated by the others' opinions of me. Regardless of how much reassurance I received, if word reached me that someone (literally anyone) had spoken about me in a negative way, I would be plunged into a dark pit, turning their words over in my mind and desperately thinking of ways in which

I could manufacture circumstances that would allow me to change their bad opinion of me.

Controlled by a guilty conscience, repetitive thought cycles would also be triggered by others' anger (and "silent treatment" in particular), and any form of public humiliation (for which my erratic, alcoholic life provided frequent opportunities) activated draining thought cycles that were both shame-driven and self-shaming in a particularly ferocious way. These were compounded by violent, aggressive thoughts that would manifest as a persistent monologue, verbally abusing my character, appearance, and behavior. Volcanic eruptions of self-loathing, these thought streams carried an unspoken, hate-filled "voice," that would urge me to harm my body (resulting in a battle with self-mutilation and bulimia). A further manifestation came in the form of heavy rumination: vicious, angry, resentful thoughts toward people in my life who had hurt me. Because I am sensitive and thus both easily wounded and easily offended, these thoughts had ample ground for colonizing my mind. Most disturbing were the intrusive barrages of unwanted sexual thoughts that would flood my mind, no matter who I was with, or what I was doing. These began in early childhood. I had no control over the thoughts. The phenomena had a profound physiological effect on me, and depending on the content, I would often be sensorially overloaded by the images, retching or shuddering in response.

I never spoke to anyone about the intensity of my thoughts because I had no experience outside of them. My sole experience of life on planet earth was that of the uncontrollable terror of drowning in the abyss of my own mind. The final form—perhaps the most dominant in my life—was that of daydream and reverie: potent, heady thought streams that would take me on adventures far beyond the boundaries of my body and the present. Long swathes of time were lost to these dramatic, compulsive, distracting, and oftentimes blissful, thought journeys, detailing me in various exalted states, whether spiritual, social, professional, or romantic. Before getting sober, people frequently called me a "spacecake," or told me that I was "on another planet." As I started doing deep inner work and began to learn about narcissistic family structures, I was able to see that disconnecting from my body and floating in the atemporal world of fantasy were the means through which I soothed my pain and escaped my unhappy reality.

A complicated childhood, an encounter with a pedophile when I was nine, and three early instances of assault resulted in depression and self-loathing. The trauma manifested as a painful narcissism that meant keeping a carousel of guys who were interested in me on rotation, but being unable to settle into a relationship with any of them. Under my flirty, flamboyant, and feisty persona, I was crippled by self-doubt. As someone who had been bullied, the development of my body into womanhood and the power that it gave me over men was like being introduced to crack. I became addicted. However, the perpetual presence of both my eating disorder and my disordered thinking imprisoned me in the inescapable reality that beneath the beauty, I was disgusting. I had a shameful secret. As a result, the heavy drinking, drug taking, and bulimia intensified.

I was desperate to escape the affliction of my thoughts, and it was through drinking that I found the strongest release: I would drink till I blacked out. I would restrict eating while partying, then would binge and purge through the comedowns, isolating for days on end until I was ready to emerge into public and start all over again. The binge eating began in childhood. Sugar was my drug. It numbed my mind and made me feel happy. I kept a diary with my weight and thigh, hip, and stomach measurements. Every day I would check my progress, making a note of the number. If they went down, I would feel elated. If they went up, I would panic. I kept this diary for many years. I craved love and closeness, but the thought of allowing anyone access to the inner turmoil terrified me. They would be repulsed by the truth of who I really was. Simply, I hated myself. Though my depleted heart yearned for love, I was not capable of allowing anyone to love me.

In response to these factors, my feminism intensified and flourished, finding expression in my academic work. I began to be mentored by a powerful literary critic and started working through, intellectually at least, the problems I had been immersed in in terms of sexual violence. I devoured feminist and queer literary theory and found a happy home in the queer community as an advocate for intersectional gender justice. Once I became more grounded through sobriety and began to meditate and do yoga, the frenetic energy was able to find an outlet that wasn't hedonistic. Life became more calm. *I* became more calm. Through entrance into the holistic philosophy of the medicine world, this process then continued.

Eat Hard

Food is not evil, but gluttony is. Childbearing is not evil, but fornication is. Money is not evil, but avarice is. Glory is not evil, but vainglory is. Indeed, there is no evil in existing things, but only in their misuse.
—St Maximus the Confessor

Eating disorders are both difficult to understand and difficult to heal. Unlike with other substances, it is not possible to stop eating altogether. You have to eat, whether you want to or not. A woman in one of my food recovery groups used to say that giving up crack was a hundred times easier than giving up sugar. The fact that it was sugar, and not alcohol or drugs, that controlled me more than anything else generated a huge amount of shame. It was just so *embarrassing*. I was addicted to chocolate. Literally. This aspect of the recovery process would come up with my therapist while we worked through the trauma that undergirded the illness.

"Tell me what you did this weekend," she began. I started telling her what had happened, piecing together the events from the weekend.

"Sorry, I can't remember if that was Friday or Saturday . . ."

"Do you hear? Even though you didn't drink anything all weekend, you still can't remember what you did *just the other day*. The sugar is almost like alcohol for you. You were out of it. I mean the things you are describing . . . it's like you weren't actually *in your body* across those days."

She was right. It had been a particularly bad weekend. I had gone to my parents' house, hoping for a period of restoration in the countryside before returning to London to work. However, I ate compulsively on the train on the way down, and on Saturday I binged from the moment I woke up. Having eaten more than I could tolerate digesting at breakfast, I had then made myself sick. Morning purging was something I tried to avoid, but some days I couldn't refrain. Following the release, I then immediately binged again, refilling the recently emptied cavity. Heart racing and head aching, my whole body was toxic from the sugar. I had a shower to try and make myself feel clean, and then I went out walking to burn it out of my system. I had spent many hours of my life walking around those fields, trying to burn off the toxins from my sugar binges. After the frenzied feeding ritual came the dogged cleansing ritual. The former was more enjoyable than the latter.

"As I was walking, I was praying. I stopped and got onto my knees. I was just praying, you know, please . . . Mother, please God, please . . . help me to stop."

She listened as I spoke.

"The walk helped, but I still felt really bad. Sometimes after I binge, I can process the toxins out, but sometimes it just . . . I just have to wait. Maybe a day, maybe two. Cleansing and purifying my system till I crawl back up to 'zero' again. But when I got back to the house I . . ." I stopped.

"I went *back* to the kitchen. I ate *more*. I actually *ate more*."

She continued to listen.

"That's the thing that I just don't get. It's such a ridiculous situation. I mean, I know the problem, I know the solution and yet—"

I looked up to glimpse her eyes widen in disbelief.

"I mean, I know it's bad, of course, but it could be so much worse—"

"So much worse?" she spluttered. "Tali, you were on your knees, in the middle of a field, begging, literally *begging God*, for mercy."

I used to tell my OA sponsor that it was as if a heavy force would descend on top of me, clouding my mind, blurring my vision, and forcing me to eat and eat and eat. Once this machine started, there was nothing I could do to stop it. *Nothing.* Dissociated, I would walk into the kitchen on autopilot and begin cramming into my mouth whatever was in reach. I would read cookbooks while binging to help block out the thoughts. By the time I was sixteen, I had read every cookbook in our house from cover to cover. I favored sugary, fatty carbs, but sometimes it would just be whatever was in my vicinity. Anything to numb the pain.[23] Anything to make it stop. Some days it wasn't there. But most days it was.

Tribes

There's a myth that we have labored under for centuries in indigenous communities and the myth is that we are a godless, heathen people.
—Uncle Rev. Terry LeBlanc

As a result of these addictions, I was determined to find healing. I didn't care about anything else. All I wanted was to be well. All I wanted was to be free. I *needed* to be free. I couldn't bear it any longer. So when the path into the heart of nature opened up before me, I was out the gate, ready to do whatever it would take. Everything in my life synthesized into this singular point of focus. A solution. *Finally.* I ran and joyfully jumped in. After so many years in the ironic disconnect of the London party scene, finding myself immersed in the heartfelt camaraderie of a spiritual family opened and transformed my internal landscape. We were not anthropologists assessing the tribal life we immersed ourselves in from positions of

---

[23] As well as binging to regulate buried pain, I also ate when I was tired, tense, angry, anxious, stressed, bored, listless, neutral, relaxed, cheerful, happy, excited, exhilarated, or just . . . content. Simply, I ate.

detached academic inquiry. The tribes we followed invited us into their homes, and we invited them into ours. They were our teachers; we were their students. But we were also friends. It was a family thing.

The relationships were also often romantic. We traveled, lived, and worked together. This intimate dynamic was underscored—for those who were aware—by the recognition that our socio-economic privileges as westerners meant a responsibility to support the indigenous however we could. I would feel an unspoken allegiance with those who, like me, used terms such as "white privilege" and "white supremacy" (this was before it exploded into mainstream consciousness). However, the interface between us westerners and the different tribes was neither the model of government-mandated legal advocacy, nor that of the NGO, nor of charities providing aid. Our support of the tribes came through our adherence to their traditions and through, essentially, providing them custom.

Within paganism, Christianity was not generally held in positive regard. Because we followed animist, indigenous spirituality and its manifold practices and rituals, we saw Christianity as the colonial force responsible for the eradication of these ancient forms of worship and the oppression of thousands of indigenous communities. The retreat I started was about recovering the indigenous practices, rites, and ceremonies of pre-Christian England, Scotland, and Wales. However, within many traditions, there existed a complex interweave between Christian and indigenous spirituality. For example, many Native Americans had integrated Christianity into their ceremonies, on the understanding that the spirit of peyote, which epitomized the qualities of perfect love, self-sacrifice, and gentleness, was the second incarnation of Christ Himself.

The harmony between the *Red Road* and the Christian gospel meant that the two traditions seemed to integrate without too much internal contradiction.[24] Although I didn't attend *cross-fire* ceremonies (ceremonies in which the fireplace was shaped like a cross and which espoused Christian

---

[24] The *Red Road* is a modern, anglophone, conceptualization of a variety of Native and First Nation beliefs, that encapsulates the desire to live in a harmonious and righteous

theology), some of my teachers in Mexico held them before I joined their community and taught their group (many of whom were young urban Mexicans, getting out of addiction and despair) according to the principles of monogamy, humility, self-sacrifice, generosity, and forgiveness.[25] However, there was another worldview, upheld by both some indigenous peoples and westerners that ran counter to this, which rejected this "indoctrination" of the tribes and the eradication of the true, pre-modern worship. Missionaries were to them the scum of the earth.

Although I loved Christ Himself, I tended toward this perspective, seeing the integration of Christianity in the liturgical life of the tribes as being founded on the tragic loss of an originary form of knowledge that surpassed the Christian religion in cosmic profundity and spiritual legitimacy. Although we had enough intelligence to understand that there was some nuance and that there were *some* Christians who had done and were doing good, we were observing the effects of Christian contact firsthand in terms of the disenfranchisement of these tribes. I had a particular interest in Native American culture and history and would research as much

---

way, in order to bring about positive change for oneself and others. This is something we would often sing about.

[25] Within the Native American Church, or Peyote religion, as it is sometimes called (though not by anyone I knew), there were fireplaces—ceremonial altars passed down generationally—that were organized around the revealed truth of Christ, with the elements of the ritual reflecting different aspects of Christian theology and all the songs sung being, for the most part, songs of Christian worship. In these ceremonies, the Bible would often be read. It is impossible to give a comprehensive explanation of the intricacies of this and other aspects of the Native American and First Nation outworking of Christian contact, and it is obviously far beyond the abilities of a book of this kind to do so in a way that does the subject matter any justice. Furthermore, it is not my story to tell. All I can share is my experience of the aspects of it that I came into contact with. Suffice to say, the relationship to Christ, within Native American and First Nation spirituality, as with all indigenous cultures that have encountered the gospel, is highly complex.

as I could, to understand, from the perspectives of the Natives, the *horrific* things that had taken place in the name of Christ.

I organized retreats for Michael, a medicine man who shared stories handed down through his maternal line, of the "hungering times." He recounted his ancestors' journeys, as entire tribes were exiled from their homeland and forced to move thousands of miles across the country into reservation camps. Trudging through bitter winter, horses were sliced open and babies packed between entrails and organs in order to keep them alive in the cold. Hundreds of thousands perished. Banned from hunting and forced to subsist on salted pork and sugar, starvation and malnutrition, along with rape, torture, and murder, were a constant threat. It was hard to remain open to Christianity as a result of hearing about the massacres that had taken place at the hands of the different waves of colonists. However, as a result of colonial contact, Protestant and Roman Catholic Christianity had weaved its way into many of these communities' customs, and we accepted and respected that (because we accepted and respected the indigenous, not because we accepted and respected Christianity).

Paganism generally values personal experience above theoretical concepts, and the hippie-influenced, neopaganism of the medicine world in which I lived promoted an attitude of ruthless openness and being non-judgmental. Therefore, there were some sensitive westerners who were sympathetic to the message of Christ though this was never in the context of the Bible as a whole. More or less, however, it was seen as a symbol of patriarchy and the terror that had been inflicted on our indigenous teachers. It was held as the reason we were separated from (and destroying, as a result) the earth. This fissure between humanity and nature was considered to be the root of all our issues, and the idea was that, through connecting to creation as we used to, we would then find the true healing we needed. Relationships with the plant spirits around which our ceremonial life was organized were the gateway to that reconnection, and the purging was the means by which we could physically, emotionally, and spiritually detox from all the negative energies, entities, attachments, and toxins that inhibited us from experiencing this uninterrupted union with nature. The primary goal of our worship was to activate ancient spiritual knowledge within us, remember our roots, and return to our originary, *pre-Christian*, state.

Mexico

Cut the desire for many things out of your heart and so prevent your mind being dispersed and your stillness lost.
—Abba Evagrius

Because of the intensity of my Buddhist studies at this time (Nick was learning Tibetan, and we were preparing for exams) and the multiple different spirits that comprised the spiritual world I inhabited, my psychic field was fairly crowded. After the two visions with Jesus, something else would come along—another ceremony, healing, or meditation experience—and so they were forgotten. All my energy was funneled into managing everything that was taking place, so I could achieve my longed-for goal of attaining financial stability and dedicating myself once and for all to one spiritual tradition. For years I had tormented myself, convinced that I needed to choose between ayahuasca or peyote. I felt sure that I couldn't keep working for both spirits. I would go round in circles but would never actually get to a point of being able to leave one behind. I was deeply in love with both of them and their attendant traditions, and so I resigned myself to the fact that I was supposed to be with both.

My kundalini practice was in the background, underscoring everything. I saw it as the base on top of which the earthy, elemental drama of the plants and their bombastic, dramatic traditions swirled. Physically, the plant work could be strong and intense. Some of the rituals would drain one of all energy, and in some cases, actually harm the body. Kundalini, on the other hand, purified from within, so it felt innate and clean. However, these inside/outside distinctions were routinely collapsed by the practices themselves—we saw ourselves as elemental creatures, made of fire, water, earth, and air. Ayahuasca was the blood that ran through my veins, and peyote my flesh.[26]

Nick and I understood that as Buddhists (though I hadn't yet taken refuge—a commitment to take spiritual "shelter" in Buddha), we shouldn't have the urge to find release and healing through plant medicine. But ayahuasca and peyote were so precious to me that despite many attempts to slow down my work with the plants, I never could. Sometimes I would manufacture circumstances that would make it impossible for me to attend a ceremony that I would otherwise attend. The result was either an excruciating night in which I regretted not being there, or a last-minute scramble to rearrange my plans so that I could, often jeopardizing relationships with the clients whose sessions I would need to reschedule at the last moment. Our *lama* (lit. "superior one," the Tibetan Buddhist term for a teacher or abbot, roughly analogous to the Sanskrit *guru*) told us that it was okay to engage with all the different spirits, Christ included, because it was good to give them their due worship. But this must always be tempered by the understanding that the highest state could only ever be achieved through self-realization. This was Buddha's example. And this is why I was heading toward taking refuge in him.

Nine months after my February meeting with Father Theophan, I went to Mexico to complete a fast in the wilderness: no food or water for four days. The night before, we did an overnight ritual to bless and protect those who were going to fast. On entering the ceremony and beginning to eat the peyote, I spoke to its spirit, requesting that I be able to experience love in its fullness—that I could feel the fulfillment and freeness of total

---

[26] It is important to emphasize the all-immersive nature of the animist worldview. Once you accept that all physical phenomena have accompanying invisible spirits, the entire world is vivified and in a state of activity. In this regard, one's entire life became that of "spirit contact." Of course, the ceremonies/meetings that we took part in, took this process to another level of intensity and were characterized by structure and ritualized protocol. However, it was commonly understood that "the ceremony of life" was the ultimate ceremony, and so the boundaries between inside/outside ritual space were blurred.

and complete, all-immersive love. I then repeated "love" whenever I ate the medicine throughout the night's ceremony. It can have a bitter taste, and focusing on your intention helps to ease it. The elders say that the plant itself is not bitter, but that westerners are bitter in heart, which is why they experience this taste when eating it.

Clearly, I was yearning for an encounter with divine love. However, at the time, my understanding of God was still very much that of an impersonal *force*. I was not yet anywhere near accepting "The Father" as the godhead. This wasn't even on the table. This force manifested through ayahuasca, peyote, cacao, kundalini, Buddha, the fire, water, music, love, food. Really anything. And everything. If you decided that something healed, then it did. The idea being that one's mind had the power to sanctify anything toward which it directed positive intentions. In my nondual worldview, God was everything and everything was God. Everything was sacred and everything healed. *Todo cura, todo sana, todo tiene medicina adentro* ("Everything cures, everything heals, everything has medicine inside"). This was one of my favorite songs. It epitomized the drive toward radical inclusivity and the merging of opposites that characterized our mindset.

In the middle of the ceremony, a friend of mine whose family was Roman Catholic (as were the families of most of the attendees) sang a song to Jesus, and I began to feel His love fill the space. The nature of these ceremonies is such that different spirits are called in all night, so this was not in and of itself unusual. However, the presence of Jesus in this moment felt different from anything else I had experienced—bright, light, and alive. Looking into the flames in front of me, something then happened that never had before. I caught a glimpse of the base of a seated *presence*. This presence had a personhood and this presence was *male*. And this was significant. I could sense that He was seated on a throne, but I couldn't see all the way up, instead only part of the feet at the base. Just like the Bible of my childhood all those years ago had described it. It actually made me laugh because it was so *wild*. God? On a throne? Never once had God manifested like *this* to me. It was a very, very unusual sensation and totally different from all the other visions I had experienced in the ceremonies I had taken part in. I felt elated.

Following the fast, I spent the remainder of November at the house of Rodrigo and Marcia, to recuperate and connect with people from the community. They were its loving leaders, and it was on their land that the ritual had taken place. Winding down afterward, I came into contact with Terrence, a healer who practiced traditional massage. The reason that I was led to practice massage myself was a nerve issue in my spine that manifested as chronic agitation in my left arm, shoulder, and neck. Desperate for relief, I was always on the lookout for very deep massage that could work into the tendons, ligaments, and deeper tissue (which feeble western massage mostly fails to do).

In one of the sessions, during which I cried the entire time as a result of the emotional and physical release that was taking place, Terrence told me to tell him what I could see. A sequence of images in which I was running screaming out of a burning house began. After bending down on the ground in front of the burning house, I then saw myself walk back into the flames, pick a baby up out of a box in the middle of the room, cradle it, and walk it out of the fire into safety. As I was seeing this image, I was feeding it and my understanding of it back to the healer: the baby was my abandoned inner child, the burning house was my childhood, and the act of my rescuing her was my healing effort—restoring the broken self to wholeness.

Continual Thirst

Let our soul always thirst for the knowledge of the truth.
—St Paisios the Athonite

Spending time in the spirit world was a regular part of my kundalini yoga practice in which I would engage with spirits, have past life experiences, and see and move energy inside people's chakras and ancestral lines. When I allowed the Hindu spirits I channeled to move through me, I would spend hours at a time astral traveling. This was also the case with the plant spirits and the other psychic empowerment techniques I engaged in. As such, the visions of Christ that took place after my meeting with Father Theophan, first in London and then in Mexico, didn't cause a shift in my perspective of spirituality as a whole.

That these experiences with Jesus were situated within my other visionary experiences was to my mind at the time—though I didn't conceptualize it as such—evidence that Christ and the Christian "path" were another manifestation of the same divine source as Hinduism, Buddhism, shamanism, and everything else I practiced. As was often the case with the teachers I met, who carried an authentic lineage and who worked with integrity, I had struck up a very close relationship with Terrence and became immersed in what he began to teach me about how to work with the body according to his tradition. As such, the vision I had before the fast got swallowed up by what took place afterward.

At this point, Mother Nature was still the highest power, and Christ fell below her in the hierarchy of creation—Christ from nature rather than nature from Christ. Although up till then Jesus was always present within my wide-ranging cosmology (and loved in huge part because He was to me the "first feminist"), there was no way that I could accept that He, as someone who only incarnated two millennia ago, could be the source of it. This was thanks in part to the many deceptive visions I had experienced with different spirits telling me as much. Several times I had been shown my personal origin story—a past life regression—by a variety of spirits, whether plant, crystalline, or psychic, and never once was Christ present as Creator of all in any of these visions. Not once.

PART ONE

Noble Truth

Buddhism is fine as far as it goes. But it does not go far enough.
—Fr Seraphim Rose

Following my time in Mexico, I felt more forcefully that I needed to stop *Lam Rim*. It was coming up to Christmas, and I wanted to make a decision before I flew to America to visit my sister and Father Theophan at the monastery (he had invited me by email after our meeting earlier that year). I had been doubting whether Buddhism was my path for the two years I had been studying the *Lam Rim*, but the persuasive power of the teachings and the lama himself meant that as soon as I was about to cancel my place, I would become scared that I was throwing away the "only" chance I had to achieve true liberation from suffering, and I would resign myself to continuing on. I remember being in the garden of our Buddhist center, the first time I told our teacher that I was terminating my study. It was August and sunlight was warming the grass beyond the shaded decking on which we were sat. I looked at the leaves fluttering in the breeze and felt a sense of lightness rising inside me. I wanted to be free from any kind of religious identity, so that I could be solely with the spirits, as I had before my relationship with Nick began. The lama told me to think about it.

Afterward Nick and I drove to my parents' house.

"I just feel conflicted because I quit my Ph.D., and now I will be quitting the *Lam Rim*. I feel like I should finish, you know, even if only to finish!"

I had spoken about it with a friend who lived in a holistic community. She had told me that I shouldn't finish something just for the sake of it. Maybe I had learned everything that I needed to from this experience, and now it was time for me to move on. This was very typical of the tantric, Taoist-influenced side of the New Age, which was all about letting everything just be as it is. Acknowledging that imperfection and uncertainty *were* the perfection and certainty that we, as humans, were naturally reaching for, that it was the answer we were seeking. Hmm. Maybe. I looked at Nick as he drove.

"Or what if I quit and then I've lost this chance and I realize it *is* the highest truth, and I try and come back. I'll be behind the whole class and will have to start again. I'll lose those two years."

"Well, nothing will ever be lost," he replied.

"You know, there are many different ways of achieving liberation. The Dalai Lama always says that people should practice the religion of their countries rather than becoming Buddhist."

"But we know from the *Lam Rim* that there is only one way. Through self-realization." I looked out the window at the passing fields.

"Whatever you decide, you will always be my ultimate spiritual teacher."

I knew he was trying to make me feel better. It was sweet of him but I knew it wasn't true. Logically. Because liberation is through Buddha's example, that's the teaching. That's what we were learning and Nick, as a Buddhist, believed that. *Had* to believe that. I mean, he was a Buddhist for a reason.

The following week I sat in the garden again with the lama and Gadan, our translator. Gadan was teaching Nick Tibetan. Nick and I were always trying to wrap our heads around how Gadan, Buddhist since birth, could study the *Lam Rim* in such depth (there were several classes, and Gadan was the translator for each study group), while at the same time drinking, smoking, and eating meat. What about the teachings! Gadan would laugh hysterically in answer and tell us stories about how he used to bury a pair of jeans and a t-shirt in the forest outside the monastery he attended in Tibet, so that he could sneak out in the evenings to go to the cinema in town and talk to pretty girls.

"Why do you want to stop *Lam Rim?*" the lama asked me.

"I am constantly in conflict. With the gurus of my kundalini lineage and the plant spirits, I have a familiarity with them. It's instinctive and just makes so much sense, but with Buddhism . . . I feel so much resistance.

It's like there is something inside me saying 'no.' Constantly. Rather than making me feel free and raising me up, instead I feel locked in and heavy. I feel that with my kundalini practice—which is like an equivalent to this tradition and a parallel (not strictly but for the purposes of my point)—I am working with the chakras, meditation, yoga, and purification. So it's already all there; it doesn't make sense to then have this separate practice on top."

He looked at me in silence.

"What do you think the chakras are?"

Uh oh. Better get this right . . .

"They're gates situated throughout the body that draw energy inward and expel energy outward. Beyond the seven main ones there are several above the crown chakra."

I went into detail explaining my work with the chakras: the different yogic techniques and the process of purifying and removing entities and impurities from the receiver's body. He seemed content with my response.

"But everything you're describing, this is all within Buddhism as well, the chakras, etc."

After a while of going back and forth—I tried to be as clear as possible, so things didn't get lost in translation—the conversation came to a close.

"Of course, it would be good for you to carry on," he said.

"You are a gifted student, and you are thinking in the right way, asking good questions."

It was high praise coming from him. He paused.

"Ultimately, it's your decision. It's all from within you. You have to decide. Maybe you will go off and find your own way . . ."

He leaned forward to get up from his chair, looked at me and raised his eyebrows as if to imply that any such attempt would, of course, be futile, and laughed.

"Good luck!"

He stood and walked back inside. Good luck. I remained fixed to the bench and looked at Gadan pleadingly. He smiled but said nothing. I didn't quit.

Samsara

Buddhism has some truths, but it has one human truth, which reaches to "zero." That is, with concentration-meditation man reaches the non-being from which we came. It is an existential suicide.
—St Sophrony of Essex

I believed in and prayed to Creator (no definite article), encouraged by the First Nation and Native American traditions I studied, which worship a singular creator. However, as a dedicated proponent of eastern teachings of nonduality, the boundary between creation and creator was very fluid. As far as I understood, the primordial *force* or *flow* was the highest source of truth. Creator as spoken of in Native traditions, was to my mind the personification of that primordial force. And that primordial force also existed within Buddhist cosmology, which is how I was able to hold these otherwise quite different worldviews together.

Within the context of Buddhism, there is no creator God. It does not and cannot exist. I was very resistant to this aspect of the dharma and found it very hard to connect my heart to Buddha Shakyamuni himself[27]—which for a person who connected fairly easily to spirits, felt strange. I always bent this teaching to fit into my experience by ascribing the self-emanating, self-originating flow of consciousness, the "beginningless time" that was held as the sum of reality in Buddhism, to be "God." As with the kundalini teachings, which are not as scholarly as Tibetan Buddhism, my understanding of God—though this is, of course, not a term used in Buddhism—was that it was the fully divine totality inside which both

---

[27] Most scholars agree that Siddhartha Gautama—the founder of Buddhism, more commonly known as the Buddha (which means "awakened one")—was born to royal parents in the Shakya clan in modern-day Nepal around 500 BC. "Shakyamuni" means "sage of the Shakyas." In various forms of Buddhism, many other past and future figures are called Buddha, so the fuller title "Buddha Shakyamuni" helps to clarify who is meant.

good and bad, dark and light, and consciousness and ignorance manifested and reproduced themselves ad infinitum. And in both cases this totality of reality was totally divine but could only be understood and experienced as such in relation to the purity of one's perception and perspective. Purity that came about as a result of ascetic effort (meditation, exercises, fasting, and purification). The purer the perception, the more you were able to break through the deception of separation (conditioning, relative truth) to experience oneness (original state, ultimate truth).[28]

Throughout our studies, I would ask how Jesus fitted within *Mahayana* ("Greater Vehicle") Buddhist cosmology.[29] Initially the lama, like the Dalai Lama, said that He was a *Bodhisattva* (an enlightened being).[30] He said that Jesus' teachings were a pure example of the compassion taught by Buddha, and that in many ways Christians were better at living this out through acts of kindness than many Buddhists. Okay. If Jesus exists within this structure, then I can continue. If Jesus can be part of this, then these teachings are true. Because I knew that Jesus was in some way true. I didn't accept *I am the way, the truth and the life* (Jn 14.6), as my parents did, but I knew that He was *real*. My parents' life was testament to it. My sister's monasticism was testament to it. Father Theophan was testament to it! Of course, this categorization of Christ denies that He is God—as there's no creator God in Buddhism—but by that point, this aspect of the Trinity about which I had learned in childhood had been buried under everything else I had been studying. And although I had never read *Living Buddha*,

---

[28] These two explanations are according to this concept within paganism and Buddhism respectively.

[29] Buddhism outlines three paths, the Three *Yanas* (*yana* commonly being translated as "vehicle" but often conceptualized as a branch), to enlightenment: Theravada/ Hinayana (lit. "Way of the Elders"), *Mahayana* (lit. "Greater Vehicle") and *Vajrayana* (lit. "Diamond Vehicle). Mahayana and Vajriyana share beliefs and practices unique to Tibetan Buddhism (which evolved out of Theravada Buddhism and traditional Bon shamanism).

[30] Someone who has generated the wish to attain enlightenment for the benefit of all sentient beings and who vows not to leave the cycle of death and rebirth until all sentient beings are enlightened.

Living Christ by Thich Nhat Hanh,[31] or watched the *Jesus Was a Buddhist Monk* documentary, their existence seemed to give credence to my theory of a Jesus-inclusive Buddhism.

I would often bring the topic of Jesus up during our debating sessions but couldn't help noticing that the subject seemed to irritate the lama. Was I being paranoid? It was very subtle, but I sensed that he wanted to move on to a different topic as quickly as possible, even though other students' questions would sometimes turn into discussions that ran on for hours. Because of my insecurity, I put this down to the fact I wasn't asking the right questions. In the eyes of my boyfriend, the lama could do no wrong, and the discussions that followed our classes as we drove home would often end with us agreeing to disagree on the existence of God. At one point the lama had spoken about how all the different spirits (Kali, Shiva, ayahuasca, etc.) were worthy of veneration, and worship even, though not above Buddha. I happily assumed this therefore meant that YHWH could also be worshiped as part of the pantheon. After I suggested this, the lama turned toward me and paused. His eyes narrowed, "No, because there is no God." And then slowly and with force. "God doesn't exist."

In the end, I took refuge. I had come to the decision on my own. I wanted to do it. Or rather, I took my inability to leave Buddhism as indicative of the fact that it was meant to be, and so I resigned myself to it. Just surrender, Tali. Surrender, surrender, surrender (another buzzword from the medicine world). I was expecting to feel a big shift following the ceremony. A shift and—peace. I had decided. I was a Buddhist. It was done. But there was no peace. No shift. A recurring argument exploded between me and Nick over the meal that we had to celebrate the refuge vows, and we drove home subdued.

I always felt extremely drained after being at the Buddhist center and was disappointed to see that taking refuge hadn't changed this. Despite what the Buddhist teachings were saying, I knew, deep down, that God

---

[31] Thich Naht Hanh, *Living Buddha, Living Christ* (London: Rider, 1996).

existed (even if I didn't use this term). But because it was buried under so many different spirit-world experiences, and because I was so enmeshed with Nick and consumed by our relationship, I was increasingly disconnected from this instinctive knowledge of God. It was only later, once I had made my refuge vow, that it also emerged that Jesus was not in fact a *Bodhisattva*—for a reason to do with the intention for generating *Bodhicitta* (the mind that is aimed at awakening)—nor could He ever be one, because His teachings are based on the notion of inherent existence amongst other things. I felt betrayed. But, as with everything else, I didn't have time to process it because I had so much else going on. And so I just kept going.

In the three-week gap between Mexico and going to America to see Sister Cherubima at the monastery, I did as many sessions as I could to cover the cost of the trip. I knew that all the work that had come my way to make it possible to go to America *immediately* after the originally planned trip to Mexico was through the hand of Christ. I could just feel provision that far exceeded my own advertising efforts. Inspired by the sessions that I'd had in Mexico, I moved into working on a donation basis, so that I had more freedom to focus on the spiritual aspect of the work—which was the thing that drove me. It was something that I had wanted to commit to for a while as making money had always been something necessary to support my service in the world but was never my goal. I tended to gravitate toward those who had a good relationship with money and was blessed by their guidance as to how to live as ethically as possible. However, the stress and the tension around money rarely abated. Everyone who was self-supporting was under pressure, and pretty much everyone I knew was exhausted beyond belief.

But the ceremonies never stopped. The prayers never stopped. The cycle of events went on and on. We would often joke about how relentless our schedules had become as a result of following the spirits full-time. Because so many in the West entered the spirit world, or "consciousness" as we called it, as a means of escaping the addiction and interior dissolution of the mainstream, much of the focus was on healing and purification: we were devout and prayed intensively, obsessively, and fervently. We were seeking release. My tendency toward filling my calendar with back-to-back trainings, retreats, pilgrimages, ceremonies, workshops, trips, and projects meant that everything I earned immediately went out again, and so I would grind and grind in order to earn enough to make it all possible. It was intense. And I was burnt out.

Living Theology

We do not want words alone, for there are too many words among people today. What we need is action, that is what we are looking for, not words which do not bear fruit.
—Abba James

Setting off to my sister's monastery in America, my expectations and what happened were distinctly at odds. I went so that I could spend time with her, see Father Theophan, and deepen my relationship with Christ. When he wrote to invite me, he had referred to time with God and time to myself. Great. I needed it. On that basis, I justified the trip as a personal retreat for me to recharge. It was an opportunity to spend time with Jesus and Mary Magdalene and to develop my practice. My sister had told me I could do yoga and meditate while they prayed. After months of intensive massaging, I was thrilled at the possibility of having a long period of time to myself, without any sessions, so I could get my body into a good place in advance of everything I had planned for my return: taking the Bodhisattva vow; beginning *Lam Rim* exam preparation; leading two weeks of womb healing workshops in Barcelona; hosting an initiation in Portugal; starting a new, Mary Magdalene-focused retreat in France; preparing to go to the forest again for medicine work; starting an online female empowerment coaching program; studying to be a doula; preparing for an

PART ONE 47

Ayurvedic[32] initiation, and further establishing the roots of my business, so that I could achieve the ever-elusive financial stability.

After reuniting with Sister Cherubima, who had calmly accepted my flight's three-hour delay as a moment of grace to read her Bible, we drove through the dark to the monastery, a former convent adjacent to a Catholic school, situated on a residential road. My sister informed me that over the Christmas feast there would be an increase in services and vigils, which I was welcome to join them for. I was definitely open to it but wondered if I could integrate a visit to a nearby spiritual community that my friend had introduced me to, into my time there. In marked contrast to the "pay to pray" culture of the western side of the medicine world, which I had come to see as the norm, at the monastery everything was free. Beyond that, it had emerged in the lead up to the trip that the abbess, Mother Syncletica, wanted to contribute to my flight, so that it would be possible for me to come so soon after Mexico. In the world I inhabited, you would be required to pay to stay at a monastery or an ashram, or to join a spiritual retreat. Yet here I was, being invited to stay for three weeks as a guest. No work exchange. No karma yoga (right action). No balancing the energy. And not only that, but *they* were spending money on *me*. I was touched.

On arrival, my sister gave me a tour of the monastery, showing me the icons that adorned the chapel walls. She stopped at one in particular. St Mary of Egypt's miraculous story of transformation took her from

---

[32] The esoteric Ayurvedic rite I had on my horizon is employed for intensive spiritual attainment. The practitioner enters a room devoid of any light, and remains there, for an extended period of time without leaving, generating internal awareness through yoga and meditation. The room contains only a bed and amenities and remains pitch black for the duration. The process is overseen by an Ayurvedic doctor, who curates a specific diet for the practitioner, sometimes involving large quantities of edible precious metals. The food is brought to the practitioner and passed through a light-protected opening in the wall. The process can last for days, weeks, or even months (without pause). On hearing about this practice, I realized I had found what I was looking for and began putting plans in place for the trip to India in which I would complete a month of this fast.

childhood "prostitution" to years of asceticism in the wild. A time in which she was made so holy that God taught her the Scriptures directly (because she didn't have a Bible—or anything else), and which resulted in her being seen levitating in prayer and walking on water by the monk who found her in the desert before she died. Wow! I didn't know that these mystical events took place within Christianity. In shamanism, Hinduism, and Buddhism, narratives of this kind were commonplace. However, I found it strange that within Orthodoxy, St Mary was described as a prostitute even though she didn't receive money.

I didn't say anything to my sister, who had never been a feminist in the way that I had, but I wondered about what abuse St Mary had experienced to precipitate such behavior. You don't just start having sex with hundreds of people at twelve years old for no reason! It's a symptom of a deeper problem. Those details weren't part of the story. It was an aspect of Christianity that felt very alien to me. Sin was so heavily discussed, but the root of these sinful actions, i.e., the trauma behind the behaviors, was not. However, her story moved me. *This* is Jesus. The Lover of the one whom society uses, abuses, degrades, and rejects. I had always felt a strong sense of responsibility to prostitutes, and I was trying to figure out how I could reach them with my work as a means of supporting their rehabilitation. Christ's love for women had always been something that attracted me, and hearing this reminded me of the tender relationship that He has with His brokenhearted daughters.

The monastery followed the old calendar and so celebrated Christmas on the seventh of January, fasting from the end of November, in preparation for the "spiritual feast"—a phrase I began to hear a lot. This meant they were only eating vegan food, which suited me perfectly as this was the diet I followed ninety percent of the time. They sometimes ate fish, but as an obedient Buddhist, I was vegetarian. Everything within the monastery was organized according to a hierarchy of eldership, and so I slotted into place as the babiest of the ducklings that trailed in a line after the abbess wherever we went.

"Aren't you finding it strange being amidst all of these nuns?" Sister Damaris, a Californian with huge eyes, asked me. She spoke under her breath, the words barely sliding out of her gently upturned mouth. She was fiery, gentle, intimidating, and innocent, all at the same time.

"No," I shrugged. "It feels natural." This was partly because this—communal devotional prayer life—was what most people in my community held as their highest goal. Albeit minus the habits, isolation, and celibacy. But it was something more than that. The monastery was a sanctified space. Here were women who had given up their entire lives to follow God and live as His servants. I felt peaceful and at rest. Three weeks with nowhere to go, nothing to organize, and no workshops to hold. No responsibilities. Time to just be.

Womb Healing

> *Now a certain woman had a flow of blood for twelve years, and had suffered many things from many physicians. She had spent all that she had and was no better, but rather grew worse. When she heard about Jesus, she came behind Him in the crowd and touched His garment.*
> —Mark 5.25–27

The next day we went to a Russian Orthodox church for the Divine Liturgy. As "church" had for the last six years meant sitting in a circle around a fire in a forest, yurt, or tipi, the process of going to an actual church in earnest felt very novel. I appreciated churches as spiritual centers and prayed in them when I came across them, but they were to my mind also symbols of patriarchal oppression, enforced labor (someone had to build them and for sure it was not the clergy), and the separation of spirituality from nature, the healing of which was my reason for living. However, these thoughts fell from the forefront of my mind as we entered a little chapel in a rented space within a typically American business park. Although the room was fairly small and simple, the harmonies of the choir, the candles and the flowers, and the beautiful icons lining the walls created a twinkly, soothing atmosphere.

My sensitivity to gender politics meant I immediately locked on to the fact that the clergy were exclusively male, that the nuns stood behind the monks, and that many of the women covered their hair with scarves. Admittedly this was something I did in ceremonies, partly because it gave me a sense of spiritual protection, and partly because it made me feel like a Babylonian medicine goddess flying through the cosmos. Being brought up in the West, however, it wasn't something I was as used to seeing within the context of Christianity. On my arrival the day before, Sister Cherubima had taken me to her cell, settling me down on the only bed in the room, a single mattress on the floor (she would sleep on the floor on a blanket). I looked around at the images of different Desert Fathers and Mothers, martyrs, and ascetics on the wall, a mix of painted icons, postcards, and—in the case of the more modern saints—photographs. For the most part, they prompted positive feelings, but there was one photo of a nun, silhouetted against a bright blue sky, that made my stomach turn. Instead of the expected outline of her neck and shoulders, there was instead the very near straight, diagonal line of her black veil, that flared directly from the top of her head to her elbows. Her shiny face smiled out the center of the black triangle in which it was eerily floating. She looked deformed. I didn't like it.

In person, however, the effect was different, and I felt my heart begin to swoon at the unique beauty of the nuns, when clothed in their formal church attire. Some of them wore tall, black, cylindrical hats—*klobuks*—from which trailed long, delicate veils, and covered their black tunics with floor-length silk mantles, tied at the neck with black ribbon. So elegant. The nuns didn't really seem to sit down, so I stood amongst them, folded within a Tibetan shawl given to me by Nick. I listened to the priest and looked at the icons on the wall. The image next to me depicted men climbing up a ladder to the gate of heaven to be met by Jesus with an outstretched hand. Below them was a pit of fire and suffering, into which people were falling, burned. The icon depicted demons fighting over some of them, trying to pull them down into hell. It reminded me of the conversation that had taken place with an Orthodox convert that Sister Veroniki had introduced me to at the monastery in England. He had spoken about the battle over the soul that takes place once we die. It is a battle between the angels and the demons we haven't yet overcome—our vices. I thought about my various compulsions and the sugar addiction that persisted despite these years of healing, therapy, and spiritual practice.

Apart from the hell-realm acknowledging Buddhists (though their hell differs vastly from that of the Bible in that it is not eternal), most people I knew in paganism assumed a placid future in which they would be absorbed back into the spirit world. Although the distinction between dark and light was much more explicit in the pagan traditions than in the nondual eastern traditions and in the New Age, there still came a point at which everything merged and became one. We would often talk about the fact that the universe was perfect and that everything was sacred. Therefore, there was nothing to fear. The anxiety, unhappiness, poverty, and mental illness that simmered under the surface of these communities told a different story, but to question why things weren't as perfect as the teachings said they were would demonstrate a lack of awareness of the truth of the totality of reality—that it is divine. Most people in the medicine world—myself included—were a combination of developmentally wounded, romantically compulsive, self-obsessed, and struggling with some form of addiction. Yet all the teachings more or less pointed toward the same thing: At its core, everything is *actually* perfect as it is. At their core, all are *actually* perfect as they are. You don't have to *do* anything. Everything that you need to be whole is *within* you. Nothing from outside can ever really *save* you. You are the master. You are the creator. *You* are God. Just breathe. Relax. It's. All. Good.

After a while, I wanted to sit down on the bench next to me but forced myself to continue standing. As if in response to this decision, a vision began as I closed my eyes. Unlike my previous experiences, which had happened during meditation or in ceremony, this image began to spontaneously unfold without any impetus. In the vision, Christ began to lead me through a "rebirthing" process, taking me back to my fetal state in my mother's womb. Rebirthing was an alternative modality that was big in my spiritual world (in fact it was something I never stopped talking about), but it was always stimulated through either a physical ritual or controlled breathing. Rebirthing tended to also be associated with esoteric, *Shakti*-focused spiritual traditions.[33] But this time it was Jesus, a male god, in unity with the Father, leading me through this intensely feminine process, and the difference was that I could feel it healing the emotional wounds of my relationship with my mother with a depth that far exceeded anything I had *ever* experienced before.

I began to cry, and I just sobbed and sobbed. After a while one of the nuns placed a hand on my back and silently pressed some tissues into my hand. The fact that it was God the Father guiding the process with such tenderness was in and of itself very healing. And enlightening. To feel that God the Father wanted to go *there*. Right into the womb. In a way, the womb was the central locus of my spirituality. It was the thing around which everything was organized and according to which everything was measured. I could only accept a spiritual tradition insofar as it honored the feminine and by default the womb: I held womb-pulsing circles, sang womb songs (intuitive sounding that emanates from the depth of the body), painted my body in tribal patterns with my menstrual blood, organized my life and all the rituals I took part in according to my monthly cycle, and all my artwork depicted women in different cosmic settings representing the stages of the monthly cycle.[34]

---

[33] *Shakti* is the female principle of the primordial cosmic power that creates, upholds, moves through, and destroys the universe within Hinduism. It is employed widely throughout alternative spirituality with varying degrees of fidelity to how it is understood within traditional Hinduism.

[34] My bohemian great-grandmother had eloped with a sun-worshiping, magic-obsessed satanist, and they had started an avant-garde publishing house called the Black

PART ONE 53

Feast

*The shepherds also came laden with the best gifts of their
flock: sweet milk, clean flesh, befitting praise!*
—St Ephraim the Syrian

Following this deep healing, we headed to the next stage of the festal celebrations—further standing liturgical prayer and chanting. Having taken part in fasts, ceremonies, and other pagan rituals, I understood the process of offering physical discomfort as spiritual sacrifice. However, everything I had experienced before paled in comparison to the asceticism of these Christian monastics. They fasted from food, water, and sleep for very long periods, worked unbelievably hard, and stood in prayer for *hours* on end. No mind-altering substances, no mind-altering states. Sober and steadfast they prayed. Praying to Jesus. Praying to God. Repenting for their sins. On this particular day, there had been a long morning vigil of standing prayer and prostration, immediately followed by the Liturgy (more hours of standing), and then another prolonged period of standing prayer. If rigor was what I had been unconsciously hunting for, I had truly found it.

As we were chanting the hymns, I was reminded of a verse from the book of Revelation, *Behold I make all things new* (Rev 21.5). When at the monastery with Sister Veroniki, she had told me that Jesus saying this to the Virgin Mary was her favorite part of *The Passion of the Christ*, and after watching the film myself, it had come to be very special to me too. As my turn

---

Sun Press, which produced the early works of writers such as Oscar Wilde, James Joyce, and D. H. Lawrence. Once I began drinking medicine, I completely stopped caring about books, and the entire world of literature became dead to me. However, I considered the menstrual artwork that I produced across those six years to be the "Black Moon Project," my way of rehabilitating the darkness of my ancestral line and breaking free from its bonds.

to chant a line approached, I realized that I would be reading a phrase that was referring to this precise verse. It was as if Jesus' hand were involved in even the tiniest of details. I was nervous to read in front of so many people I didn't know, but as soon as I started to say the words, peace came over me, and I felt like I was flying. My sister then began to sing a hymn, and as Christ's name came out of her mouth, I started to cry. Watching the nuns sing these sweet, tender, and *innocent* words touched me.

It was so genuine. In earnest they were worshiping Jesus. Having grown up in a Pentecostal Christian environment, in the years between then and now anything to do with the evangelical way of talking about "Jesus" made me cringe. It was claustrophobically cozy. Uncomfortably close to home. Too evocative of Sunday school, church camp, and not being allowed to go trick-or-treating. Of rules. Of being good. Of being *weird*. I called him Yeshua. Maybe Christ. But Jesus? No. But here I was in earnest with them. Singing. Crying. The words flooded over me, and I sobbed and sobbed. Every so often a nun would come and place some more tissues in my hand. After a while of their singing and my uncontrollable crying, I went into the bathroom to weep into my lap in private. The release was immense. I felt so light and clear. I felt pure.

Father Theophan offered a word about the mystery of Nativity—the side of the feast that is lost in our worldly way of celebrating Christmas. Although I understood what he was saying intellectually, I couldn't accept it. How could the Spirit be separated from the world in such a pronounced way? In my understanding they existed as a continuum with the physical and manifest on one end and the spiritual and unmanifest on the other but . . . a continuum. For them to be distinct would mean that the physical wasn't spiritual. That there was duality. That there was separation. That everything *wasn't* one. If everything wasn't in essence one, then by extension, everything couldn't be divine. Standing in rows, we then began to sing praises. Well, they sang—I observed and joined in where possible. Coming from a way of life in which spiritual songs were sung according to the flow of the energy while sitting in a circle round the fire, the central focus of much of our worship, it felt very unnatural to stand in lines, reading the words from a book.

Shouldn't we have learned these songs, so we were able to sing them as the Spirit moves through us? God was the trees, the clouds, the wind. Shouldn't we be unifying ourselves with the setting sun? I wondered how these songs could be true if they weren't spontaneously overflowing from our souls. Sacred song was central to the oral traditions I was immersed in and was the thread that weaved community, culture, and spirituality together. But here we were standing inside, with the doors and windows closed to the world outside. I wondered how this could possibly be closer to the truth than my organic, ceremonial experiences of divinity.

In the ceremonies I attended, we honored the elements. They were the means by which we experienced our Creator: Grandmother water, Grandfather fire. They were the elders, and they were everything. Here they were not everything. Here they were *not* the focus. Some of the songs referred to the sun, moon, and stars, which made me happy; however, the emphasis was unarguably and unequivocally on "the Lord." Although my heart was open to Christ, my experiences of Him were of someone nourishing, healing, nurturing, and loving me. Lordship felt so patriarchal and sort of—feudal. The way these praises focused "up" and away from nature reactivated the negative conception I had that Christianity was a hyper-masculine, disembodied thought system that had displaced our original, elemental, and *embodied* spirituality, and which was, therefore, the source of all our woes. I was thoughtful. But this conceptual train of thought kept being rudely interrupted by how lovely everyone was being to me. So soft, open, and welcoming. I loved everyone.

I was confused, however, by the violence of the words. I was a Tibetan Buddhist who lived according to the understanding that reality was governed by the inescapable law of karma. This, therefore, meant that you should not hurt any sentient being for any reason. According to the dharma, all sentient beings—humans, spirits, ghosts, animals, gods, hell-beings, and demons—needed love and compassion. We were taught that it was through giving them love and compassion, and only through this, that we could free ourselves from our negative karma and therefore free them from their negative karma. The prayer of the Buddhist was that all sentient beings would be reborn as a human, so that they would have the right conditions to be able to then generate the means of becoming a Buddha—the highest goal.

From the moment I had arrived at the monastery, I had struggled with the concept of "the enemy," the term used most frequently by the nuns. Having been on such an intensive diet of "you create your reality," the idea of willingly defining God's divinity in relation to an opposing negative force felt like a self-defeating enterprise. Karma also played a role in this, the generally understood idea being that our words have a karmic impact, and as such, they should be directed toward a positive outcome in whatever way possible, as negative words meant a negative result. In the elemental traditions outside of Buddhism, this same idea cropped up, though often in a less tightly formalized manner. I once overheard an elder talking about how a person's ascension into a higher realm of consciousness would attract a higher proportion of dark spirits, "as they too want to come to the light." This perspective permeated every area of my spiritual understanding, forming the basis for a holistic worldview in which every spirit was working toward the same goal.

The term "enemy" not only necessarily implied opposition, but beyond that, an opposing force that was held in some kind of contempt by the person speaking. Shouldn't we love the enemy into repentance? The concept of a spirituality that invited the adherent to reach toward sanctification through relationship to God while at the same time maintaining a negative attitude toward that which was of a lesser level of consciousness baffled me. It seemed to me that these dark feelings toward the enemy would inhibit you from rising higher toward God. If God was love, and God was the Creator of everything, then by extension everything was love. Including this so-called enemy.

PART ONE

Water

Return to dust that which is dust...
—The Life of St Mary of Egypt

On arriving in America, I had told Sister Cherubima that I had been addressing Father Theophan as my "Father in Christ," in our email exchanges, and that he would call me his "daughter in Christ." "So, he's your spiritual father!" she exclaimed excitedly. Yes! I mean . . . I guess. I hadn't really thought about it. I wasn't yet sure exactly what this entailed, but I knew how safe and special the relationship with him felt. Father Theophan (whom I naturally began to call simply "Father" as the other nuns did) had arranged for us to have a meeting the next day, so that we could talk about everything that had been happening. The nuns told me to write down the points I wanted to discuss, not to waste any of my time with him. Because of Father Theophan's humility, I hadn't really realized the importance of the role he played in the monastery. Observing the way the nuns spoke about him made me understand that the moment that was about to take place was not to be taken for granted.

On my sister's instruction, I noted down some of the Psalms that I was struggling with from the Psalter (basically all of them), and we set off for his monastery. As had been the case with all of the people who had come into my life in the role of spiritual guide, I was constantly watching him, scanning, scanning, scanning: Where's the flaw? Where's the chink? Where's the weak point? Where are you not healed? Where are you not free? Father stood in wait as the car pulled in, his bony, delicate hands folded over one another, and his head bowed. Feet protruded from beneath the hem of his well-worn, but well kept, black cassock. Both his hands and feet seemed much too large for his body. He was tiny. Leading me into a small meeting room, Father Theophan then spoke with me for three hours—I later found out that meetings usually lasted thirty minutes!—asking me to tell him my life story. He never pushed a position or perspective on me, but rather encouraged and affirmed me, responding to all of my questions with deep and heartfelt answers.

He explained the necessity of allowing Christ to enter ever more deeply into one's being, so that the "pouring" of grace that moves down through the person into the world can take place unobstructed. This was sanctification, and it was this process through which the Desert Fathers were made holy. This crucifixion of the fleshly self, the egoic self, continued until death. I felt that Father Theophan understood me, and that beyond that, he loved and accepted me exactly as I was. In response to my admission that I didn't feel worthy of the love and care he had for me, his face broke into a wide smile and he replied, "Oh, you are so worthy." On my request, he then told me the stories of St Mary of Egypt and St Mary Magdalene in greater detail, and I noticed that he seamlessly slipped into using the term "hypersexuality," which I had been using to describe my work with those dealing with the consequences of sexual abuse, rather than the biblical "harlotry." I found this a testament to both his intelligence and compassion. As I was leaving, he took his icon of St Mary of Egypt off the wall to show me and then placed it into my hands, to take home as a gift. He also gave me three books that he had written and explained that I needed to be gentle and not push myself too much during my stay.

Driving back to the monastery afterward, Sister Cherubima told me the story of the Samaritan woman, whose *five husbands* (Jn 4.18) symbolize the fruitlessness of using romantic love as a stand-in for the holy love of God. When Christ meets her at the well from which she has come to draw water, His divine searchlight exposes her spiritual malaise. Honing in on the root of her pain, He tells her that *whoever drinks of the water that I shall give him will never thirst* (Jn 4.14), because the water that He gives will become a *fountain of water springing up into everlasting life* (Jn 4.14). After she begins drinking *His* Holy Spirit, the emptiness she has been filling with romantic obsession is instead filled with God's divine love, and she never thirsts again.

"You know when we were reading Mark earlier," I turned to face her as she drove, "I suddenly realized how old the little girl was when she died—twelve years old." It was at this age that my bulimia started. It was also the age I was assaulted by a group of boys at my school.

"This is exactly what I felt as well!" she said.

"Whenever I would read this passage, I would always ask the Lord to bring you back, because I feel like it was at twelve that the devil really came into your life and took you."

She had been tenderly thinking about me and praying for me all this time. While Father was talking, I had also noticed that the timeline of St Mary of Egypt's story mapped exactly onto my own life—at twelve the destruction began and for seventeen years it lasted. As my sister spoke, more details of everything that had happened began to fall into place, and I realized that the idealized self-image that I held and imagined everyone else saw was not in fact what others experienced of me. My sister didn't think that I was fierce, free, and empowered. From her perspective I was a sick little girl who was under the devil's power. Surprisingly, this brought me peace. Throughout the day, a tiny gap had opened in my mind, allowing for the possibility that maybe everything *wasn't* sacred, that perhaps there *was*, in fact, absolute darkness, that maybe there was, after all, an enemy.

Back at the monastery I sat and chatted with some of the sisters by the front door. Sister Eleni and Mother Syncletica swept in, having completed a run of administrative jobs in the city.

"You're back!" Sister Eleni said in her melodic Californian.

"Missed you." She leaned against the back of my chair and put her hands on my shoulders.

"How did your meeting with Father go?" I turned in my chair to face up to her.

"Oh, I missed you too! And yes, it was just amazing."

"Oh yes," she said, gently sweeping her hand through my hair as she gazed down at me, "you're just *radiant*."

Purification

> *The ones who seek the divine gifts and insights while being immersed in the passions are in proud and foolish delusion. First, one needs to work on cleansing oneself. Grace is sent as a gift to those who are cleansed from the passions. And they get it quietly, at the moment that they don't notice.*
> —St Nektarios of Aegina

Father Theophan often talked about being cleansed, sanctified, and restored by the word of God. I began to understand that for Christians, Scripture was their "medicine." It was the healer. It was the purifier. It was the thing that transformed them. My sister had given me her small leather-bound Bible as a gift when I arrived, and following the meeting with Father, I felt a ferocious urge to read it. I didn't pick it up immediately, but I felt it in the corner of my room. It was alive. Father Theophan later told me that this was the Holy Spirit. He had also spoken to me about how through regular reading of the word of God, the entire physical, mental, and spiritual body can be redeemed. Then going on to read more regularly across the days that followed, I realized that every phrase was utterly beautiful, a poem in itself. This was the Bible? This was news to me . . .

During the times of personal study that then began to take place at Father's suggestion, I would feel the tender and loving power of the words wash over and through me. The idea of being transformed internally through the consuming of certain sacred words was, to my mind, similar to what I did with the Medicine Buddha *sādhanā*:[35] a sequential meditation executed through chanting and *mudra* (symbolic hand gestures used in

---

[35] *Sādhanā* is a spiritual practice designed to help the practitioner transcend the ego. It is found in Hindu, Buddhist, and Jain traditions.

ritual) that summons a spirit in order to merge with it—in this case Medicine Buddha, the healing Buddha. I was thrilled at this further evidence that Tibetan Buddhism and Christianity were "two sides of the same coin" and was excited to tell Nick. What was important about this comparison—which was later nullified by several fundamental points—was that it illuminated a dynamic whereby energy was being engaged for transformation. There was, of course, prayer in the Christianity of my childhood, as well as worship and teachings. But not *this* kind of prayer. There hadn't been any of this complex, multi-layered, liturgical *process*.

The Orthodox seemed to pray non-stop: Matins; the First, Third, Sixth, and Ninth Hours; Vespers; Compline; and the Midnight Office. On top of which was Scripture reading, prayer, and prostrations, and all different kinds of fasts, feasts, vigils, services, and Liturgies. Every day without fail the monastics took part in these prayers as a means of strengthening and purifying their internal landscape. Or, "girding the spirit" and "eradicating the passions," as Mother Syncletica put it. The more time I spent with them, the more the murderous, bloody, violent language of Christian asceticism entered my lexicon. By focusing their wills on God, the myriad and often conflicting drives of the self were tamed until eventually they were killed off completely—resulting in total obedience to God's holy will. Although the content of obedience was something I was familiar with as it was a part of some of the traditions I was involved in, the way Christians talked about it in such explicit terms made me uncomfortable. Why does God *want* me to submit to Him? Doesn't He want me to be empowered?

Following afternoon prayers the next day, a painful dynamic from the past arose between my sister and me. However, something new happened. Rather than defending my actions in response to her words, despite feeling that I was the one who had been hurt by the interaction and was justified in my reaction—the trigger for the distress—I knew that I needed to be quiet. If I could just put my needs to the side and allow her to share without saying anything, then I could demonstrate to her that I had really changed (we had been estranged for several years prior to my coming). As she spoke, both our eyes started to flood with tears, but I remained silent, allowing her to share everything and forcing myself to witness the pain that I had caused her. I felt the grace of the Lord in that moment, creating the space necessary for the healing to take place. After we spoke, I felt light, but I was also raw and exposed. I tried to continue on with the events of the day, but I couldn't move on from what had happened. Unable to stop the tears, I took refuge in the bathroom to cry alone. It felt cleansing. Sitting with Mother Syncletica that evening, she began to spontaneously speak to me about the Samaritan woman, the same Samaritan woman about whom my sister had shared.

As she spoke I felt as if several other chambers in my heart were being opened and the crying intensified.

"Sorry, I just—"

"I will leave you, so you can rest a bit," she said gently as she stood up. Sister Damaris, who was also wiping away tears, translated.

After they left, I completely lost control and went to my room. Face down on the floor I cried like I have never cried before. The Lord gave me an image of the wounding in my little sister's heart, and the intensity of the pain made me convulse. It was so intense. But it felt so good at the same time. Because it was the truth. True love. Christ showed me how my insecurity had hurt her. As a "left brained" introvert, she did not process emotions externally in the way that I did, and growing up I had often painted this aspect of her as deficient, unwell, and wrong, my rapid-fire psychoanalytic accusations running rings around her startled silence. I sobbed on as this image of her pain moved through my body. The Holy Spirit had dissolved a blockage in my heart.

PART ONE

Opening

If someone has come to know God by the Holy Spirit, his soul will burn with love for God day and night, and his soul cannot be bound to any earthly thing.
—St Silouan the Athonite

The monastery had a powerful ability to force pain and trauma that was buried within me to the surface. I was familiar with this process because this is precisely how the retreats and ceremonies I ran and attended worked. However, what was unusual was that the spiritual atmosphere was not mechanically generated through breathwork, movement, ingesting plants, invoking spirits, or as a result of being immersed in nature. There was just a consistent sense of peace and safety. The morning vigil held by the nuns at four contributed to this, as I would be woken by their angelic singing at the end of their prayers. I felt like I was waking up in heaven. Then I bought some earplugs. I wasn't quite ready to get up before dawn. I was also getting used to the materials the Orthodox used to consecrate their spaces and observed their equivalents in the world I came from. They used golden censers to burn frankincense, myrrh, and rose, while I used clay, ceramic, or wood with copal, sage, and pine. They prayed to the Father, Son, and Holy Spirit; I, immersed in Native traditions, to Creator, Great Spirit, Great Mystery. They repented for their sin. I purified my karma. I was delighted to come across Orthodoxy's doctrine of *theosis*—the sacred union between God and humanity—the *marriage supper* (Rev 19.9) of the Bridegroom and the Bride.

To my mind, it was simply the Christian version of the dissolution of duality that all the spiritual traditions I followed were geared toward, none more so than Buddhism. My sister explained that what differentiated it from eastern traditions, was that rather than union through self-generated revelation of inherent divinity, there was instead grace-driven deification through the relationship between human activity and God's uncreated energy. She emphasized that the Christian merging did not eradicate the unique imprint of either the human person or God. Her correction of my understanding irritated me, but I managed to maintain equilibrium, increasingly aware of how arrogant and touchy I was. The monastery was exposing subtle behaviors through one event after the other. Conscious of the pain my mood swings had caused people in the past, I was determined to become humbler and for this defensiveness to die a quick death.

I was softly falling in love with the mystery of Orthodoxy, of the ancient faith—the gift Christ had given the world through His crucifixion. I loved its depth, its beauty, and its emphasis on contemplation and meditating on the Scriptures. I was becoming accustomed to standing in my cell for hours on end, reading the Bible, or doing the Jesus Prayer with prostrations.[36] I loved the discipline and the severity and the way the entire Liturgy was sung. I loved the ruthless self-denial, the purification through asceticism, the "eating" of the holy Scriptures and how Christians, much to my surprise, seemed to be the ones who were actually going through the ego death process that New Agers were so fond of talking about. According to my vocabulary at the time, Orthodoxy appeared to me to approach spirituality almost . . . shamanically. They burned incense to purify spaces. There was an awareness of how thoughts affect the material world. They fasted. They prayed for hours on end. They held vigils all through the night. Music was present on every occasion. Healing was taking place constantly, though this was rarely processed verbally as it was in my world.

What was entirely new to me, was that everything, every single thing, was stated in relationship to God. Nothing positive that took place was *ever*

---

[36] *Lord Jesus Christ, Son of God, have mercy on me, a sinner.* The Jesus Prayer is central to the *hesychastic* tradition of Eastern Christianity, in which believers seek *hēsychia* (divine quietness) through contemplation of God in uninterrupted prayer. The prayer is repeated both aloud and internally, when sitting or during activity.

due to personal merit. It was always from God. God was the only source of goodness. I first encountered this self-displacement at the monastery with Sister Veroniki, where asking the monastics how they were would be met with, "Thanks to God, I am good," or simply, "Thanks to God," and a firm nod of the head. Here in America, this continued on. A typical response to a compliment would be something like "God gives us the ability to try, we fail, but His grace carries us through." Whoa. Sister Eleni's reply to my request that she tell me her life story was, "It's very boring." Any postulated future activity would always be prefixed with, "God willing." If something good happened it was because of God's grace. If something bad happened (following attribution to the enemy or the "power of the flesh"), gratitude would be given for the opportunity to partake in the Lord's holy suffering. Things didn't "fall into place"; God put them in place. Things didn't just happen. God *made* them happen.

I started to notice how my vocabulary was drenched with phrases that elevated the self. No one self-healed in Christianity. God healed. No one manifested in Christianity. God gave. We weren't gods and goddesses. We were helpless humans. We weren't the sacred source of reality. Our spiritual blindness inhibited us from comprehending the truth of reality. The answer wasn't within; the answer was the word of God. We weren't the creative source of life. We were created. We weren't divine. We were sinful. They didn't talk about the strength of their spirit or their force. They talked about their lack of spiritual progress and their weakness. Positive feedback was rationed to diminish the possibility of igniting vainglory. In my world, you were encouraged to follow your heart at all costs. But the monastics followed the Bible's teaching that the heart is corrupt and that you should obey God's commandments. The concept of posting pictures of oneself praying online was incomprehensible. It would attract demonic attack in the form of vanity. "Liking" someone's self-congratulatory social media post would cause them to sin by encouraging pride. This was humility. *This* was spirituality.

Goddess Complex

For all have sinned and fall short of the glory of God.
—Romans 3.23

The day began at four, and I attended the entire morning vigil. After my jetlag wore off, I started to sleep later and would normally miss the whole thing. In the days before the feast of Nativity, however, I would inadvertently wake at the same time as the nuns and try as I might, I could not go back to sleep after they began. I felt that it was a signal from the Holy Spirit that it was time for me to begin developing these muscles, and so I surrendered to it. There was something exhilarating about getting up this early to pray, watching the sun rise as the day dawned. Afterward the sisters would return to their cells while I stayed awake doing yoga stretches (the chronic back pain continued).

On Father Theophan's instruction, I took breaks from the daily activity, and if I had done enough work on my back to be able to lie still without too much discomfort, I would read one of Father Theophan's books. Reading about knowing and experiencing God, I winced at the mention of how the increase in homosexuality and abortion was being used by the enemy (a concept I was still troubled by) to destroy humanity. I loved and trusted Father with all my heart, and I was not surprised by the perspective—I had been brought up by a pro-life campaigning Christian—but it made me angry that it would be presented in this way. Although I had left some aspects of feminism behind on entering the spirit world, I was still very much dedicated to serving women in every way. I considered myself a "sacred feminist," someone who works for equality but who believes that such work will only be realized through coming to an understanding that life is sacred, and that it is only through relationship with the divine that true gender equality will be achieved. I never thought that abortion was *good*, but I vehemently believed that women had a right to *choose*.

PART ONE

Growing up, I had been enraged by the obsession that Christians seemed to have with abortion. I just couldn't get my head around marching for unborn babies but not marching against wars where thousands of women and children—and unborn babies—were killed every day. Or being pro-life while also being pro-capital punishment, pro-torture, or pro-whatever other violent thing, Christians (self-proclaimed at least) inexplicably seemed to fervently support. Or dedicating one's entire life to preventing abortions—the result of which was unsafe abortions, incredibly hard lives of single motherhood, having to carry the child of one's rapist, expensive private abortions, or in some cases death—while seeming to have no particular care for women's wellbeing or health outside of this, or of gender justice in general. It seemed to me that pro-lifers spent more time trying to prevent abortions than they did trying to help women. In those days I saw the Church as a whole as a mafia that profiteered from pedophilia, as a result of what had taken place in the Roman Catholic Church. The subjection of women to this constant stream of abuse, judgment, and legislation without infrastructure had an almost fetishistic quality to it. The fact that it was the same institution that had colluded with *clergy who raped children* was a hypocrisy I couldn't accept.

Entering into the world of healing, my awareness of the sanctity of life increased, and I no longer held abortion to be a right. Although the concept of a "human right" was always held up to scrutiny within academic feminism, in general parlance and popular feminism it was commonplace. Entering into the spirit world, the discourse around rights fell away totally to be replaced by the idea that everything in life was a gift. However, this was only within the respectful confines of the medicine world. Within the context of secular culture—which historically subjugated, terrorized, and marginalized the tribes from whom these teachings derived—the discourse of rights was used to fight for protective legislation. It was only through campaigning and advocating for rights that indigenous cultures had any hope of being protected from the theft and abuse of governments the world over.

Within the spirit world, childbearing, birth, maternity, and motherhood were revered as divine. However, people still got abortions and my clients with abortion trauma, in which the abortion itself had often taken place before they began exploring their spirituality, were numerous. I was always surprised when women from within my community got abortions *after* beginning their spiritual walk, but my focus was always on how I could support them. A lot of the healing work I did was about helping to heal and integrate the blockages (physical, emotional, and spiritual) that resulted from abortion. As my practice evolved and intensified, I started performing healings in which I would help them integrate the trauma of the abortion. I would "extract" the imprint of the fetus that was lodged in their spiritual body, which I saw as being the thing causing blockage, guilt, grief, or lack of abundance, guide them through the process of mourning and letting go, and I would then return the fetus back to its source. The matrix I used for my channeling work acted like a vacuum that would suck out impurities, entities, energetic debris, and the psychic imprint of the aborted fetus. I would watch them be hoovered out of the person by the spirits, to be metabolized.

The client would then be left clear(er) of the trauma and would be able to continue on, freed from guilt and with energy flowing in the area where there had previously been density in the tissue, on however subtle a level. I would use my voice to help guide the energy and would go into a trance, telling the person what I was seeing and its connection to their ancestral line, which I would also be cleansing, while singing different songs that would encourage healing. Sometimes all of this would be done while I sat in meditation. Later I integrated this into deep massage, working on their lower abdominal area with my hands, while doing all the above. While I lay on my bed reading Father Theophan's book, I still held what I did to be a force for good in the world and considered that the spiritual power that led me in this work was the same Holy Spirit that was moving through them as they prayed in the chapel.

The Heart

Behold, I stand at the door and knock.
—Revelation 3.20

After falling asleep during the break between services, I returned to the communal area of the monastery to join everyone. It was the thirty-first of December. At a small table in the center of the room, Father Theophan, who was visiting the monastery for the day, spoke as one of the nuns translated. The way they sat and organized themselves was in itself a lesson in courtesy and humility. Although I tried to work with people who were humble and focused on supporting indigenous communities, an unfortunate number of wounded people consumed by a need to dominate others took leadership roles in the more promiscuous and money-focused side of the medicine world. You always knew when you were in their orbit because everyone else's insecurity would be triggered, and a subtle (or sometimes not) atmosphere of performance prevailed.

Before coming to America, I had started to get a group of women together to begin calling this behavior out through our interconnected communication networks. Everyone was getting fed up with the proliferating scandals and the shame they were bringing on the medicine's name. I knew, however, that my narcissistic desire for attention, acknowledgement, and social power, meant that I was very susceptible to the charms of these personalities, and so I avoided their circles, having learned some hard lessons at the start of my journey. Entering into the sanctuary of Christ's domain, the atmosphere was completely different. The monastics went about their actions with reverence and modesty. Heads bowed rather than heads held high. In the world I inhabited, "meek" was not an adjective that people readily associated with themselves. Powerful? Sure. Wild? Frequently. Strong? Of course. But meek? That would be no. Meek meant subservience. Meek meant not knowing all the answers. Meek meant . . . weak.

Father Theophan spoke about being cleansed through prayer, and as he was talking, I realized that Christ was requesting to enter within me, in order that I could be sanctified. I felt like I was learning about the extent of Christ's transformative power for the first time. I had never heard anyone speak about how Christ's godliness worked in our beings in a methodical, all-encompassing, restorative way before. That *He* would move through every part of us, redeeming and transforming everything within us that was broken and in need of cleansing. It was the (perceived) lack of all of the above available to me growing up in the pretty much secular, but still vaguely Christian, modern West, that drove me to seek out healing in other cultures, traditions, and practices. Suddenly everything I had been working toward was being offered to me. But through Christ! Because what differentiated what Father Theophan was saying from the impersonal pagan conception of transformation, was that this cleansing and sanctification was specific to Christ—it came through Christ and Christ alone.

He then continued to explain that we needed to yield to Christ's request to enter our hearts. He would approach every person's heart, and it was up to us, whether we would permit Him to enter, in order that He could do His therapeutic work. You could not do it yourself. My whole world revolved around everything coming from the self. The higher self, yes, but the self: self-healing, self-care, self-realization . . . My worldview was predicated on the idea that we have within us everything that we need to become an enlightened, all-powerful, divine being who has the capacity to create reality, overcome adversity, eliminate suffering, and to even conquer death. In other words—to become God.

As Father spoke, the depth of Christianity opened up before me. It is an infinite depth. So *this* is what it means to be *born again* (Jn 3.3). To let go and accept Christ meant to really, truly, and completely die to who we were. To die to the identity we have been holding on to. Holding onto so tightly. Father Theophan spoke about Christ's indwelling and how the

PART ONE

deeper He cleansed and purified, the more we were able to grow spiritually. Elevated to this position we would then be able to partake of the heavenly joy, joining the saints and the angels. Although some people in my community spoke about heaven, people tended to use other terms to denote the afterlife, which didn't carry the same triggering religious connotations. I suddenly felt the reality of the pain and suffering within me and how much I needed cleansing. Despite my line of work, I was not at peace. I was not whole. Father Theophan's words caused a shift in my perception. An awareness of what redemption in Christ truly meant, and what Christianity was actually about, took root within me. Instead of seeing Jesus as a discrete entity in the midst of a vast spiritual expanse, I suddenly saw *Him* as the vast, atemporal cosmic expanse, out of which the spirits (with their associated religions) emanated, and to whom all were subject.

Father Theophan continued speaking, and I began to have a vision. Death. In a huge dark space a large boat with many different levels floated into view. The color of the space, if space can have a color, was a deep, dark brown, and the boat was gold, but completely transparent. I understood that the boat had arrived to carry us to judgment. After being transported across the formless expanse, it presented us before Jesus. He was gold, but the gold was not static or hard. It was shimmering, as if made up of trillions of distinct particles of light. Everything in Him was alive and glimmering. Everything else was dark. He was seated on a throne, and before Him stood the space of judgment. His left forearm was raised, and His head rested in His hand. He looked deeply distressed, weary with the reality of what was taking place. The just judgment of His children. He emanated grief, and I could hear a sound, a kind of groaning, radiating from the pain in His heart as He sat on His throne. It was so real. It was the truth.

The vision completely contradicted everything I had been learning in my Buddhist studies. The *bardo*—the intermediate stage between death and rebirth—is central to Tibetan Buddhism. Through disciplined meditative practice, the student aims to control the stages of his or her death process in order to influence his or her rebirth. For those who are more advanced, possibilities would begin to open whereby one would also be able to influence other people's death process. The lama I had been studying under was qualified to practice *phowa*, an advanced Tantric practice of this kind, whereby the practitioner controls where he or she goes during and after death. This process can also be performed (for a price) on behalf of a less spiritually advanced deceased person as a post-mortem ritual. The fact that our teacher could do this was held by us as a mark of his proficiency. It was considered a skill that far exceeded the highest hopes of most Buddhists. To master death was the crème de la crème of Tibetan Buddhism. It was to master all. Or so I had been taught. But there was none of this here. No masters. No methods of transcending death. No godlike tantric adepts. Everyone was simply human. *Everyone* was under judgment.

He Revealed Himself to Me

The human spirit lies open to God alone, for it is a fathomless depth.
—St Seraphim of Sarov

Father Theophan returned the next day, in order to spend more time with the nuns. I was beginning to understand that he was not normally around as much as he was during this particular period, which was why the daily schedule of the monastery had been changed, to accommodate his visits. That afternoon I returned to the chapel, in order to have some time of quiet reflection. Above the chapel altar, there was a large icon of Jesus looking out into the room. I started to look into Christ's eyes, and after several seconds the icon started to talk to me, "Tali, Tali, Tali." Immediately a shift took place and I felt that I was in a continuum with the Christ of the icon. It was as if He were speaking to me directly, and there was nothing separating the reality of what was inside that icon from what was holding me in place in the room. I then saw Him take me up into His arms and hug me, His stature enveloping me. I was not able to see His face directly—it was as if I were standing diagonally to the side of Him and the person He was hugging.

In the vision I was hysterically crying, wracked with grief. He continued to hold me firmly and steadily as I manically writhed around in His arms, resisting His love. I couldn't let Him hold me because it was too painful. The strength of His love hurt too much. But He remained steady and continued to hold me. Impurities started to come out of my body. His love was forcing them out of me. He continued to hold me as more and more of this dark matter lifted up off the surface of my body. I watched myself being held by Him, weeping. I felt that He was showing me how He had removed the seven demons from Mary Magdalene (Mk 16.9; Lk 8.2). With the information I now had regarding the process of sanctification, I wondered if the removal of these seven demons was symbolic of how Mary had allowed Jesus to enter every part of her in one movement, precipitating a total and completely unique transformation.

Growing up in an Evangelical household, we had often had communion services at home. With Orthodoxy it was different—only a priest could prepare the Eucharist. Attending a Liturgy that evening, a very strong sense of the Holy Spirit began to overwhelm me. Every Liturgy we had attended had been very special, but this evening, all my senses were electrified, and I was alive to every sound, taste, and scent. I watched the nuns take Communion and thought about the way in which the pagan "sacraments" of the different plants were distributed by the shaman. Although this context was obviously new, the process generated the same atmosphere of heightened awareness and hyper-focus. As the nuns returned to where we were sitting, Sister Cherubima walked up to me and silently pressed some blessed bread into my hand.[37] I put it in my mouth

---

[37] Blessed bread, called *antidōron* in Greek, is given to communicants after receiving Communion and is also distributed at the end of the Divine Liturgy. It is not Holy Communion, but it is blessed and holy (unlike Communion, it is often shared with non-Orthodox who attend the Liturgy).

and as I swallowed, I began to feel the bread vibrate as it moved down my throat. Intense heat then expanded out from my stomach, warming my entire body. My whole body began to shake, my vision became blurred, and I broke down in tears.

The third vision then opened from the bread inside me. I could see the world before me, suspended in space. Out of the right side of my vision, a huge cross started to descend from heaven toward the earth, as if moving on top of me and then lowering in front of me, so that I was looking down at it. Jesus was spread upon the cross, and He was looking up toward heaven. As the cross moved through the cosmic expanse toward the earth, it caused intense waves in the atmosphere and everything shuddered and quaked. The cross started to spin as it continued its downward descent, the outstretched arms creating vortexes of energy on either side that spiraled out into space. The cross then penetrated the earth's surface, causing the whole planet to shake. Fire, rock, and rubble exploded outward at the point it pierced. The base of the cross drove down into the earth's surface, drilling through it as it continued to rapidly spin.

I then heard the words, "I am the root, I am the ground, I am *the* nature . . . I AM." It was not audible to anyone else. My entire body was vibrating with the vision and in that moment I understood. Jesus is God. God is the Creator. Creation, although of God, is separate from Him. It alone cannot save. My understanding of nature immediately, completely, and irreversibly shifted in that moment. Jesus is the Lord of nature. He is the King of kings and Lord of lords. Nature exists in—and because of—Him, but He far exceeds it. Nature is created. He is *uncreated*. Through Him, and through Him only, could I be one with nature, because *He* is the source of nature. *He* is Mother Nature. He is the source of *all* life. My eyes opened.

PART ONE

Vision

The physical world is morally neutral and may be known relatively well by an objective observer, but the invisible spiritual realm comprises beings both good and evil, and the "objective" observer has no means of distinguishing one from the other unless he accepts the revelation which the invisible God has made of them to man.

—Fr Seraphim Rose

I was overcome by a sense of my sin. I knew I had sinned against God. I had rejected Him and His word. Deceived, I had lied. I was a false prophet. Later standing in my cell, I started to pray. As I began to speak, my voice broke, and I started to sob, "Heavenly Father, I stand before You so naked. I have sinned. I have sinned against You. I have rejected Your love because of my pride. I have even hated You. Please forgive me. I am so sorry. I love You. I give my life to You." Later I heard the nuns discussing "nakedness" and the need for spiritual clothing, and I realized there was a theological discrepancy between our understanding. As a nature dweller, I saw nakedness as a good thing. When I had prayed about being naked, I had said it with the intention of communicating that I was exposed and vulnerable, that I was raw and honest before God, but not that I needed to be clothed. I had meant that I was free. But when the nuns discussed their need to be clothed in spiritual garments, it was in reference to Adam and Eve in Eden and the skin coverings God made for them to hide their nakedness (Gen 3.21), apparent to eyes that had been opened by sin. But maybe it didn't matter. I was praying to the Father—remembering that Fr Theophan said He does not heed spoken words, but rather the words of our hearts. My heart was broken, and I was sure that God could feel it.

Through these visions, the deception I had been living under was exposed. Following the earlier visionary experiences prior to coming to the monastery and what was happening now, there was a shift in their breadth and depth. I could see three stages of visionary experience, each one distinct from the one before. The visions that I had experienced through plants, magic, and psychic empowerment, all had a unifying quality (even if their content differed from tradition to tradition). Although up until that point I hadn't experienced them as such, they suddenly seemed "horizontal" and finite. Their range—although including multiple dimensions, portals, and realms—was limited to the cosmos.

Obviously the cosmos is beyond our spatial understanding, which is why people feel that these visionary experiences reach as far as can be reached. These visions also tended to involve a kaleidoscope of colors, patterns, and different vibrational frequencies specific to the geographical or spirit-world dominion of the power they served. The visions I then experienced once Jesus entered into this sphere differed simply in that He was present in them. The atmosphere remained the same, but He was absolutely nothing like any of the other supernatural creatures, gods, goddesses, spirits, symbols, or structures that frequented my spirit-contact experiences. Following the womb-healing vision in the church and what followed in the retreat, this then changed.

The veil that had been obscuring my sight was completely lifted. There was now a uniformity to the visions that separated them from everything before. My pagan visions had the quality of fluorescent light amidst darkness. But now everything was gold. No other animals or spirits were ever present. What differentiated these visions is that they were *heavenly*. These visions felt far beyond the scope of my perspective, as if I were just getting a glimpse into something much, much bigger. I had no control over what happened within them. I couldn't visualize anything into being, or guide the spirit who was manifesting, or cause one aspect of the vision to expand by honing in on it. There was also a stillness to them, and a vastness. Suddenly everything was turned on its head. As a pagan, I had held the visionary experiences of the plants and traditions I had been part of as the supreme knowledge. Knowledge that was hidden from the uninitiated. But in Christianity nothing was hidden. The truth wasn't a secret; it wasn't *occult*.

Although I was accepting of Christianity in a general way, because I believed all devotion pointed to love, I felt that the religious images, symbolism, and teachings of Christianity buried—in an effort to dominate—the original truth of the spirituality of the world, each country having its own primordial tradition. The native practices of the West were considered to have been in decay for longer than those of less modernized areas of the world, because of the spread of Christianity, but they were understood to still exist, if only often in a fragmentary state. Recovering these ancient practices was my life's work.

But now this tightly held dichotomy between authentic, nature-based spirituality and false, man-made Christianity had been shattered. Actually, Jesus was the source. *Christianity* was the source. The earth and all that was in it came later, out of Christ, as a result of Christ and not vice versa. I thought about Genesis, *In the beginning God created the heavens and the earth* (Gen 1.1). Although Christ became incarnate thousands of years after creation, He existed before the world was even created because *All who dwell on the earth will worship Him . . . the Lamb slain from the foundation of the world* (Rev 13.8). I now understood the true meaning of the verse, *All things were created through Him and for Him* (Col 1.16).

A vision from Christ is not a Christian version of the visions that come through paganism. A vision from Christ is the *original* vision. It comes from the uncreated light of Christ. These visions are what the enemy tries to replicate in the many false religions he uses to distract us from coming into contact with Christ. I thought back to the vision I had experienced during the ritual healing with Terrence, when in Mexico. It was a very powerful experience. There is only one problem. No Jesus. At the time this vision made sense to me within my spiritual context. Looking back at it following this encounter with Christ, however, it's a clear example of how the deception works. Its harmful power is not in that it is always explicitly against Jesus, but that it suggests that redemption and genuine healing are possible without Him. Likewise for all the other religions I had come into contact with. Through this I understood. Christ's visions were the blueprint. All other visions were *counterfeits*.

Throughout my stay at the monastery, I had been looking at the online profile of Doreen Virtue, a former New Age psychic whose conversion to Christianity had caused shock waves in the alternative community. She was fairly famous for her tarot cards and had authored multiple books on angel communication. All of her posts were Christian, but it was not the syncretistic Christianity she had espoused before her conversion. She spoke about how she'd had a vision of Christ and had converted immediately, as a result. When I first heard about her conversion, I thought it was strange, but that there was also something wonderful about it. But visiting her page soon after and seeing the Sunday school images of Jesus surrounded by flocks of lambs, I was overcome by the same sense of claustrophobia and nausea that I then experienced during the first visions with Christ in London.

Following what took place at the retreat, however, I returned to her profile and suddenly everything that she was saying made sense. Her posts started to convict me. Direct in her approach to spreading the gospel, she shared message after message about the deception of the New Age versus the truth of the Bible. Although I had hoped to be offline during the retreat, I considered it topical reading. Her conversion and evangelism were still causing shocked, baffled, and incredulous online responses in the pagan community. Generally, everyone was saying that she had gone completely insane and yet, there I was, agreeing with everything that she was saying! She frequently quoted Deuteronomy on practicing magic and as I read, I felt as if I were being slammed in the face. Witchcraft garners its energy from the devil. It is evil. It was like waking up from a dream. What was I if not a witch? God did not differentiate between white magic or black magic, between healing or *brujeria*[38] (witchcraft) as

---

[38] *Brujeria* is the Spanish term colloquially used within the pagan world to describe witchcraft that is negative in intention. Most people considered themselves to be invested

we did in my community—all magic was strictly forbidden and was *an abomination* (Deut 18.10) to the Lord.

Light

I am the light of the world. He who follows Me shall not walk in darkness, but have the light of life.
—John 8.12

After seeing Christ, everything else became dark. All the different roads I had been walking were suddenly exposed for what they truly were—roads to death. I saw the different traditions as different paths interlinking and weaving, all pushing toward the same direction: heaven in the distance. But rather than that being the final point, as it had been before this encounter with Christ, I now saw a boundary that stood between the end point of the paths and heaven. At this point, the roads that were not directed toward Christ all violently swerved to the left. It was only those on the path that led to Christ who then moved forward into heaven. Everyone else went to hell. Driving back from the retreat, a client who owed me payment for a womb healing sent me a message saying that she had transferred the money. I messaged her back immediately. "Please send me your bank details. I am sending the money back to you. Thanks for understanding." I didn't explain any more. She messaged back asking if I was sure. Yes. I knew I couldn't accept the money. Now that I had encountered the true light of Christ—the real, holy, original, pure, and loving

---

in healing only—so too with black magic and white magic. However, witchcraft was not seen as a bad thing in and of itself: the ethical value of any magical act was determined by the intention and outcome, not from the practice itself, for the simple reason that all spirituality was considered to be magic. Furthermore, the term "witch" was an honorific given to many of the elders and employed, partly for political reasons, by many women for self-descriptive purposes.

light of heaven—I was starting to see the light of my world as something else—darkness in disguise.

Later that night, the scales fell from my eyes (at that point I also learned that this saying comes from the Bible). I looked at my websites, one for the wild feminine retreats and the other for my individual sessions, and I felt estranged from their contents in a way that I never had before. On my wild feminine website, I had hundreds of photos taken by an artist friend with whom I worked. Although the natural landscapes were beautiful, and the photos themselves were formally gorgeous, as I sat flicking through the images, it was as if all the life had been drained out of them. Instead of the fire spirit that I had lovingly tended, and to which I had sung, I suddenly saw a very powerful demon hiding amidst the flames, aping the presence of God. Recollecting memories of channeling chants in ceremony, a practice that used to bring me immense joy, I became aware of what was taking place spiritually. High ranking spirits in the unseen realm used plants to locate, groom, and then work through humans in order to extend their spiritual tentacles down into the manifest world. The fragile egos, auras, and boundaries of the traumatized people who worked with medicine or came for healing made it all the more easy for them to disseminate this supernatural knowledge through them. As I looked at the photos, I saw my healing work through new eyes. It had not been helping the women I served in the way that I had thought it had. Because only God could heal. It could only come through Christ.

I stood up from my laptop and walked to the doorway of my room. It was about ten in the evening. Most of the nuns had gone upstairs to their sleeping quarters. The guest rooms were the only bedrooms that were on the ground floor. I was the only guest. Someone was in the kitchen, turning off the lights. I heard the final click as Sister Cherubima emerged out of the darkness. She was carrying a tall, plastic cup and holding a phone charger. She looked at me and waved silently before beginning to ascend the staircase. She stopped and turned.

"Are you okay, Tal?" she asked, her brow furrowed. I was just standing there, staring at her in silence.

Was I? I didn't know. I felt . . . strange.

"Yeah . . ." I answered, and then nodded with vigor.

"Okay," she turned. "Night."

I watched as she walked up the stairs. And then she was gone. I looked across the tiled floors to the chapel. All the lights were now off, except for the overhead lights in the atrium that connected the guest bedrooms to the chapel. Across from the bedroom door was a wall of black glass. I stared at my reflection and then went back inside the room. Getting ready for bed, I dressed as quickly as possible and curled up into a ball under the covers, looking out into the room until I fell asleep. I usually slept on my other side, but I couldn't leave my back exposed that night. I needed to face the room as I fell asleep.

The next day, my understanding of the channeling work I did completely flipped. I had received many initiations connecting every cell of my body to the spirits I served. My entire system was overrun by these forces. During the most recent training, we had been empowered to work with a particularly powerful angel. I began to research him, checking the online explanations against the Bible itself, as instructed by Doreen Virtue, who had gone through a similar process with some of the angels she had previously communicated with in her work. I came across site after site that would begin with biblical verses about the angel, but which would then broaden out into different New Age descriptions and histories of the angel that clearly had nothing to do with the Scriptures. I loved healing with this spirit as the power he gave me in sessions brought very potent results. After I had been initiated to work with him, I had noticed a big shift in my practice, which was then confirmed by the intensity that he brought to the sessions I did while under his power. But I now knew that this spirit I had been worshiping was not a biblical angel. He was not one of God's angels. Therefore, he, *it*, was a foreign *spirit*. In other words, it was a *demon*.

A chill moved through my body as the reality of what I was connected to dawned on me. I messaged Father Theophan telling him what I had realized, and I asked if I could be baptized as soon as possible. He responded immediately, telling me that he was so happy to hear what I was saying. When he had first seen my website earlier that year, he had been extremely alarmed and deeply troubled by what I was doing but "dared not" say anything, for risk of offending me. I was completely astonished by his self-control and trust that Christ would reveal the truth to me at the right time. Plans for me to be baptized were put into place.

However, I was very unnerved by what I had been shown, and I felt on edge. It was less noticeable in the daytime, but that evening, as soon as it began to get dark, the awareness that I had been immersed in a tangibly real spiritual underworld rose up inside me. As I began to fall asleep that night, I felt the presence of a dark figure outside my window, black from head to toe. It wore armor, totally covering its face and neck, and a black, floor-length cloak. But it was not made of any kind of material from this world. It wasn't human. It was all of an alien substance. It stood outside the ground-floor window watching me through the shutters and breathing heavily through the grates that covered its face. I knew that it had been sent by the power that controlled the channeling lineage I was part of. My former master, furious that I had given my life to Jesus, had sent this servant to scare me. I lay completely still, repeating Jesus' name. I was terrified, but I knew I was safe. It was finished. Christ had rescued me. I was free.

Heresy

God became man, that man might become God.
—St Athanasius the Great

Over the next few days I continued to research my former world, trying to make sense of what had happened. I listened to Doreen Virtue interviewing Christians regarding the way occult practices had intercepted Christianity. I read her posts on yoga, meditation, Reiki, astrology, tarot, and channeling, and I looked up everything that I had been studying.

PART ONE

Everything that she and the people she interviewed said made total and complete sense to me. Everything that was being said would sound completely insane to everyone I knew, including my boyfriend. I came across a chilling website that detailed the process of energy harvesting in tantra. The website interweaved the tantra of Gnostic Christianity with that of Tibetan Buddhism, and it was very specific to the teachings Nick and I had been receiving from our lama. The website talked about the seven churches and how they pertained to the seven chakras. It was similar to that of New Age Hinduism, which taught about the biblical creation story in relation to the chakras. So this is how the enemy worked. He created counterfeit religions around false gods that simulated the journey of the human soul, from separation to union with God. But they're fake. Because Christ is the only means through which the human can bridge that separation. He is the only way *back* to God. He alone offers eternal life.

Although Nick welcomed what I was sharing, the Buddhist dissonance posed a problem. I held back as much as possible when we spoke, as I didn't want to hurt his feelings, but I was very freaked out by what the Lord had shown me: Tibetan Buddhism was in essence death magic. It was all about death. On that everyone could agree, as this aspect wasn't hidden. But what was different was that I now no longer saw death as sacred and beautiful. Death was a result of sin, and sin came from the devil. It was not holy. *Life* was holy. As I continued praying and processing, I realized that all eastern religions were actually different methods of magic. Anything to do with reincarnation and empowerment equated to magic because it worked with spiritual energy that was not sanctified by God. It was just a more refined form of magic—working with different principalities and powers—than that practiced in elemental witchcraft. Although God looks at the person's heart, according to the holy Scriptures, the practices themselves are all evil in the eyes of God. They are evil because they draw their power from the satanic realm.

I had three different upcoming retreats and as a result, the people I was working with were contacting me, so we could book planning meetings. I couldn't do any of them. They were all connected to the realm of darkness. Even the women's retreat that I had coming up, which was centered around Mary Magdalene, which was so dear to my heart, would not be possible. Everything involved magic. I wondered if I could do them without practicing magic, as I didn't want to let everyone down, but it would never work. I had to cancel everything. *Everything*. It took me several hours of difficult conversations, but the Lord poured His grace down into every interaction. Everyone was very understanding, responding with enthusiastic open-heartedness, typical to those I was close to in my community. And then it was done. I also responded to many messages from people requesting links and leads for magical practices in different countries to help them on their journey. This was something that I had always loved doing, but newly aware that I had actually been inhibiting people from coming to know the true God, I responded, saying I was no longer involved in that world. I told them I had given my life to Jesus, and I recommended the spirituality of Christ and the early Church! Such is the aversion of my community to Christ that most didn't even respond.

Joining the nuns, I approached the kitchen island at which Mother Syncletica was standing with Sister Eleni and Sister Damaris. They were peeling grapefruits from the tree in the garden. Every time Mother Syncletica dug her oval thumbnail into the skin, a light mist of the acidic juice escaped, coating the front of her hand and the counter beneath it.

"Talitha *habibi*! How are you?" I glanced at Sister Eleni and pointed from myself to Mother Syncletica, to see if she would be happy to translate.

"Um, so, there are many amazing things. But also, I am just . . . realizing so much!" Sister Eleni translated into Arabic. Mother looked at me and nodded in encouragement.

"I've suddenly realized that I have been practicing witchcraft. For *years*." As I said the word "witchcraft," she crossed herself, observing me with her penetrating gaze.

"Well, not *witchcraft*, witchcraft, like, I wasn't practicing sorcery *on* people, I wasn't hurting people, you know, I mean, just, all these pagan practices, they're magic, they're . . . witchcraft."

Sister Eleni was translating and was quick to communicate the nuance. Mother Syncletica nodded to indicate her understanding.

"Don't worry, don't worry, I understand," she said in English. She then began to speak in Arabic, and Sister Eleni translated.

"When I first met you with, I kept very quiet. I was listening and asking, 'Jesus, Jesus, please show me where she is bound,' so that I knew what I needed to pray for."

She put down the grapefruit and placed both hands down on the counter, shifting her weight from one foot to the other.

"The Lord showed me something of this," she indicated with her hand, "and I began to pray that He would reveal the truth to you."

She had been praying for me all this time! The sense of being held and known by her and Father Theophan to the point that they cared enough about my wellbeing to dedicate their private prayer time, free of charge, to my salvation, was another demonstration, amongst the many that were taking place, of Christ's incomprehensible love.

"And now He is showing you! Glory to God!" Sister Eleni translated, smiling.

Another sister approached and began to ask Mother Syncletica about elements of the schedule for the upcoming months. Spirituality and administration were never far apart in the monastery. Mother Syncletica responded to her questions and then turned back to me and began again:

"Were it not for the fact that you have to leave because of all the work you have coming up, I would invite you to stay with us for everything—"

"But that's the thing," I cut in.

"I have canceled everything. Everything that I had planned. All the retreats. All my work. It's . . . over." She stared at me, shocked.

"*Everything?*" Then triumphant.

"You are like Matthew the tax collector!" Her eyes filled with tears and she grinned. Then her face became serious and she looked into my eyes.

"This . . . *this* is Jesus."

The Jesus Way

But the water that I shall give him will become in him a fountain of water springing up into everlasting life.
—John 4.14

The future had radically changed shape. Although we cannot fully know what the future holds, our plans do to some extent dictate the events that are going to follow. Multiple things were ahead of me, but the thing that had been held as most certain of all, was the continuation of my relationship with Nick. But suddenly everything was different. Everything had been transformed in the fire of God's grace. I felt like my entire life had been scorched by Jesus' divine light, and the only elements that now lived were those that were acceptable to Him. My life no longer belonged to me. In that moment of conversion I had given it to the Lord. It was a sense of total liberation. I had lost my life, and in losing it, I had become free.

It was in light of this that a totally new horizon opened up before me. It was stunningly beautiful and determined entirely by Jesus: His will for my life, His commandments for humanity, and His principles as laid out in the Scriptures. Everything just felt so clear. In the case of my relationship with Nick, painfully so. Unless he was willing to join me in this, I would be going into this new life without him. An argument between us later ensued after an evening Liturgy. I mentioned that I had read the article about hostile magic in Tibetan Buddhism and was now able to comprehensively understand the tantric deities and spirits we worshiped as a result. I didn't mean to say it. It just slipped out. My boyfriend pleaded with me to prefix my views with, "My belief is this, and my belief is that." This was, of course, a totally reasonable request. Having come into contact with the living reality of Jesus Christ, however, there was in my mind no doubt *whatsoever* that He was the truth. I *knew* He was the truth.

Buddhism's refusal to acknowledge absolutes (whether in terms of truth and falsehood or good and bad) was blocking what had previously been an open channel between Nick and me. Jesus was *the* truth. The highest, ultimate, absolute truth. For me. For *everyone*. I couldn't pretend otherwise. Of course, I knew not everyone, or in the world I had come from literally *anyone*, saw Him this way, but I now knew that He was. Even though I understood that it appeared disrespectful, oppressive even, to believe that all that contradicted this fact was a lie, I did. To say that this was *my* truth would be to subtly voice opposition to Jesus' statement of divine identity: *I am the way, the truth and the life, no one shall come to the Father except through Me* (Jn 14.6). However, I chose my words carefully, to make sure my boyfriend felt heard and that both our perspectives were welcome. Which they were. It was just that I no longer believed that they were equally true.

I had spent years denying God. Growing up, I had been embarrassed by my parents' Christianity and rebelled against it through heavy drinking and drugs—unconscious responses to ancestral issues, childhood trauma, and the assaults I had experienced. Embracing evolution and feminism, I had disposed completely of God the Father. Reeling from the pain of both my inherited trauma, which at that point was still buried under my addictions, and my own traumatizing experiences, my rage at the masculine meant I could never come to terms with a Father God. My lack of progress in the Twelve Steps had partly been because of this—every time the word "God" was mentioned in the texts, I shut down. Although critical of science's assumption of a rational, human subject, my psychoanalysis and deconstruction-informed literary studies meant further rejection of (and scoffing at) the concept of a loving creator.

Toward the end of my degree, my spiritual yearning stubbornly pierced through this regardless, finding nourishment in self-help literature, mindfulness, and Buddhism. These fed my extremely hungry heart's need for sustenance and healing though they were at odds with the nihilism of my academic discipline. After that first experience drinking ayahuasca, in which the spirit had forced me to look at the darkness of my inheritance and my wounding around femininity, a vivid world that far exceeded the limited parameters of the intellect exploded, replacing my analytical reality with the feeling-focused, experiential knowledge of the spirit world and all that extended from it. The academic paradox of searching for truth while believing that absolute truth does not and cannot exist was—temporarily at least—shoved to the back burner. Although this nature-focused study of divine consciousness was undeniably spiritual, God, in this context, was not the God of the Bible.

Although we found truth in the Bible, it was taken as a given that the Scriptures had been intercepted, edited, and censored to distort the true message of God. Maya, the friend who had introduced me to plant-spirit worship, had a deep yearning to meet Yeshua, and she and I would obsessively research the ecumenical councils to show that the truth of Christ, as expounded by what I had now learned were different heretics, had been stamped out by the militant Fathers who ran the Church. We had misinterpreted the humble, self-effacing attitude of the Christian as ignorance and had taken it as a given that the Fathers did not have the spiritual maturity to comprehend how it was that the practices that made up our ritualistic counter culture—witchcraft, sorcery, divination, necromancy, spiritism, spellcasting, and mediumship—were in fact the correct (and most spiritually advanced) means of entering into communion with Christ. We believed that we understood the Scriptures in a way that Christians self-evidently didn't, and within this context, Jesus was accounted for through the identities of Buddhist monk, tantric adept, Bodhisattva, ascended master, or divine masculine counterpart to the "goddess" Mary Magdalene.

As a result of having selectively read the Bible passages that corresponded to my favored practices, I had created my own Christology that posited Jesus, along with Mary Magdalene, as the source of the magical lineage I was part of, which itself had evolved out of the cult of Isis.[39] Moses and the burning bush were to my mind the talking fire spirit whom I worshiped; the tree of life and the tree of knowledge of good and evil were different plant medicines; the serpent in the garden was the creator goddess; and Moses' bronze, fiery serpent was the Bible's way of describing kundalini activation. Different spirits across different traditions supported this theory through deceptive visions aligning my channeling practice with ancient Egypt. In a sense there *is* a connection between all these traditions even though they manifest in geographically distinct locations. It is the same religion—the underworld of fallen spirits that oppose Christ and seek to destroy the eternal kingdom of God—manifesting in a variety of ways. What was now clearly *not* true, however, was that Jesus was in any way part of it: *Then He healed many who were sick with various diseases, and cast out many demons; and* **He did not allow** *the demons to speak, because* **they knew Him** (Mk 1.34). Christ alone has the ability to overcome the power of spirits ("demons") because Christ alone is God. And although we *humans* often don't know that Christ alone is God, the *spirits* do, and that is why they fear Him.[40]

Darkness was accounted for through our therapeutic experiences. After all, if there weren't negative forces, there would be nothing to heal. However, this was predicated on an understanding that darkness always had the opportunity to be transformed into its opposite within the impersonal force of atemporal reality. If eternal consequences following death were believed in, they were rarely discussed or taught. The emphasis, because paganism elevates the power of one's mind in creating reality, was on how the darkness was perceived, and what positives could be drawn from it. Although paganism encompasses a vast number of different traditions and lineages (with the New Age taking bits and pieces from different

---

[39] Almost every occult tradition I was part of featured, found a way to accommodate, or felt a need to explain Jesus in a way that it didn't for any other religious figure. Why?

[40] See also: Mt 8.31–32, 17.18, Mk 9.25, Lk 11.14, Acts 16.18.

pantheistic, panentheistic, polytheistic, and monistic lineages and traditions), all were united in disavowing Christ's supremacy, and every single tradition I entered into rejected an absolute division between good and evil. What instead took place was a continual merging of opposites: masculine and feminine, life and death, *God and the devil*.[41]

Having spent so many years criticizing God, denying God, mocking God, or repurposing God to fit within an accepted spiritual worldview, an inner resistance to the discourse of relative truth that permeated modern culture and the medicine world jubilantly arose. However, the very essence of my relationship with my boyfriend was our shared occultic spirituality. It was how we met, what we did together, and where our future lay. In that we had been united. Except now we weren't. Meeting the person of Christ had meant a 180-degree shift in my perception of the spiritual world. Where I had seen light, I now saw darkness. What had been good was now bad. What I had held as God was, I now knew, the devil. It was like we no longer spoke the same language. He had been the one to voice the shift. Over the final few days of my trip our communication continued as normal, but a shared awareness that something had changed and that the effects of this change were irreversible silently and painfully underscored our every interaction.

Completion

God is here. God is everywhere.
—Abba Bessarion

As we drove through the desert, I looked out across the dusty expanse and thought about the different tribes that had traversed the land prior to first contact, and the atrocities that had taken place—the land

---

[41] *God is light and in Him there is no darkness at all* (1 Jn 1.5).

grabs, the mass rapes, the slavery, the mission schools, the hangings, the dehumanization at every turn. Did people care? No one ever seemed to talk about it. Before I had come to America, I had wanted to start a project to support Native women who had been trafficked. Maybe Christ would make it possible. Unable to share what was in my heart, I asked the nuns about their stories of exodus out of the world.

It had now been six days since the conversion, though it was really more of a reversion, since I was returning to my original state as a child of God. Within the space of three weeks a totally different life than the one I had planned to live had opened up ahead of me. A life entirely devoted to Christ. I was completely certain that whatever He wanted of me was the only thing I was to do. But the knowledge that I was going to leave Nick pressed on me, and the freedom I was feeling was shot through with pain. However, I was filled with a level of peace I had never experienced before—ever. I had spent the past six years saying it without its being true, but everything was now actually *in its place*—I was home. After attending a Liturgy in celebration of the Nativity, I anointed myself with holy water and put on a floor-length white dress, embroidered with blue birds. Gathering with the nuns, Father Theophan anointed me with blessed oil, and I reiterated my intention to consecrate my life to Christ. As I spoke, one of the sisters began to cry, and I realized the immensity of what had taken place. I was giving my life to Christ. I was becoming an *Orthodox Christian*. It was a miracle.

PART TWO

I Belong to Jesus Now

*Then people went out to see what had happened, and they came to Jesus
and found the man from whom the demons had gone, sitting at the feet
of Jesus, clothed and in his right mind, and they were afraid.*
—Luke 8.35 ESV

I was due to arrive back in England on the anniversary of the first time Nick and I met. We had made a plan for dinner in central London. As my father had said of my mother, when she had left their relationship following her conversion (he converted two years later, and they then married), "It was like she had met the ultimate man." Partner, friend, confidante, teacher, master, healer, counselor, Lord. All the saints said that whoever encounters Christ and responds to His call will always choose Christ—He will always come first. I had wondered if there might be a period of reckoning between Nick and me, in which we would process everything that had happened, secretly hoping that Nick would see the renewal in me and through it miraculously become open to Christ, so that we could enter into this new life together.

But Christ, doting and self-sacrificially loving, but also firm and straight to the point, had other ideas. He brought the moment about immediately. After Nick reiterated that he was not open to Christianity, I realized that it was the end. We spoke about everything beautiful that had happened in our relationship, grasping each other's hands as we looked into each other's eyes, tears pouring down our faces. The four-course meal we had ordered to celebrate remained completely untouched. As we sat together late that night, I felt as if all the blood had been drained out of my body. For the first time in my life I truly understood the meaning of spiritual sacrifice.

The next day I went to my father's seventieth birthday party alone. I had risen early to complete my morning rule, having barely slept as a result of how late Nick and I had stayed up talking. It was understandably too much for him to join me following what had happened. It was a huge party, with two hundred of my parents' oldest friends—most of whom were Christian—whom I hadn't seen since childhood. As I stood welcoming the guests, one person after the other came up to me, grinning and excitedly congratulating me on the good news of my conversion. I tried my best to smile. I had no idea who most of them were. After years of living completely outside my parents' Christian community in the counterculture of the medicine world (which to most Christians was simply hallucinogenic drug taking and witchcraft), I was suddenly in the fold, in the family. I, Miss Anti-establishment, was now part of the church club? It was truly surreal.

I was sure that I could not proceed in any direction except directly toward Christ, but I was devastated and in shock at the reality that Nick and I were no longer together. We used to have this joke that we would come and find each other in the *bardo* and help each other achieve a successful rebirth. Every other minute I would remember that we had just separated and would feel a kick in my stomach. After telling my older sister, she took me into a side room, and I cried in her arms. I spoke to people as best I could, but it felt like my entire body had been stripped of its outer layer of skin and completely drained of all its energy. I then found a corner of a room that was hidden from the party, put my head in my lap, and sobbed.

An hour later I was found by two of my family's oldest friends, whose daughter I had grown up with. I didn't really want to talk to anyone, but I felt that there was something unusual about the way that they had both arrived by my side silently, administering some kind of Christian medicine to my soul, so I unwrapped myself from my shawl and spoke to them. Seeing my reddened eyes and puffy face, they began to pray, lifting me up to the Lord. Although this, like so much of my new life in Christ, made me cringe internally, I was again struck by the living, breathing relationship Christians seemed to have with God through prayer. Judged on outward appearances, you would never have known that they were in a state of constant communion. The fact that it was hidden from sight seemed to make it all the more special.

Over the next few days, I dealt with the fact that Nick and I were no longer together. The sweetness of this new life, and my relationship with Christ, carried an aching loss. Through this process of having to give up what I loved, I was able to understand the paradoxical dynamic between sacrifice and sanctification that encapsulates the path of the cross. I could feel that there was a light inside me that was sacred, and that I had a responsibility to guard its flame, and despite the magnitude of what was happening, I felt calm. The pain was present, but underneath it was tranquility. There was only one goal: to deepen in love with Christ and to do what I could to encourage Him to draw near. Suddenly life was very simple. Anything and everything that fed that end began to fall into place in front of me forming a path toward this new heavenly destination. Anything that detracted from it began to fall away.

Cleansing

And a number of those who had practiced magic arts brought their books together and burned them in the sight of all. And they counted the value of them and found it came to fifty thousand pieces of silver.[42]
—Acts 19.19 ESV

Immediately following our separation, Nick went to stay elsewhere while I prepared to move out. I had hoped that we would have a period of time together, so that we could at least integrate what had happened by talking about it, but I trusted in him and in the Lord that it was better this way, painful though it was. I felt a deep quietness in my mind. Calming the mind is the well-known goal of mindfulness practice.[43] However, it generally comes about sporadically and as a result of discipline, perseverance, and consistency. But something else had happened. It was as if Christ had swept away my thoughts. I have never experienced anything like it in my life. I *was* thinking things, but not that much beyond what was happening in that precise moment, if that. I would sit for long periods of time in a state of total stillness. On top of this solid seabed rolled waves of intensity, first in relation to the turbulent process of exiting the spirit world and second

---

[42] Whatever its exact modern equivalent, fifty thousand pieces of silver is intended to communicate a considerable amount of money.

[43] Although all the different traditions I explored had ways of explaining and managing thoughts, perhaps none more than Buddhism, it was only through studying the Scriptures—and the Fathers' teachings on *logismoi* (sinful, afflictive thoughts)—that I found clarity regarding the *essential* nature of these types of thoughts—through explanation of their lapsarian source. Buddhism teaches that there are negative thoughts that need to be overcome and how they come into being. However, it doesn't cover in depth *why* such a phenomenon exists in the first place and in so doing equip you with the tools to overcome it. See Ana Smiljanic, *Our Thoughts Determine Our Lives: The Life and Teaching of Elder Thaddeus of Vitovnica* (Platina, CA: St Herman of Alaska Brotherhood, 2013).

because of the heartache engendered by the breakup, but these would subside and silence would return. For very long periods of time, I felt like my thoughts had literally been turned off. Peace.

During those first days back in the house, the Holy Spirit began to cleanse my surroundings of everything connected to the spirit world. This meant cleaning out pretty much everything that I owned. I deleted my wild feminine website, took my business off Google, and deleted the associated email accounts, my blog, and everything to do with channeling on my website. I was happy to delete my Facebook, but it meant losing the women's group I had created, which had over six hundred members from around the world. I wondered if maybe I should keep it, so that I could share the good news with them. I weighed the pros and cons as my finger hovered over the button. That's a lot of women who need to hear the gospel . . . I hesitated before finally clicking delete. God wanted a totally clean slate. I dragged the shortcut of my favorite TV show into the trash—it was pirated, and, therefore, it was theft, and then I moved through the flat packing up all the different items I had acquired and accumulated over the past years. There were three altars in the house: an earthy-plant altar, a healing-crystal altar, and an altar to Buddha. Everything Buddhist belonged primarily to Nick, so I didn't touch any of his things, but I began to dismantle, cut up, bin, and bag everything that was mine.

It is impossible to describe the sensation of becoming aware of—and fearing—the kingdom of darkness as a result of encountering the light of Christ. To the outsider, you just look as if you have gone mad. But my eyes had been opened to the fact that not only did the satanic realm exist (distinct *from*, as opposed to as an extension *of*, God), but that it established its authority over places and people through objects. In the previous years I would float around the house, surrounded by all those things, completely relaxed. The house was my nest as well as a healing space, and I had always felt totally safe there. I thought of the hours I had spent in the shrine room channeling and chanting. Or the times I had sat late into the night, journeying and singing with the spirits. Never once did I feel fear. There or in any of the other spirit-contact situations I had been in. Because we believed that everything existed within a continuum of love, there wasn't really anything to actually be scared of. But now that I had stopped working for the enemy, the entire spiritual realm had turned on me. Because the enemy had lost me, he had no reason not to attack me. Christ had lifted the veil of deception that had caused me to see goodness and life where there had actually been darkness and death.

Everything to do with my channeling practice had to go first. I piled up all the healing objects I had collected, hundreds of pounds worth, and completely dismantled my plant-worship altar, which was in the center of the house, building a new one for Christ, with Orthodox icons, candles, Christian books, crucifixes, my Bible, and some fresh flowers. The ambience of Orthodox ecclesial objects was still very alien to me, but with that established I felt slightly more safe. Jesus is the king and ruler of all. Although the house was still technically an enemy territory, every spirit in that house knew that I belonged to Christ. Through reading the Bible, I had come to understand that the battle between the kingdom of heaven and the kingdom of darkness plays out through establishing territories in the unseen realm that manifest in the physical realm. I thought back to the way Jesus steadily increased His authority over the spiritual field I inhabited through the introduction of the crucifixes into my channeling grid. It must have enraged the enemy to powerlessly observe this spiritual switchboard, hitherto his dominion, be repossessed by Christ, gradually and then eventually, totally.

I continued through the house, cleaning out every enchanted object that was connected to the spirit world or to idolatry in some way—clothes, jewelry, drawings, postcards, talismans, charms, images, tools, artwork, throws, crystals, books, statues, instruments. Everything was put into trash bags and placed in the shrine room to be thrown away. As I was clearing through our bedroom, I moved toward a cardboard box in the corner of the room. As I opened the box and put my hands in, an intense rush of energy hit me, and I screamed and jumped backward. The box contained

Nick's *kendo* (a martial art) battle outfit. I stared at the box in silence. After a while of thinking about how bizarre my life had become, I psyched myself up to pick it up and put it in the spare room. I walked backward out the room, so that my eyes remained on the box before shutting the door.

As soon as it became nighttime, I then began to feel an intense aversion to the shrine room. It was full of Buddhist statues and wall hangings. Previously my favorite room in the house, everything inside me was screaming out against its contents. I tried to make it feel more friendly by lighting the altar lamps, but after a while I couldn't take it anymore and shut the door, making the sign of the cross and praying Jesus' name over it, as the New Age converts on YouTube had instructed. Despite this, whenever I walked past the door, I would feel a kick of fear and speed up. Although the evenings were otherwise peaceful, I could never fully relax, aware of what the shrine room contained.

Spirits

Sorceries or other evil arts and all such things are services of the devil; therefore shun them.
—St Cyril of Jerusalem

Throughout the week, I listened to people who had converted to Christianity from the occult. Coming across an amazing sequence of talks, I completely forgot how spiritually far away I now was from everyone I knew, and I sent them to a close friend with whom I had been chatting. He had told Nick that it sounded like I had "found God," and that this was all that he himself wanted. Because of his enthusiasm and the texts we had exchanged—and because of how open minded he was—I thought that he would receive the videos well. A huge mistake. Less than an hour after I had sent them, and we had spoken about which sequence would be best to watch them in, an email thudded into my inbox. My heart started to beat rapidly as I read his words: a fierce rebuttal of everything that was being shared, laid out point by point. After pausing to calm down slightly, I started to message him to explain things corresponding to my understanding. "So according to your Bible I am going to hell?" The way in which you answer that question has the power to end a friendship for good. It was a difficult conversation.

Some understanding was found, but essentially, there was a huge chasm between us. I had barely shared anything with anyone since the conversion, as I was aware of how explosive Christ's words were for those in my community. It saddened me that this was my friend's first experience of me following the conversion. Had we met in person, I would have been able to explain things in a more edifying manner. I repented for my impulsiveness and asked God to give me the discernment and grace to share with people according to what was right for them in each moment. Following this incident, I was extra vigilant about how I spoke about Christ. I was aware, however, that my days of being respected within the alternative community were more or less over. The Bible says what it says. It is not up to me as a Christian to alter it in order that I am not rejected for sharing its message. But the Lord was not asking me to work in this way for Him yet. I was aware that my responsibilities during this stage of my growth were simply to feed on the Scriptures and to completely surrender in His loving arms. The rest would come in due course.

In those first few days, I studied the apologetics website of Steven Bancarz, an influential New Ager who had met Christ.[44] He had abandoned the spirit world to share the truth of what was taking place in the unseen realm, and he wrote about what was happening during psychic empowerment practices such as astral projection. I realized that through meditation I had been opening myself up to paranormal attachment. Because of the beliefs I had previously held around sexuality, I took it as a given that I would often have hyperintense experiences of intercourse

---

[44] Steven Bancarz, *Reasons for Jesus*, <https://reasonsforjesus.com>, February 28, 2020.

with spirits in the dreamworld, for extended periods of time throughout the night. It was simply a normal part of my life. However, the articles explained that astral projection opens up one's psyche in such a way that different types of unclean spirits can come and feed on you when you are sleeping (or meditating).

I had been spiritually raped. The devil had come into my life, deceived me, lied to me, abused me, stolen from me, and left me for dead. As the reality of what had been happening sunk in, I felt overwhelmed by a sense of "dirtiness." I looked down at my body and thought about all the ways in which I had opened myself to this kind of feeding, and of all the different dark spirits that had been inside me. This sense of spiritual violation activated the memories of physical and emotional violation that were still stored in my body, and I called Sister Cherubima crying, telling her what I had seen. She listened intently, comforting me. With each new realization of the darkness of my past, Christ further freed me from the binding of my former spiritual ignorance.

After this, I stopped looking at anything to do with the spirit world. Each time I did, it would activate a very specific atmosphere within me and in the space around me—a physiological, as well as spiritual and emotional, experience. I needed to cut off the past, not reawaken it. My sister encouraged me in this, telling me that even though it seems benign, seeking this kind of information "gives the enemy a foothold." I was beginning to understand that the devil did not care if our thoughts toward him were positive or negative; as long as our focus was on him, then he had won our attention—attention which should be focused on God.[45] I messaged Father Theophan explaining what had been happening, and he confirmed that this kind of information, although Christian in content, was feeding the enemy by nourishing my attachment to his world. I had only just

---

[45] "When our mind is wholly directed towards God, all questions cease. There remains only one question: how to have in oneself, and to keep, the Holy Spirit?" St Sophrony, *Words of Life*, 62.

escaped. I needed to be immersed in Christ, and Christ alone, until I was instructed otherwise.

After stopping watching the videos, the feeling of unease around certain areas of the house diminished and I began to feel better. The next morning, I opened the door of the shrine room and allowed the light coming through its window to fill the house. I thought about Nick and how much I loved him. He was a beautiful child of God, and his heart was full of love for everything in this room. Yes, his love for God was intercepted by Buddha, but the *love* was real. It was just misdirected. Focusing on that love put an end to that period of fear and unease. Despite what was taking place on an emotional level with regards to the loss of my former life, I continued to feel the consistent presence of the Lord, guiding me as I made those first steps. During this period, a lot of connections ended organically. I had deleted my Facebook and WhatsApp and with them lost contact with a vast number of people.

Despite my medicine community being those with whom I spent the most time, the Holy Spirit guided me to cut contact with the majority of them. We were just too far apart. I pledged that I would come back for everyone who had ever been under my care at any point. I saw all my clients and those whom I had looked after as my "babies," and I knew I had a responsibility to tell them the truth, regardless of whether they would accept it or not. But to do this effectively, I needed to immerse myself in Christ. I needed to become a dwelling place for the Holy Spirit, so that anything I then said about Christ would have a better chance to break apart the deception that they were under. Unless I became a living example of the truth of Christ, it would just be words. It would not be life giving. The Desert Fathers emphasized the necessity of entering the inner desert through intensive fasting and purification, in order to be established in the Spirit. And St Paul, following his Damascene conversion and a short period of "first flush" evangelism, entered the Arabian desert in preparation for his ministry (Gal 1.17). I knew I was being called to do this. Without reservation.

Something I had read again and again in people's testimonies was that the Holy Spirit, once welcomed into a person's life, had the power to repel those who did not want to come to the light of Christ. Far beyond my control, this was taking place. I felt the Lord firmly pushing away some of those with whom I had been closest. I tried to be as still as possible throughout, so as not to reactivate connections that God was killing. As a way to guarantee that I was following God's will, I held back completely, trusting that if He wanted me to speak to someone, he or she would contact me of his or her own volition. Those with whom I did speak kept telling me that they were so happy that I had found "my truth." Although I appreciated the enthusiastic sentiment, after a while it began to grate.

Having spent years holding together a range of different religious outlooks and worldviews *and* following the teachings of Buddha (who teaches that there is no essential truth), would I really have given up everything to follow another path that was only as true as everything else? If Christ had no more of a claim to truth than anything else, then why would I have left my business, my spiritual community, my studies, my friends, my house (my favorite place in the world), *and* my boyfriend? Leaving him meant losing our entire life together. Would I have given that all up for just another, partial, discrete truth amongst many other truths? Would I really have given it all up just to follow *a* path? And beyond that, why would I, a convinced feminist immersed in the worldview of the twenty-first century postmodern world, choose to give myself over entirely to a religion that embodied all that I had so passionately stood against?[46]

I expect the contention—of course, you weren't succeeding doing so many different things and mixing all those traditions. Of course, rushing around like that you were going to burn out and not progress. Of course, you weren't going to become enlightened living like that! Definitely, I had

---

[46] With thanks to Dan Buxhoeveden for conceptualizing this final point in such eloquent terms. I couldn't have put it better myself. Which is why I didn't! Thank you for allowing me to use your words.

too much going on. But there is a reason why I was able to integrate all those elements into my practice without any serious metaphysical dissonance beyond the fact that I was overstretched. There is a reason why weed-smoking hippies chant *Hare Krishna* (a famous Hindu mantra). There is a reason why Jungian psychotherapists talk about spirit animals and recommend practicing yoga. There is a reason why the Tibetan Buddhist pantheon includes Hindu and Shinto deities. There is a reason why Qi Gong teachers attend plant-medicine ceremonies. There is a reason why New Age healers do Tai Chi. There is a reason why Reiki practitioners use tarot cards. There is a reason why kundalini yogis venerate Sikh gurus. There is a reason why rebirthing coaches read Sufi poetry. There is a reason why Taoist bodyworkers hold new-moon cacao rituals. And there is a reason why Orthodox Christianity does not mix with *any* other religion, spiritual tradition, or lineage. There is a reason.

The Jesus Prayer

Peace I leave with you, my peace I give to you; not as the world gives do I give to you. Let not your heart be troubled, neither let it be afraid.
—John 14.27

Calm. This is the word Nick used to describe me when we had dinner together. He noted that I seemed much less anxious. From the moment that I arrived at the monastery, peace had entered my heart and, to my surprise, despite leaving and returning to London, it hadn't left. Huge shifts were taking place during this period, but I felt completely at ease. I was experiencing firsthand that *the peace of God, which transcends all understanding, will guard your hearts and your minds in Christ Jesus* (Phil 4.7). As my preparation for Baptism continued, I acclimatized myself to the relationship between the human and the natural world as understood within Orthodox theology. Up to that point, my center had always been nature,

Mother Earth. Spending time in creation was the thing that healed me. What the Lord had opened my eyes to see, however, was that nature was the Spirit-breathed *vessel* through which *He* transmitted life. If I honored, cared for, loved, and gave thanks for creation as an expression of the Creator's majesty, tenderness, and compassion, then this relationship would bear spiritual fruit. But if I worshiped nature as the source of life itself, then I cut myself off from the oxygen of Christ. Christ, the incarnate Creator Spirit who is the source of all life. Nature was only alive so long as it was inspired—*breathed*—by the Holy Spirit.

Worship of Christ will (or should) always sanctify our relationship with creation—God's gift to us. Worship of nature, on the other hand, can only bring about a partial sanctification of our relationship with God, because true union with God the Father can only come about through relationship with the Son, Jesus. I previously resisted this equation because the division felt unnaturally overt. Every spiritual tradition I had taken part in tended to dismantle the distinction between the created and the uncreated, the earthly and the heavenly, and the material and the invisible, to bring about merging. As had my previous literary and philosophical inquiries. Yet what I was experiencing with Jesus was an *enhancement* of the division.[47] Although Christ comes down into the depth of our human hearts to minister to us, there is a distinct gap between our humanity and His divinity. By becoming incarnate He spiritualized matter, into which death had entered as a result of the fall, opening up the possibility for us to then ascend higher toward Him. Or, as St Athanasius puts it, "God became man so that man might become God."

What was transformative for me, however, was that I was beginning to understand that this elevation of a person's spirit can only come as a result of a gift of grace from above. This was completely different from everything I had experienced. All the traditions I followed emphasized that light

---

[47] See the instances of God "separating" in the creation narrative, Genesis 1.4, 1.6, 1.7, 1.14, 1.18.

was generated through internal effort. If the light was self-originating, what other means could one access it except through oneself? But the saints taught that proximity to the light of Christ had the effect of heightening one's awareness of his or her sin and darkness, rather than absorbing it and thus neutralizing it (as in the guru-master model). In paganism, there is no distinction between a shaman and a saint—they are understood as the same phenomena manifesting in different ways. But because the saints were given the gift of experiencing the authentic light of Christ, their unveiled eyes could perceive their sinfulness and mortality, and the separation from His divine holiness that resulted from it. The paradox is that this humility and self-abnegation was the very thing that sanctified them and made them Christ-like.

Having contacted Sister Veroniki on my return from America, I prepared myself to return to her monastery for another retreat. I felt the Lord's hand present in the way that the plan had unfolded, as I had in everything that had taken place since I got back from America. Returning as a believer, I was connected to the monastics in their shared worship of Christ in a new way. Continuing the structure established while in America, I rose early to complete the small rule Father Theophan had set for me, before attending the daily services in the main chapel. Beautiful icons, a mixture of muted pigments and gold leaf, adorned all its walls. One afternoon, I went to the oldest chapel in the monastery to pray the Jesus Prayer: *Lord Jesus Christ, Son of God, have mercy on me, a sinner.* Monastics (as well as pious laity) repeat the prayer throughout their working day in obedience to St Paul's instruction to *pray without ceasing* (1 Thess 5.17).

The room's dark wood felt steeped in the power of the thousands of prayers of those who had quietly sat within its walls. Later in the refectory, following a meal during which ascetic literature was read aloud by one of the nuns, I began to have another vision. I could feel the way in which chanting the Jesus Prayer had cleansed me, allowing light to enter my heart. As we ate in silence, listening, I started to see Christ peacefully traverse the refectory ceiling above us. As I observed this movement, my

PART TWO

eyes remaining open throughout, I felt myself filled with His light. Experiencing that light made me understand more deeply what was meant by the term "the uncreated light of Christ." Why it is that His uncreated nature differentiates Him from all the other spirits. The spirit world is filled with light, hence its attractiveness. Furthermore, *Satan himself is transformed into an angel of light* (2 Cor 11.14). But whereas that light is *created*, light that is a reflection of the light of God, Christ's light, is *uncreated* and is the source of all other light.[48]

Praying with my mother on the phone that evening, I suddenly realized the degree to which my ignorance regarding the nature of Christianity had poisoned my perception of her spirituality. She prayed for a long period in the early morning, chanted the Jesus Prayer throughout the day, and then prayed again at night, *every day*. All this time I had sought out practices as far away from that with which I had grown up, thinking that through them I would find the truth of God. Working in the liminal spaces as an intermediary between the physical and spirit world, the elemental healers judged themselves (and one another) on the strength of their spirit and on their "force." While immersed in this way of thinking, Christian obedience to the Bible was held as evidence of

---

[48] This increase in understanding dovetailed with a new perspective on occultic and *spiritist*, as opposed to heavenly and *spiritual*, visions. As mentioned in part one, the majority of the visions I experienced through sorcery were characterized by the appearance of fluorescence (typing ayahuasca or peyote visions into your search engine will give a vague indication of what they look like), a quality that was completely absent from the heavenly visions I then experienced. What blew my mind was that when I researched what fluorescence actually is, the answer demonstrated that what is taking place on the level of spirit can be understood through science itself: the light of fluorescence is light that has been absorbed and which is then emitted. It is second-hand. Like natural fluorescence, the light of witchcraft is not the uncreated light of God but is rather light that is created by God, that has then been appropriated by the evil one for his purposes. Satan can transform himself into an angel of light, but the light itself will always be created and finds its origin in God, because God alone is uncreated.

fundamentalism and a lack of maturity: Sheep was the word commonly used. Sheep, who were asleep.

As I stood watching my mother, however, I realized that the strength of the Christian was entirely invisible to the outside world—it came through obedience to God. To His word, to His commandments, and to His statutes. I thought guiltily of the times I had assumed that because someone was Christian, his or her spirituality was weak, dry, and stagnant. The Lord was opening my eyes to the fact that the hidden treasure of a dedicated prayer life entirely invisible to the outer world pleased Him far more than outward expressions of spiritual aptitude. It was for this reason that He tells us, *When you pray, go into your room, and when you have shut your door, pray to your Father who is in the secret place, and your Father who sees in secret, will reward you openly* (Mt 6.6).

Although I hadn't spent a huge amount of time thinking about it, I wondered how my visionary experiences fit within an Orthodoxy that seemed quite hostile to such phenomena, in the context of the average person. I emailed Father to again discuss the nature of some of the visions that had taken place. I felt particularly close to St Sophrony, as a result of his teachings on eastern religions, and wanted to make sure that my experiences lined up with the enlightened wisdom that he and other hesychasts espoused in their ascetic writings regarding the necessity of discernment in the context of unusual, supernatural experiences. Their warnings against being deceived by the devil through the imagination were repeated for a reason. I had already voiced the concerns that I had, and that I had often heard spoken of by New Age converts, regarding the potential dangers of confusing deceptive demonic experience with genuine mystical experience. Although firmly in agreement, Father shared examples from the lives of living Orthodox elders and those with whom they'd had contact, to demonstrate that in some special cases, miraculous experiences were something witnessed in contemporary Christianity. Father assured me that, although very unusual, the visions were symbolic, and that they were gifts from God, which would be used for His purposes, and so I proceeded in peace, grateful that the fulfilling love of Christ meant that visions, as an end in themselves, were no longer something that I was actively seeking.

As I prepared to leave the monastery a few days later, Sister Veroniki advised me not to share all the details of my testimony with people. Of course, I could tell them what had happened, but it was better to conserve the sacred energy of the visions and encounters I'd had, in order that they could nourish, heal, and illuminate me from within. If someone wanted to pray for me and support me in the Spirit, then this was not a problem. But she explained that if someone was just asking out of curiosity, verbalizing everything would dissipate the grace that was dwelling inside me as a result of what had taken place. It was too special to waste. Her words clarified something that I had been feeling, but that I hadn't conceptualized in words.

As someone prone to oversharing—especially when under pressure—I had felt obligated to explain to those close to me why so much was changing. But the process had often been very draining, especially when the person's reaction was negative. I had spent (and probably wasted) a lot of time translating my experiences into yogic, Buddhist, and New Age terms, in order to help my friends understand what was happening. I wanted them to understand how deep and immense Christianity truly is, but it was a mistake. When discussing the issue with my parents, they quoted the Gospel of Matthew: *Do not throw your pearls before swine* (Mt 7.6), simply meaning that the context must be correct and blessed by God for it to bear fruit. It was the second time I had received this message. As I was preparing to leave America, Sister Eleni had turned to me and gently warned me not to share what was happening inside me with anyone. Yet.

The Narrow Gate

*I have come to my garden, my sister, my spouse; I gathered my myrrh with my spice,
I have eaten my honeycomb with my honey; I have drunk my wine with my milk.*
—Song of Songs 5.1

Returning to London, I emailed Father Theophan to ask if I could begin confessing to him. I had to accommodate the reality that for Christ, an intimate relationship exists solely in the context of (heterosexual) wedlock (Mt 19).[49] Although I understood that immense care was required, I wondered how humans were supposed to live up to this standard. When in America, I had brought the topic up with Father Theophan who had spoken about two people coming together to unite in love, but not because of lust. When he had said the word "lust" in that context, I flinched slightly. Isn't lust a good thing? Isn't lust natural? Despite wondering this, I had accepted what Father Theophan had said because I trusted his experiential wisdom. He was so open and down to earth. He also had a medical background and so was able to talk about the body in intense detail, thus rooting his knowledge of sanctification in corporeal reality. I knew that what he was saying didn't come from a place of undealt-with cultural conditioning or sexual repression, but rather through the living experience of Christ's formation within him. As a result of this grace, he was always able to answer my inquiries in a way that left me feeling both heard and respected.

Within all my former spiritual traditions, fasting from sexual activity (at certain points or for certain reasons) was connected to spiritual growth.

---

[49] So *that's* why it's called wedlock. It is locked—secured, fixed, protected. Across this period I began to understand that the reason Christians held marriage in such high regard was that they understood that mortal marriage is rooted in the sacred marriage that exists between God and His creation, or, as the mystical writers of the Hebrew Bible put it, His *səgullāh*, "treasured possession."

PART TWO

They were all ascetic lineages. However, in those traditions, there was no concept of the fall. Through Orthodoxy, I was beginning to see that sex itself had become corrupted in some way by that primary rebellion—which is why it required so much safeguarding. What was clear from the time I had spent with these ascetics, however, was that the sexual complexes most westerners imagine precipitate religious celibacy were not something that I saw any evidence of. In fact I had been pleasantly surprised to see how frank, open, and unaffected the elders had been on the infrequent occasions that the topic had arisen.

As I was immersed in the purity of monastic life and reading the Bible daily, the Holy Spirit began to reveal why it is that Christ instructs against—what is described in the biblical idiom of the New Testament as *adultery* (Mt 5.27), *fornication* (1 Cor 6.9), and *sexual immorality* (1 Thess 4.3). Life is sacred because God is the source of life. Sexual energy has life-giving power. Therefore, it must be treated with a level of respect, and reverence even, that reflects this reality. In paganism, despite being a spiritual community, broken hearts, serial cheating, anxiety, depression, reluctant polyamory, unplanned pregnancies, abortion, sexually transmitted diseases, single motherhood, broken homes, plastic surgery, infertility, domestic violence, porn addiction, compulsive masturbation, violated boundaries, and hungry hearts starved of true intimacy were more common than not.

Well protected in marriage or in some cases transformed solely into spiritual energy (such as in the case of the monastics or those called to celibacy) sexual energy, *life force*—a term from my former world but one that is in this case entirely appropriate—could become a force for good in the world. Father Theophan had told me that after a certain point of renunciation, sexual energy is transmuted and begins to flow through the believer as spiritual, rather than biological power, enabling ever deeper levels of communion in worship. Abstinence, chastity, purity. Taken in earnest, these were completely foreign words to me before Christ, but suddenly I began to see how it was through them that becoming *truly holy* and thus becoming *truly free* was a possibility.

As my relationship with Confession deepened, a tug of war took place between my mind and my heart. The philosophical question of whether Confession had the power to create, as opposed to alleviate, guilt surfaced. Was this some kind of twisted, religious self-flagellation? All my work on the wild feminine had been about letting go of culturally inculcated shame and the sense of being deficient. Suddenly I was down on my knees, vocalizing every single thing I had done wrong that day and asking for mercy. Spiritually, however, I could feel something beautiful and mysterious taking place within me when I confessed. The Christian practice of *submitting to one another out of reverence for Christ* (Eph 5.21) meant entering the holy mystery of Christ's humility before the Father. This was the example we were being given. I imagined the fierce, free-spirited women I had worked with, in disbelief, seeing me in this state of vulnerability, earnestly confessing my sins to God before going to sleep, crucifix in hand. It required me to surrender to the wisdom of something much greater than me.

Toward the end of my time in the medicine world, I'd become increasingly fed up with the corruption and abuse of power I observed around me. Similarly, though the dynamic was more complex because it fed into my own egoic desires *and* my desire to be loved, I had become disillusioned by the fact that a lot of my male teachers' feelings toward me tended to devolve into romantic attachment. A phenomenon that both pleased me, because it meant that I was worthy and equal to them in some way, while also disappointing me, because it meant that they weren't holy and that they couldn't, therefore, help me in the way that I needed to be helped. Then I met Father Theophan.

PART TWO

Exodus

Filled as I am with my own opinions about things, I am not able to receive anything from God.
—Elder Aimilianos of Simonopetra

During this period, I experienced what it is like to (voluntarily) enter social exile. Word would occasionally reach me regarding the conversations that were taking place at gatherings across London: the stifled laughter, the hushed incredulity, and in some cases, the outrage. Dinners that I used to attend with those that I had grown up with, and who were, by all accounts, friends. People whom I loved and by whom I was (as far as I was aware at least) respected. I did not permit myself to inquire beyond whatever stray comment was shared, but my mind would automatically paint a vivid picture, collaging all the culinary and atmospheric elements that comprised my old social world: the spread of middle eastern vegetarian food; the organic vegetables from the local health food market; the pretty, second-hand, mismatched crockery; and the friends streaming in at different times, from occasionally high powered, cultured jobs, in and around London.

Whether in academia, fashion, art, music, journalism, charity, the food business—or in my case—the alternative health world, we were all unified by a foregrounded social vision, predicated on the diluted communist principles of the ultra-progressive left. But having broken ideological rank, I was no longer one of them. I was instead the topic of their dinner party conversation: a *freak*. Yoga, meditation, earth worship, ecstatic dancing, tantra, witchcraft even, could be—and had been—faithfully accommodated. All had a certain bite to them, and the provocativeness of my wild spirituality had replaced that of my wild partying without providing too much conceptual dissonance, plus many of my friends came to me for sessions and attended my retreats. But Christianity? *Bible* thumping? This was unprecedented.

I was acutely aware of the fact that to many of those I knew, I was no longer a wise, wild woman; I was now just weird. Jesus' love was enough to mean that this process wasn't painful as such, but it was strange, occasionally uncomfortable, and frequently surreal. From the perspective of my former circle, I was now spiritually aligned with the slavery apologists, witch-burners, and indigenous tribe-destroying missionaries of the world. There was nothing I could do to change this. Christianity is vast and Orthodoxy little known. The teachings of the desert and the saints, of the one, holy, catholic, and apostolic Church, have nothing to do with any of the above but the characterization of Christians within my community and a lot of the wider world was that of sexually repressed, homophobic white supremacists who *hated* nature and wanted to destroy it. Through this I learned hard and fast that being misunderstood (a pet peeve) was an important part of growing in the spirit: God knows the truth, and that is all that matters.

Being misread without collapsing internally or justifying oneself was a fundamental part of Christianity. Christ Himself was utterly rejected. It is sacred because it means dying to the ego. As a Christian I was no longer attractive according to the world's standards, but I knew Jesus, and that is the greatest gift that it is possible to receive. The division between the spirit and the world was clarified through this process. Confessing that Christ is Lord marked an invisible boundary between me and those who did not, and through this I was able to really understand why Christianity emphasized the distinction between the earthly and the spiritual. The world was created, temporal, and—as a result of human pride—fallen. The Spirit was uncreated, eternal, and holy. *Spirits* that did not explicitly and avowedly serve Christ, served the world. The world served the devil. It is for this reason that Christ tells us, *I will not speak with you much longer, for the ruler of this world is coming and he has nothing in Me* (Jn 14.30).

Through submitting to this separation by entering into Christ's Body, the way I then related to the world shifted. The misunderstanding around Christianity is that this shift precipitates a way of relating to the world that is negative. That is life-*denying*. Rather, through connecting to the true source of life, I felt able to relate to the world in a way that affirms the living truth of reality. The reality that creation did not create itself, but that it was created by the Creator who has a divine mind, heart, and personality even, and who wants to have an intimate relationship with us. As I would read daily, *Know that the Lord, He is God. It is He **who has made us, and not we ourselves**. We are His people and the sheep of His pasture* (Ps 100.3). In the past, the masculine pronouns would have been enough to make me check out, but looking beyond them, I was now able to see that a creative and tender relationship based on sacrificial servanthood epitomized God's merciful love.

Pilgrimage

As for anyone practicing incantation or sorcery, he shall be allotted the time of a murderer.
—St Basil the Great

I was starting another pilgrimage. But rather than occult ceremonies at sacred sites with pagan priests, witches, and healers, I was traveling to churches and monasteries in France, Germany, and Norway, with a group of my parents' Christian friends, some of whom were Orthodox. It was my twenty-ninth birthday. Lily, one of my closest friends, met me at the train station before I left. We had been friends since we were eighteen. Incredibly kind and loving, she had been my rock through addiction and recovery, and my ensuing journey into spirituality and wild womanhood. She was a cheerleader for my life, as I was for hers. We had accompanied each other through so many different stages of development, both having similar tendencies, healing goals, and backgrounds. We had worshiped "the Goddess" together and were incredibly close. She was my closest friend. But my conversion had caused a seismic shift in our relationship. I had been shocked by the negativity of her response, having imagined that this revelation would, as with everything else, bring about a beautiful new chapter in our shared spiritual journey. That we would begin a pilgrimage into the heart of the Father together. On that point I had been naive.

Loving as she was, she had come to see me off and give me a birthday present, despite the fact that she was not in agreement with my decision to leave Nick and begin this new life. She never forgot a birthday—or anything else important. But I knew her heart wasn't in it. I knew she didn't support me and that she wasn't happy for me. It hurt but I knew it wasn't intentional. I knew she *wanted* to feel that what was happening was a good thing, and I wanted her to feel that way too, but she didn't. That was the truth of it. Faithful to the end, she stood on the other side of the barrier as I went through security, waiting for me to get on to the train. A complex mixture of emotions played out in her changing expression as she waved. I wanted her to understand that what was happening was good. That it was the best thing that had ever happened! I now had the possibility of true salvation, the thing I had been seeking. But my heart belonged to Christ now. We no longer spoke the same language. It was just . . . different. There was nothing that could be done about it. Disturbed by this new and totally alien distance between us, I waved and blew her a kiss before running to catch up with the group and get on to the train.

On the third evening of the pilgrimage, I came across an article about the occult written by a former New Age cult member who had been attacked by, as he put it, a coven of witches from within his order. The event had brought him to Jesus and to Christianity. The writer explained that a lot of the philosophies, practices, and beliefs of the New Age had been repurposed by worshipers and adherents of Lucifer. In order to draw more people toward Lucifer, they had worked toward feeding a more sanitized version of occult spiritual practices to the masses. He wrote about mediumship, channeling, astral projection, nature worship, tarot, non-duality, astrology, self-realization, manifesting, visualization, affirmation, and the chakras.

As I read, realization dawned on me that most of what I had been practicing was luciferian. Luciferian spirituality was not outwardly dark in the way that satanism was, but it drew its energy from the same source. The enemy works through different modalities that can be divided into—supposedly—distinct categories, in an almost infinite number of different ways, hence the thousands of different esoteric traditions and lineages. It is for this reason that luciferian mysticism is such a powerful trap for the spiritually curious—there is always something new on the horizon enticing the mystical seeker forward in his or her quest. Maybe *this* tradition will be the thing that finally delivers the health, wealth, and happiness I have worked so hard for. The writer spoke about chakra-balancing practices and the fact that they opened the door for the adversary. The Holy Spirit doesn't need our chakras to be "open" to enter our being. As our Creator, the Holy Spirit does not access us by mechanical means. However, there is someone who benefits from the energetic opening that results from these kinds of psychic exercises . . . the devil.

I felt my blood run cold. A lot of my healing work had revolved around the chakras, as did all the tantric practice I engaged in. I thought of the womb work I did and saw how instead of healing women's wombs, I had been opening them up to the unclean spirit realm, enabling possession by demonic forces. I had literally been doing the *exact* opposite of what I had been trying to do. Following the encounter with Christ at New Year, in which He had lifted the veil and revealed His divinity to me, I had carried on womb pulsing, reasoning with myself that if I disconnected what I was doing from its Buddhist source, it could work as a secular physical release practice. However, on the occasions when I had done it, I'd had the disturbing experience of the spirits of the lineage attacking me while I pulsed on top of the client. So forceful was one of the attacks, that I had to stop the practice altogether midway through the session. I managed to smooth out the process as much as possible, so that the client didn't really realize what was happening, but vowed to never do it again, as a consequence.

As a result of what I had learned from Father, I now knew that Christ works through our embodied mental, emotional, and spiritual system, which in Christian terms is conceptualized as the *members* (1 Cor 12.12), uncovering, balancing, and sanctifying them at an appropriate pace and in a way that is safe. But this process can only come about as a result of each person's personal relationship with Christ. Any activity of this kind that is driven by spiritual practices that conflict with the revealed truth of Christ and with the commandments is de facto satanic because it is driven by a spirit other than the Creator. I thought anxiously about all my friends who practiced yoga, meditation, and other forms of chakra opening.

The article then went on to talk about how these occultists offered worship to, and eagerly awaited the coming of, the liberator Lord Maitreya. I froze as I read the words. Lord Maitreya? As in Lord *Buddha* Maitreya? Buddha Maitreya was the Buddha who was to come after Buddha Shakyamuni. I knew that western occultism took inspiration from older eastern religions, but the fact that those who indirectly worshiped Lucifer through adherence to the principles of self-mastery and self-realization believed that the next spiritual epoch would be ushered in by the arrival of the same powerful being of light that the Buddhists awaited threw into sharp relief everything that the Lord had been showing me with regards to the interconnectivity of all spirit-world practices. Maitreya was who Nick was waiting for. I started to freak out and began crying, thinking about whether or not I should call him to tell him. I wanted to rescue him from what he was unknowingly involved in.

I spoke with one of the group, who wisely urged me to remember that I didn't need to *do* anything, except to keep moving toward Christ. Christ would take care of Nick. I just needed to keep focused on Christ. That night I lay in bed completely unable to sleep. Destabilized by what I had read, I thought of all the spirits I had been in contact with throughout my life. My mind raced through memories of luxuriating in their patterns and vibrations, and the sensations I experienced as a result—that they existed was enough to convince me that they were good. Throughout the years I had been in magic, I had spent *a lot* of time contacting spirits in ceremony. All ideas that I had held (and taught) about mastering and controlling the spirits were simply fantasy. In offering myself up to them as one of their vessels, I had given them permission to do in, and through, me whatever they had wanted.

My deep mind was saturated with the psychic, emotional, and physiological imprint of their presence, their touch, their taste, their scent. It had never crossed my mind that they were *all* part of a supernaturally well-orchestrated master plan, the only goal of which was to delay my coming into contact with Christ, the one true God, and with Him, everlasting life. I eventually fell into an uneasy sleep, and the next day I contacted Mother Syncletica to tearfully confess. Comforted by her words, and touched by the pain she expressed at hearing me in such a state, I dusted off (as the monastics say) with some of the Psalms and stopped reading material to do with the kingdom of darkness. Father Theophan had already told me that Christ would reveal everything that I needed to know to help those who are deceived through internal and mystical means, not through reading and watching information of this kind.

Temple

The entire life of the Church, the entire tradition of the Church, all of human history, from the creation of Adam and Eve to the Second Coming of Christ, are contained within the Book of Psalms.
—Elder Aimilianos of Simonopetra

Throughout the pilgrimage, I continued to rise early to pray alone before the day began. Something mysterious took place when the early mornings were offered up to the Lord in prayer. Although I felt physically tired, my spirit felt more activated and alert than when I slept later. As I read the Gospels, I could feel the words coming alive. Sometimes as I was reading, I would feel as if the page were opening in front of my eyes, and I was falling inside the words. The Desert Fathers and Mothers taught that the believer must *eat* the Scriptures in order to be nourished by them—they are our vitamins, minerals, nutrients, and roughage—and one abba taught that if one turned the pages of the Bible with enough affection, it was possible to see baby Jesus swaddled within them. The way the strict asceticism of the desert was combined with such a tender relationship with Christ and with the Scriptures touched my heart. In the monastery in America, I remember glimpsing Sister Eleni picking up in distress, gently patting, and then tenderly kissing her *Bible* after she had dropped it. And on another occasion, I glanced over at Sister Damaris during prayers, to see her gazing lovingly at the crucifix she was holding in her hand.

I loved the deep, sensitive, and passionate way that the monastics related to Christ. It was a tenderness born out of the rigor of their willingness to give their entire lives to Him. Father Theophan had once spoken about the relentlessness of the monastic routine, and during my prayer times on the pilgrimage, I experienced in a small way its inescapability first hand. Prayers varied from day to day. If I was focused and my mind was empty, the words would become liquid, and I would receive insights into phrases that had otherwise been invisible or obtuse. The word of God would talk to me. If I was willing the time to go more quickly, on the other hand, I tended to "slide" across the surface of the page, reading passively and not fully tasting the words or their meaning. The result was less insight and less of a shift in how I felt from start to finish. My sister had described praying the Psalms as a "wash." Every time I found myself beginning to daydream, I would bring my focus back to this, tuning into the way the heavenly words were showering my soul from above.

Having been in a monastic environment for so long, I noticed that being suddenly surrounded by laity during the trip meant that energy related to my identity as a woman began to rear up. This started a battle between wanting to focus solely on Christ, on the one hand, and thinking about men, on the other. The monastics were present in my mind, representative of total sacrifice for spiritual growth. Now, however, I was also being given an insight into the spiritual life of these lay Christians, who were either single, engaged, or married, and immersed in the joy of family life. Alone in my room, I listened to a recording of one of the conversations I'd had with Father Theophan, in which he explained what it means to be consecrated to God and to have an intimate relationship with Him. True and everlasting intimacy that far exceeds what can be achieved by two humans alone.

Father Theophan spoke about the fact that to enter more deeply into this intimate relationship with Christ, we had to let go of the personal delights we were grasping for, so Christ could draw us closer to Him. Because it is through being purified in this way, that we, as His bride, are then able to not only feast on Christ's peace and His bliss, but also to be admitted into an inner sanctum in which He would allow us to share in His *agony*. As I listened, I felt like I was being given a taste of Christ the Bridegroom, the only person who could truly complete me. I was aware that I had gained such clarity as a result of Christ's having released me from the spiritual binding in which I had been enmeshed, and that I felt internally free, in a way that I never had before. Meditating on this grace-filled teaching during a Liturgy that evening, I allowed the words to wash over me and cleanse me.

Warfare

Beloved, do not believe every spirit, but test the spirits, whether they are of God.
—1 John 4.1a

The next day, I experienced a demonic attack. A group of different elemental spirits that I had encountered during a sequence of earth rituals in Wales were doing everything that they could to dislodge me from my newly established, but still fairly fragile, position in the Spirit. The attack had started in the morning during my prayer rule, and no matter what I did, it *would not stop*. When talking with someone or engaging with the group, the heavy, oppressive energy would lift, but as soon as I started to pray, it would engulf me, and I would become drowsy and begin to dissociate. I tried to remain focused with everyone but was so distracted that after a while I had to go outside. I stood in the rain, breathing in the fresh air and asking God for help: "Please help my mind, body, and soul be freed from this tyranny." The situation persisted into the evening. I went outside again into the dark, wet night, and rested my forehead against the trunk of a tree, repeating the words of the Jesus Prayer. Eventually the oppression subsided, and I felt that it was safe to return inside.

However, the heightened energy of the situation had made me feel ungrounded. I wanted to be anchored by the presence of another person, but I went to the prayer room at the top of the house alone instead and bent down on the raffia carpet floor. After a few minutes of kneeling there in silence, I remembered a conversation I'd had with Sister Damaris when in America, about how Christ ministers to us in the broken places of our being, and I began to cry. I then began to pray, facing the image of Christ mounted on the wall. Jesus Christ, please cleanse me. I asked the Lord to help me make peace with the patriarchy of Christianity, so that the matriarchy of paganism—which still felt to me much more reasonable—and the spirits that went with it might lose their grip on me. Following this moment of communion with the Lord, everything became normal again and I returned downstairs.

Standing in prayer afterward, a vision then began. I saw Christ before me, seated on a throne, shrouded in heavenly light. Everything about Him was made of light. His robes were glittering, sparkling, and shimmering with life. I could only see a sliver of His face because He was facing away from me. He was giant in size, His throne a temple in front of me. I looked up at Him as life flowed down from His robes. The corner of His prayer mantle spread out toward me into a huge pool of living water. I was on the other side of this lake of life, and in the vision I knelt down and began to drink from the pool of water. The vision continued as we prayed, and each word I spoke filled my mouth with such sweetness, I felt like I was drinking honey. I felt this sweetness pour over me, drenching me in the honey of His love. I luxuriated in His holiness; my entire interior being cleansed with the purity of His living words.

Worship

The four living creatures, each having six wings, were full of eyes around and within. And they do not rest day or night, saying: "Holy, holy, holy, Lord God Almighty, who was and is and is to come!"
—Revelation 4.8

We ended our pilgrimage at a tiny Protestant monastery in Norway, inhabited by just four nuns. They had been sent to start it as a mission outpost of their larger monastery in Belgium. The monastery consisted of a smattering of raised wooden buildings in the middle of a flat expanse of rural land, bright white with snow. Nearby was a vast river, which streamed around iced-over islets. We had arrived in the middle of the night, and as soon as I stepped out of the van into the velvet silence of the Norwegian countryside, I fell in love. I had never seen so many stars before. Early the next morning, I went to the monastery's small chapel to pray. All the buildings shared the same bright Scandinavian aesthetic. Wood burners kept the monastery's assortment of little buildings cozy, while frequently opened windows meant that the rooms were consistently rejuvenated by a thorough circulation of fresh air (an alien concept to my Jordanian monastics). I was in heaven. I sat in the back row of the tiny chapel. It was quiet.

In accordance with Protestant theology (and Nordic minimalism), there was very little in the chapel, except for a large, wooden cross above the altar. The cross, the pews, the piano, and the walls were all carved from the same pale wood, the mimicry of which was both immensely satisfying and deeply calming. At the foot of the cross, one of the nuns had placed three pale-pink roses, tied into a posy. The only other object in the chapel was a life-size white dove, which was suspended from the ceiling by a piece of string. It floated in front of the cross, as if in flight. Despite the joy I was feeling as a result of being in such a beautiful place, I was not entirely at ease. During one of our stops in France, we had met up with some other families, and I was attracted to one of the unmarried men who had joined our group.

Suddenly, different emotions had begun to swirl inside me, and they had followed me all the way out to Norway. I had told Father that I felt that the Holy Spirit was drawing me, temporarily at least, into retreat, away from the possibility of a relationship, in order that He could do a specific work inside me. As soon as the encounter at New Year had taken place, I had been, as Mother Syncletica put it, "running in the spirit." But the result was a tension—between the Spirit, on the one hand, and the "flesh" (i.e., my former ways of judging, feeling, sensing, perceiving, and cognizing), on the other. This beginning of the falling away of my old man was an experience that was entirely unique. It wasn't *painful* necessarily, nor would I describe it as *intense*, as pagan purification is physically, emotionally, and in every other way.

The descent of grace was not like anything else I had experienced in this world. Nothing can compare to it because there is nothing else like it. It is light. It is life. But it did feel . . . strange. I realized that I was getting a glimpse of St Paul's teaching regarding the way in which the *outward man* perishes but the *inward man* is *renewed day by day* (2 Cor 4.16). I clasped my hands together, and rested my forehead on them, closing my eyes. Father had spoken to me about the sequence of stages that characterize the mystical journey, beginning with purification, followed by illumination, and finding completeness in union. The *theosis* that I had been unconsciously trying to achieve, through however misguided means—whether ascetic or hedonistic—prior to my conversion.

    The tension of this unwelcome but dizzying new attraction had been building for some days now, and I began to sob. As the tears streamed down my face, a vision began. In the vision was a valley, with a river running through it. On the hill that I, the viewer, was facing, there was a path upward, toward a line, on the other side of which was a swathe of bright light. At the boundary point between the hill and the light beyond it there was a ring of fire, standing upright like a doorway between two worlds. Next to it, however, was another track that also started down at the river. But on this path, there was not just one ring of fire, but one after the other, moving upward toward the boundary line. I understood. Each ring of fire symbolized a passage through death that resulted in divine union. On the path on the right, this happened once, at the end of the journey, at the point of biological death. On the path of the left, however, that moment of union with Christ, happened at the *beginning* of the journey, before death. On the right-hand path, it was the final step. On the left-hand path, however, it was *step one*. Life with a man or life with Christ. Both paths were open to me. I sobbed and sobbed, uncomfortably aware of what it was that Christ was inviting me into.

    That evening, I returned to the chapel. I had spent hours reading Scripture, as the Desert Fathers prescribed, praying the Psalms, and doing long sequences of prostrations, and I could feel that my spirit was completely activated as a result. Life on earth felt very far below me as I padded silently across the chapel floor. I was wearing a pair of knitted, alpine booties that each of the guests had been given at the beginning of the retreat. They had pom poms. A single lamp was burning in the middle of the altar space, lighting the cross from below. I kneeled on the floor and became very, very still. As I looked ahead, a second vision gushed open before me, like spreading myrrh, to flood the chapel, and I saw a vast, dark expanse, the same in quality and color as that in the encounter at New Year.

There were rows and rows of people, each made up of particles of light, shimmering and flaring. Each person was kneeling in their place, equidistant from those around them. Ahead of me in the distance, beyond these rows, was a throne. Christ sat in the center of the throne. His entire being gleamed, the same in quality as the people, though His stature was of a different dimension entirely. Vast. The kneeling figures bent over and then raised their upper bodies, their arms lifting upward with a shout, before again immediately bending prostrate before the throne. They were worshiping. The movement was ongoing and took place in *perfect* unison, but at the same time it moved in ripples across the expanse. It seemed to exist in a temporal frequency that was entirely distinct from anything I had ever encountered. On and on they worshiped. Glinting. Flickering. The burning worshipers and the burning throne. It was terrifying.

The Unseen

Someone passed sequentially through Islam, Hinduism, Buddhism and black magic. In all these religions at the same time he did magic. As soon as he became Orthodox, he wanted to practice it along with this magic, but he was unable to do it. From this he realized that magic is the foundation of all religions, and that religions are dead, their leaders are dead, but Christ is the living God.
—St Sophrony of Essex

Following the pilgrimage, I returned to London to pack up my belongings and move out. Nick was abroad. It had been two and a half months since the conversion on New Year's Day. After my things had been collected by my parents to be taken to their home, Nick returned and we said goodbye for the last time. I was due to stay at a friend's house until I was able to return to America, and as I made my way there via two massage clients the next day, I looked down at the small suitcase I had with me. On the road again. *Sojourner.* I had always been comfortable having a fairly flexible state of address, but I had pathologized this as a deficiency resulting from trauma. But maybe this is just how God had made me, ready for a life lived in Him. In many ways followers of Christ are total hippies in their attitude to where they live and how they will earn money: on the wings of the Spirit. Father Theophan frequently spoke about the need to overcome our obsession with planning out the future. When firmly situated within Christ and a life of prayer, everything necessary for one's salvation would be put in place. It was just down to us to remain wholly and completely focused on Him.

I settled into this new season and began to naturally wake before sunrise. But instead of trying to go back to sleep, as I would have in the past, I instead began praying, a candle flickering in the blue morning light. Bit by bit, my rule increased and some days, I would also read one or two of the Gospels, standing for the duration. I wasn't obligated to do this much yet, but I wanted to allow for as much cleansing as possible. After praying in this way, I felt amazing—centered, energized, clear, and sometimes elated. What I had to become accustomed to, however, was the fact that as someone who had converted to Christianity out of deep immersion in the occult, an easy start in the kingdom was not something that was permitted to me. Thankfully, during this period, things were generally steady in the daytime, and the only thing I had to contend with when awake was a demon rushing up to attack me in the psychic realm as I was dropping off to sleep. After saying the Jesus Prayer, I would feel His protection around me, and things would stabilize. However, when asleep, I was much more vulnerable, and it was in the dream realm that the consequences of my renunciation of magic and the spiritual powers that drove it were felt most acutely. I was in a war.

The spirits had different means of approach. One of the most common was a form of liturgical coercion, in which they would try to get me to participate in practices in the psychic realm that I no longer engaged in. On one occasion, I was standing in the middle of a field, surrounded by several huge fires. My whole body was aglow with the light of the fire in front of me, and I felt its heat on my face and hands. I looked into the mesmerizing flames, aware that I was dreaming. Many hours of my life had been spent next to the fire, tending it and contemplating its mysteries. It was my favorite place to be. Precious substances were then pressed into my hand, as I was encouraged toward the fire. Automatically my arm raised to make an offering, but instead of praying to the spirits and releasing the substances into the fire, a declaration of Trinitarian sovereignty poured out of my mouth, and I dropped the offering on the ground, before snapping awake, my heart beating. Each time this form of warfare occurred, the Holy Spirit gave me the words, actions, tools, or abilities—in the dream sphere—to escape each trap.

Perhaps the most destabilizing (and disgusting) were the instances in which spirits would approach me in disguise and draw me into some form of union with them, in order that they could attack me from up close. In another example, I found myself in a luxurious temple space, adorned with billowing silks and shallow pools of water. Another figure was in the space with me, and across the course of the evening, showered me with affection, holding my hand and guiding me around the temple. Again, I was aware that I was dreaming throughout. After—what felt like—hours of floating around together, the figure rapidly approached me and began to kiss me. At the exact moment that its mouth touched my mouth, I felt sharp fangs rip into my lips and tongue, and I jolted awake, as the spirit manifested its true, demonic form, rapidly clawing at my face, hissing and screaming. This became a pattern for my disturbing nighttime encounters with the spirits.

Although I was officially cut off from the spiritual side of yoga, I reasoned that as I tended to practice at home, I could still do the physical practice itself and avoid any *mudras* (ritual hand gestures) or poses that were connected to a specific Hindu deity. Throughout this period, I had been doing mostly mixed-movement and therapeutic sessions in order to avoid traditional yoga, as well as the sequence of moves I had perfected over the years to deal with my back, shoulder, and neck issues. With a whole day free ahead of me, I excitedly planned a sequence of exercise and self-massage in order to release the pain, prior to the weeks of physically strenuous massage work I had coming up.

Having done a couple of hours of tension release, I then did a class with a teacher whom I had always followed. The sequence was focused on core strength but had been interspersed with a few goddess poses. In order not to connect with that energy, I skipped them, continuing with what I was doing. At the end, concluding that I had successfully carried out an occult-free exercise routine, I lay flat on my back, resting after the exertion. As I lay there, however, I felt something landing on, and then in, my chest. I tried to ignore it but immediately began to feel very drowsy. I wanted to get up but found myself completely unable to, locked into a kind of waking paralysis.[50]

After a while I managed to get up and go to my bedroom, hoping that the feeling would pass. I really wanted to be free from this demonic influence. I was due to go out for dinner that evening but was overcome by intense drowsiness. I spent two hours reading the Bible to try and shift it, but I remained completely trapped. After showering in the hope it would change the situation, I prepared to go out to meet my friends. I felt terrible. Before meeting them, I drank tea in order that the caffeine (which I usually completely avoided) would lift the drowsiness, but it didn't work and I continued to feel cold, clammy, and on edge. The next day I woke

---

[50] Sleep paralysis is something I have experienced throughout my life. It was only through the witness of Christians who had converted from the occult, that I began to question why it was that I regularly experienced such a thing, as well as flying, underwater breathing, teleportation, entity communication, being fed by "characters" in the dreamworld and paranormal attachment. I deduced, from comparative conversations with others, that these were not in fact "normal" dream experiences but were rather the consequence of demonic influence and engagement with occultic practices. If you have all of the above but have never practiced magic, it is highly likely that someone in your ancestral line has.

up and was shocked to see that I was *still* in it. I then prayed as many Psalms as I could bear to and after several grueling hours, the sensation finally disappeared.

I emailed Father telling him what had happened, and he confirmed that its disappearance as a result of praying the Psalms was evidence of the fact that it had come from the satanic realm. As a result of this episode, I realized that the physical side of yoga can never be severed from the spiritual. Whether you believe in (the existence of) the spirits you are worshiping through yoga is irrelevant to the spirits. As long as you are worshiping with your body, and therefore giving them permission to dominate you and exercise invisible authority over your soul, you have already given them everything that they need. It looks innocent—and is perhaps the most widespread of all eastern practices—but it is not. As I was no longer under the spell of the powers that govern it, they had no reason not to attack me as violently as they could.

I had been a servant of yoga for years, a useful vessel for the dissemination of its teachings. Because Christ had opened my eyes to the truth, however, I had become useless. More than that, as someone who now belonged to, and served, Christ, I was a target. I messaged Father Theophan telling him that along with cutting off all forms of yoga, I was also eliminating all traces of womb work from my therapeutic practice. He was ecstatic to hear that the Holy Spirit was opening my eyes to the fact that a battle between dark and light was being waged over our souls.

Following my return from the pilgrimage, I had felt the Lord's hand bringing me an abundance of massage clients, so I could earn enough to cover the costs of the next trip to America. The extra money that remained once I had booked my flight was set aside as a small buffer for when I would return. It would give me a bit of money to cover the lag period before I could then book up more sessions and earn again. However, despite having made all that I thought was needed and some more, more work kept coming my way. Covid was beginning to intensify and I began to wonder if I would be able to get through the US border in time. Two days before my flight, they announced that the US border would be closing. My flight fell just after the restriction began. I went on the website to try and change my flight seeing that the last available outbound flight had risen by £500 since the announcement. *Now* I knew why God had brought me all that extra work. Thanks to that money and what my parents kindly offered to lend me, I was able to book the flight. It was a race—one missed step, and I would be shut out of America for as long as the virus continued. I *had* to get baptized. Everything in me was focused on this one moment that would cut, permanently, everything from the past. As my taxi pulled up to the monastery two days later, my body finally relaxed. By God's grace I was home.

Wilderness

Demons love fullness, drunkenness, and bodily comfort. Fasting has great power and works glorious things. Fasting is feasting with angels.
—St Athanasius the Great

I had entered the desert. The *inner* desert. The Orthodox lenten fast, the longest fast of the divine calendar, is a preparation for Christ's Resurrection. The intensity of the nuns' daily rule was amped up with the addition of more stringent fasting and an increased number of prayers, readings, and services. I told my sister that I planned to join the sisters in everything that they did. "Yeah," she answered, "I mean . . . what else are you going to do." Quite. The monastics had begun fasting a month before. As had been the case when I was there at Christmas, the diet was vegan. Apart from myself, there was one other guest: Aleja, a Brazilian missionary, who worked with tribes in the Amazon.[51] It was testament to the changes

---

[51] What a *coincidence* that she was there at the same time as me.

that had taken place within me that, despite my wariness, I was able to approach her with an open heart and was happy—and relieved—to find that she was kind and thoughtful, and that she understood the necessity of cultural sensitivity in the context of Christian mission.

As Great Lent progressed, it helped me to remind myself that I was standing directly before God as He sat on His holy throne, whenever I felt my energy lagging during prayers. Christ was in the room with us. The knowledge that the living God of heaven was watching us at all times began to alter my actions, thought processes, and choice of words. This was not out of fear of discipline and judgment, but rather out of love. The universal veil that had been blinding me had been lifted to reveal that Christ was right there before me (as He is for us all). It changed me. It had become so very personal. Any bad behavior on my behalf could no longer be dealt with through far off karmic recompense. Daily repentance, to *Him*, was required. Giving an account of everything that had happened throughout the day in the presence of the Holy Spirit was an evening practice prescribed by the Desert Fathers, and Mother Evgenia, who reminded me of Mrs Tiggy Winkle, had told me to talk to Jesus at all times.

"Whatever is in your heart, whatever you are thinking or feeling, whatever pain you have, talk to Him, talk to Him!"

When I had visited at Christmas, I had asked Sister Cherubima how the different mothers expressed their love for her, and she had given examples of something each had done, with each instance communicating something of their personality.

"And what about Mother Evgenia?" I asked.

"Well, I know Mother Evgenia loves me, because she tells me all the time," she shrugged. She sat up in her place and became more animated. "When I first arrived at the monastery, she would come up to me and be like 'I love you, Cherubima, I love you!'" She impersonated Mother Evgenia's mannerisms and her little scooting laugh.

PART TWO

The next day, as I walked toward the kitchen, I passed by Mother Evgenia as she descended the staircase. I stopped and smiled as she got to the bottom stair.

"Ooh, Tali!" she greeted me; she spoke only a little English. She laughed, tilted her chin down, and pursed her lips, before raising her eyes up toward me, smiling.

"I love you," she pointed at her heart and then at mine.

"Yes," she nodded.

"I love you." She giggled and clasped my hand in hers, squeezing tightly. She pulled me toward her and placed a delicate kiss on my forehead. I felt like I had struck gold.

I began to practice the discipline of emptying the contents of my heart and mind into Christ's hands throughout the day, inviting Him into the difficulties that were taking place within. My ego, so keen to problem solve, control, and dominate, would be planning, thinking, and strategizing. But I realized that I didn't need to waste time doing that anymore. I had spent so many years of my life imagining and planning future experiences, and then worrying about these projected future outcomes, for them to never even happen. Now that I knew that Christ, as opposed to an impersonal force, was holding me, I could truly relax. In a conversation with Sister Cherubima, I told her that when I felt overwhelmed, I would picture myself leaning backward onto Christ and allowing Him to carry me.

"Yes!" she exclaimed excitedly. Then leaning back in peace, "This is all that we are required to do." She gazed out of the window, the corners of her mouth turning upward ever so slightly. "This is all that He wants."

Fast

*Our great work is to lay the blame for our sins upon ourselves
before God, and to expect to be tempted to our last breath.*
—Abba Anthony the Great

As much as I had hoped that Great Lent would placidly float past as a result of this new understanding, it was not true. Again, the monastery forced things within me that needed to be healed to the surface. Issues that I had thought long dead—such as unhealthy behaviors around eating—reared up violently. Speaking to Father Theophan about the rabbit hole I had fallen into with food, he confirmed that it was natural that the enemy, furious at having lost me as a servant, would be attacking me in the areas in which I was most vulnerable. The conversation ended that period of out-of-control eating, a reminder of the hell that my life had been when separated from the love of God. In anticipation of Pascha, I followed the monastics' lead, focusing on repenting for everything within me that inhibited Christ's formation. It was beautiful observing the way in which the nuns attended to their prayer responsibilities as guardians of the whole world, praying on behalf of all those who were sick and in need. The spread of Covid and the introduction of lockdown measures increased the potency of what was taking place within the walls of the monastery. This was not a game.

After my jetlag wore off, I found getting up at four in the morning increasingly difficult. I would manage for several days, hating every minute of it, before hitting a wall and giving myself permission to turn over and go back to sleep when everyone left for the chapel. However, as I continued to fight this morning battle, I began to understand more deeply why it was that the monastics woke early. What shook me was the realization that the overlap between pagan night rites and the Church's night vigils was not coincidental. My *maestros* had taught me that three in the morning was a sacred portal, because it was at this time of the night that the universal forces are at their most potent. It was not formulated in this way in Christianity, but the fact that three in the morning was "the witching hour," was. Which is exactly what Sister Cherubima had said when we had discussed the topic. I hadn't shared my understanding regarding the universal portals, but realizing that three o'clock was understood to be a significantly intense time of night from the perspective of "the other side," the Church, it clicked. Oh, so three in the morning really *is* a portal. The Church's night vigils take place in order to mitigate the effects of the same dark powers that I had worshiped.

"And do the mothers refer to that? About the fact that witchcraft is at its strongest then?" I asked.

"No," she laughed. "They're too pure. They don't think like that."

When the link between these two things dawned on me, the reality of what had happened in me leaving paganism to become Christian was thrown into sharp relief. It felt incredibly surreal to realize that I was now praying *against* all the people from the past whom I loved. Or that most of their prayers were actually magic spells, and it was precisely *this* that Christians were combatting through *their* vigils. It was just so strange, going from there to here. The revelation that the destructive capacity of the foreign spirits local to a particular area, directly correlated with the number of Christians who either were or weren't in prayer at any given moment, made concrete the fact that prayer has a palpable role in the battle that is taking place in the unseen realm, and the role that the Church plays in maintaining spiritual equilibrium, from country to country.

Another reason why it was so important for me to pray before the sun rose—and why it was so hard—was that the demonic forces in my ancestral line were most aggressive during this time. I had come to see the morning vigils as a spiritual battleground in which the heavy power of magic was fought by the joyful cries of praise. The vigils were frequently unenjoyable, but if I missed them, this battle would otherwise be taking place in the dream sphere. Unconscious, I would not be able to offer much in the form of military might. Another aspect related to lessening the power of the "flesh," an ontological correcting of the imbalance whereby the physical dominates the spiritual. By breaking the sleeping/waking pattern of the world, Christians can proclaim their role as servants of the kingdom.

Father Theophan emphasized the importance of waking early by explaining that it was necessary that one gather the "heavenly manna" that was waiting for the Christian at this time. In waking before dawn, the believer could offer up his or her day to God. Not offered in this way, it gave the devil more room to sow seeds of discontent. In fact, Father said that if the day was *not* dedicated to God in this way, it by default belonged to the devil. I experienced this firsthand by how dazed, spaced out, and spiritually fatigued I felt on the days in which I chose to miss the vigil to sleep in. Across that period, I discovered a park nearby and would go there after I had done my chores to sit under the willow trees. Sometimes I would read, sometimes I would sing, or sometimes I would record a voice note to send to Carina, the one friend with whom I continued to speak regularly during the fast. One day I said a special prayer, a little nervously because of what might happen, asking Christ to enter into the deepest wounds of my past, as I felt Him knocking there.

Holy Week

By the sign of the cross all magic is stopped, and all witchcraft brought to nothing.
—St Athanasius the Great

During Holy Week, the morning vigils started at three and would go on some days for as long as ten hours. Most days this would be then followed by other services. The day would continue on with more Scripture

PART TWO 137

reading and prayers, and then dinner. The sleep deprivation began to work on my heart like a sweet tonic—I felt like I was floating. During my pagan life, there were often scenarios where I would have little sleep for consecutive nights as a result of ceremonies and rituals. What was different here, was that there were no mind-altering plants being imbibed. Ceremonies had always been quite easy in a way, because once you connected with the plant spirit, your time/space awareness shifted and the energy of the medicine carried you through the night. Sometimes for several nights in a row. This was much more intense. Waking in the dark we would head to the chapel to begin the vigils that would go on for hours and hours on end. Nowhere to run, nowhere to hide. Just you and the word of God.

One morning, after doing hundreds of prostrations in my cell, we headed to church. Dizzy with dehydration, I left the service to go and lie down in the adjacent dining hall. Just as I was beginning to relax into sleep, Sister Damaris jolted me awake.

"It's the moment when the cross is adorned with red roses, and the women are being invited to partake! Come! Come!"

I did not feel like standing up—at all—but forced myself to follow her out of the refectory and back into the service. Still feeling unsteady on my feet, I wove rose stems between the lattice and thought of Abuela Carika, my spiritual teacher from the mountains outside Mexico City. I nicknamed her *Abuelita Forza* (little grandmother force) because of the strength of her love and because of how powerful she was. When I told her that I had given my life to Jesus, after a long pause, pregnant with questions that she wasn't going to push me to answer, she responded, "Well, Christ is the master of the universe."

I think there was shock and disappointment that my conversion meant my leaving behind the medicine world. When she was in England, she would stay at Nick's and my house, and we would spend the weeks together cooking and singing. I learned so much from her. She helped support me in my retreats, leading the rituals as their spiritual elder. Like many of those of the North, Central, and South American indigenous population, she was Catholic, and Christ and the Virgin Mary had been integrated into her cosmology in a way that did not exclude her native traditions. Despite the implicit judgment that she might have felt by this radical change in my beliefs (which didn't exist in my heart), her warmth and wisdom meant she had continued to shower me with love, regardless.

Whenever I was near flowers, I always thought of her and the rose baths I would have at her house in Xochimilco. Although practicing divination with the petals after the bath was no longer necessary, because I was now in Christ and He alone held the keys to my future, the ways in which I had learned to interact with the beauty of nature alongside her was something that I treasured. As I continued to weave the flowers into Christ's cross, I thought of her daughter Delicia, and granddaughter Marisol, and the young girls in her town whom I had befriended. I would receive texts from them on WhatsApp (which I had downloaded again), sharing photos from their *escaramuzas*.[52] Maybe one day they could all come and join me out here in the desert. I wanted them to meet Father.

Resurrection

Death is transfiguration.
—Elder Gabriel Urgebadze

As a result of the stringent fasting and intensive schedule that the Church prescribed to draw believers into the potency of Christ's Passion, by the time the end of Holy Week approached, I was in an elevated and electrified state. "You're just flying, aren't you," Sister Cherubima laughed, rolling her eyes with affection, as we sat listening to Mother

---

[52] *Escaramuza* is an all-female sport within the Mexican equivalent of rodeo.

Syncletica explain that Baptism is a mystery of which all believers are to partake, not just the person being baptized, late on Friday night. I was. I could feel a divine flow of energy coursing through my body. After we were dismissed, I prepared everything for the coming service. I would be baptized on Holy Saturday, in the tradition of the early Church. Mother Syncletica had arranged for a floor-length white robe with a gold cross embroidered on the front to be made, and I had been taken to the local supermarket to buy white clothing. Sister Cherubima had given me the delicate white skirt she had worn for her Baptism several years earlier, over which I was going to wear a fine, ankle-length, white cotton cardigan that I had bought when in Barcelona.

Before we had left for the service, Sister Eleni quietly beckoned for me to come to the door of her cell. She gave me an icon of St Macarius the Great and a book on the necessity of retaining devotional love for Christ. Following the morning Liturgy, we filed into the refectory, to wait for the baptismal service to begin. Father Theophan was with us. Mother beckoned for me to go over to where they were sitting, so that Father could speak to me. He explained the order of events and then told me I could make a final Confession before the moment of transformation, if I wanted to. I nodded eagerly. There were some things I needed to clarify. They got up and walked me over to the corner of the room, out of earshot of the other nuns, who were sitting in silence.

Mother Syncletica sat down, shimmying into the back of the chair (once she sat down, her feet no longer touched the floor, tiny as she was). Father Theophan stood beside her, bending forward to create a private sanctuary in which I could confess. I kneeled on the floor in front of them, looking up at their faces. Mother was grinning (she was always grinning when sitting next to Father), and Father looked down at me, smiling, his eyebrows furrowed slightly in preparation for the Confession.

"Does it need to be specific, or can I just speak of what's been going on, because there are a couple of things . . ."

"Just whatever is on your heart, my dear daughter," he said, in his gentle, rasping voice. "Whatever you want to tell your Father and Mother, feel free. Take as long as you want."

I nodded and began to speak.

After being baptized and wrapped in piles of bright white towels, I was led to the middle of the nave and anointed with the holy *myron*. The boundary between the physical and the unseen felt very fragile. As the priest applied the chrism to my forehead, I began to see clouds streaming in and out of one another above me. Blue sky emerged between the clouds as they rapidly merged and parted, revealing the delicate movement of rich, white plumes that fluttered in harmony with the movement of the wind and all that was taking place in the chapel below. The open heaven pulled my heart upward into the radically open sky. I was then dressed in the white garments for the procession and my first Communion.

In Orthodoxy, one receives a new name in Baptism. Father Theophan and Mother Syncletica had prayed separately about what it would be, both receiving the same answer: *Anastasia*. Greek for "resurrection," the name communicated both the blessedness of my paschal Baptism, and the miraculous transformation that precipitated it. It also introduced me to Saint Anastasia the *Pharmakolitria* ("Deliverer from Potions" in Greek), who is revered as a healer and exorcist, and who had come into Christianity through paganism. The word used by Saint Paul for "sorcery" in the New Testament is *pharmakeia*, which denotes drug use or, more pertinently for me, "dealing in poison." The term was applied to the ritual use of plants divination, spell casting, or healing. Through this detail, I understood that Christ, in His sovereignty, had been present throughout everything that had taken place and had known exactly what path I would take, and where it would lead. I felt myself enveloped in Christ's love. He was in everything: present, past, and future. Sitting with Father and Mother after the service, Father spoke about the mystery of spiritual covering in the life of the newly baptized.

"Because your life in magic was a 'naked' life in the spirit, you were completely exposed and without any spiritual protection," he started.

"But the sacred covering that you just received in Baptism, the mystical, inner garment, will have significant effects on what takes place in the spiritual realm."

Referring to St Paul's teaching on the importance of making sure that our spiritual nakedness is covered by Christ, he explained the rage that the enemy felt at the fact that I, one of his former servants who had always been "kept naked," had been delivered from the occult. A deliverance that meant that I now had this holy garment to cover my inner man.[53]

"If this garment that we receive is allowed to extend, it will transform our inner being, changing our thoughts and our emotions, until all our senses are transformed," he said, his face lit with peace as he spoke.

"*Then*," he said, "God will release your calling. Your true calling, Anastasia, supported and activated by *His own* anointing. Then you will make a *real* difference in the lives of women. *Then* you will be able to really help your generation."

The explanation complete, he turned to Mother Syncletica and rapidly translated what he had said into Arabic. She smiled and nodded slowly as she listened, and then she looked at me, and grinning, nodded vigorously. We then discussed what was going to happen next in the deepening of my education and immersion in Christ. We spoke about marriage, celibacy, and taking monastic vows. The richness of the wisdom they had acquired through their years of asceticism provided the perfect answer to my questions of what it was that needed to happen and when—continue the daily steps of prayer, prostration, and soaking in worship and according to Christ's will, all would become clear. We decided that after returning to England to renew my visa, I would then come back when next possible, to continue studying the living theology of Christ.

---

[53] *For in this we groan, earnestly desiring to be clothed with our habitation which is from heaven, if indeed, having been clothed, we shall not be found naked. For we who are in this tent groan, being burdened, not because we want to be unclothed, but further clothed, that mortality may be swallowed up by life* (2 Cor 5.2–4).

Magic

The world is passing away . . .
—1 John 2.17a

Through the removal of the obstructive idols that had been inhibiting me from directly communing with the Spirit, I was now able to drink from the divine source of life. Jesus' restorative work in my soul had cleaned through a blockage that had inhibited me from creating. In the months leading up to my conversion, I had started to put in place a plan for my artwork. I had a whole exhibition's worth of pieces in my mind but never actually created any of them as a result of how scattered and burnt out I was. But in the deep time of the monastery, in which the lack of any outside stimulus encouraged the pouring forth of all that was hidden within, I began to draw again. Our immersion in prayer meant being drenched in a constant stream of life-giving words that I would then translate into art. The project I had been working on prior to my conversion was a selection of portraits of myself as different tantric goddesses. There was a goddess in particular whom I worshiped, whose egolessness was communicated through the act of her cutting off her head so that her female servants could drink her blood. An image that then figured in the menstrual art I produced as a means of reclaiming and celebrating the otherwise denigrated natural cycles of the feminine body.

Through my conversion, however, these beliefs began to change. The first thing that happened was that the Lord showed me that my womb was an idol. I honored the womb above all else. It was because of the ostensible lack of womb wisdom in Christianity that I had rejected it so violently. But in that moment of insight, I realized that unlike Christ, who had died on the cross for me, my womb would not be able to save me from death. I know it sounds kind of stupid, but if we elevate something above God, then this is the life-giving power we are imbuing it with, however unconsciously. Later in the monastery, the second stage of this transformation took place. A memory of myself in the forest, offering my blood to the earth and using it to paint my body came to mind. But instead of seeing vitality and regenerative power as I always had, I suddenly saw death. The forest, I, and my blood were all dead, drained of color.

When I had arrived at the monastery for my second stay, I had decided I would continue the process of the total abandonment of everything I had known prior to my encounter with Christ, as an exercise in letting go and trusting in the Lord's wisdom. Because menstruation had been part of my idol worship, I decided I would not do anything I previously had when on my period, as a means of offering Christ repentance for my former life. With severe cramps, I pushed through my tasks, praying and asking God for help. Speaking with Father Theophan about what approach I should take during this time of the month, he encouraged me to be very gentle with myself, to take as much time as I needed to integrate all that had been happening since the conversion, and to drink lots of fluids. It was, he said, a "season," in which one was to take extra care of the body. He emphasized that Christ was doing a deep, restorative work in every area of my being, including, if not particularly, my womb.

Through all the changes that had been happening, however, I found that I was no longer drawn to create art depicting menstruation, but instead the blood of Jesus, the ultimate source of life. In this I noticed a pattern that had taken place between my conversion and my Baptism. Symbols that had once been central to my previous world reappeared, but in the context of Christ. Instead of menstrual blood, I was now painting Christ's holy blood. During my Baptism I had been anointed with holy oil, and the stripes mirrored the marks painted in honor of a particular deity, in the pagan rituals I had taken part in. During my refuge vows, the lama had cut some of my hair as part of my initiation into living under Buddha's authority. As I was declaring my willingness to be united with Christ, my hair was again cut. Also my voice, which had previously been a tool used by the enemy to direct my worship away from the living God, began to chant holy songs of Christ' divinity. I shared my thoughts with Mother Syncletica. "Yes," she said. "Because Christ is redeeming all the parts of you that were stolen by the enemy and restoring them to their intended original use, when they were given as gifts during your creation." This cosmic homecoming was another reminder of the way in which Christ knew me better than I knew myself.

My sister had described the monastery as a universe in itself, in answer to my question of how it was that she could stay inside it for so long without leaving. This was something I then experienced myself on becoming one of the planets in its solar system. The monastery also had its own particular time quality. A spiritual-psychological process that might take six weeks to be worked through in traditional therapy would be completed in a twenty-four-hour period. Time seemed to expand in direct correlation with the contraction of our geographical location. This dynamic between limitation on the one hand, and opening on the other, characterized Christianity more generally. However, I soon started to feel very trapped by the pressure of the monastery and the sense of a life ahead of me entirely devoid of opportunities outside its walls. Beginning to feel the heat of my voluntary isolation, my mind began racing toward the future. I'm a people person—I thought—I need to be out in the world. As the tension began to rise within me, I became increasingly claustrophobic. Just as I was beginning to hatch a plan to escape, Father Theophan spoke to us about how our generation was imprisoned by the false freedom of self-fulfillment. He said that it is only through Christ and the cross of self-denial that genuine freedom can ever be experienced. As he spoke, I began to cry, waves of ecstatic peace flowing over my heart. I saw an infinite horizon ahead of me, with Christ's golden light radiating across the sky.

As someone who had struggled with addiction, I knew the mechanism of escaping pain and suffering only too well. It is what addicts do. Entering recovery, I had started to explore the subtle behaviors that underpin the addictive cycles themselves: the existential emptiness, the deep wounding, the low self-esteem. Complexes that then drive the addict in their fruitless attempts to use created substitutes, whether edible, snortable, or in some cases, fully human, to fill the aching void that can be filled by God alone. Reading Genesis, I began to see how this urge toward ending the solitary confinement of a fragmented psyche disconnected from the Father, the source of life and blessedness, pointed directly back to Eden. The idea of a deep chasm within, that one tries to fill—the famous "hole in the soul"—is a fairly common way that repetition compulsion is conceptualized, in popular discourse as much as in therapeutic practice. I had always understood this as being the initial disconnection from the source of all life, the archewound, of which all other traumas were a later iteration. Which is true.

What the Bible offered, however, was a deeper explanation of how and why this came about in the first place. Most importantly, what it also offered was its solution. By placing the importance of the *personal* relationship at the forefront of the discussion, Christian theology offered a means of salvation that would result in the desired completeness: being made whole again. The radical element of this was that the single means of this taking place was through a relationship with the person of God. The divine energy of God that permeates every part of the cosmos is not enough to fully transform the originary wound. Only through willingly interacting with God's person as articulated through the Son can the fissure be permanently healed. Because it is through the falling away from the relationship between humanity and God in the garden that the wound came about in the first place.

Throughout the lenten fast and the period of feasting that followed, I observed the way in which Christ drew behavioral patterns, toxic cultural conditioning, and early trauma to the surface in order that they could be addressed. Like many whose boundaries had been routinely violated, my understanding of where they lay—and what I, as a human being, had a right to do or not do, if they were transgressed—had been scrambled. Sensitive as I also was, I tended to pick up on other people's emotional states very easily and would be affected by them, often to a destructive extent. Although a gift in some respects, it frequently led to my being "swamped" by other peoples' feelings, engendering mental and emotional confusion. Blurred boundaries. One highly sensitive trait that plagued my existence was guilt-driven, stress-inducing, hyper-awareness of other people's anger. Eager to smooth over even the most hair-thin crack of conflict, I would anxiously manufacture circumstances in which I could ingratiate myself with (or apologize to) the relevant person, as a means of easing my discomfort.

In psychotherapy, this would be called a "low distress tolerance." This effort toward grounding myself through verbal communication was something I thought I had moved on from as a result of the inner work I had done during my pagan life. However, it had just been suppressed by the fierce persona I had developed in response to the unconscious repulsion I felt toward my sensitivity.[54] Once the Holy Spirit began to gently push at the edges of this mask, the stress and anxiety began to overwhelm me again. But rather than talking things out "American style," as the Jordanian mothers put it, it was monastic discipline to instead go to one's cell whenever one had an issue and then, after much prayer, *maybe* talk it through with the concerned person, *if* it was still absolutely necessary. Being forced to do this taught me two very important things. One, prayer works. Two, the more I submitted all my interpersonal interactions to Christ, the more the Holy Spirit was able to bless my relationships. One problem after the other was resolved simply by talking to the Lord.

---

[54] Those with perceptibly high sensitivity are more prone to stress, as their systems are easily overloaded by too much sensory input. Understanding how significantly this impacted my experience of being alive only came to light through Christ. Growing up I just thought that there was "something wrong with me," that I was "a cry baby," and later, that I was "crazy."

Air

> *Only the religion of Christ unites and all of us must pray that they come to this. Thus union will occur, not by believing that all of us are the same thing and that all religions are the same. They are not the same . . . our Orthodoxy is not related to other religions.*
> —St Porphyrios of Kavsokalyvia

Through entering the consecrated space of the monastery, my understanding of what was taking place in the unseen realm and the way in which I had been deceived were clarified. When in the airport on my way back from the pilgrimage, I had walked past a cosmetics shop. At the front of the store was a big stone Buddha statue. Although pretty standard, I realized something new—this statue was marking a spiritual territory in the physical realm. Through the pilgrimage, the difference between the spirit world and the unseen realm had been brought into focus. The former was only part of the overall picture, while the latter included reality in its entirety. As well as YHWH, there is a heavenly host of different ranks of spiritual beings and angels who are immortal. After God created humans in His image and they rebelled, death entered creation ending the unbroken connection between humanity and divinity. They were now separated by sin. God's holiness is so perfect that it is not possible for anything negative, dark, or unclean to exist within Him and as a result, we, so long as we are sinning, are separated from Him, the God of love.

Growing up, I had always perceived this dynamic to be predicated on a kind of moral, psychological judgment—that the moment of cohesion between humankind and God is about to take place but God looks at us, sees our sin, and then callously says "no." In this understanding, which is how a lot of people see the situation, God is the one who appears to be actively rejecting us, as opposed to us rejecting God through our refusal to repent. The way I had seen it in the past was that the world and its ways were the standard while God, in His total purity, the deviation. Isn't this the metaphysical foundation upon which all arguments against repentance, sobriety, and chastity are based? The idea being that sinning is *natural* and thus must be okay. However, it is only natural in a worldview that doesn't involve the fall. The Fathers of the Church teach us that our natural state is actually our prelapsarian state, while the sinful state is our "conditioned" state. Because the fall is roundly not accepted, the fact that humanity tends toward sin is used as a legitimation for sin itself. The idea, therefore, is that we are desperately trying to reach a level of *unnatural* (and by implication unhealthy) perfection, in order to be able to live up to God's strict standards. With failure to do so resulting in punishment of everlasting damnation.

Through meeting the Lord and His love, I began to understand that actually it is the world and its sin that is the aberration. Returning to the edenic state was the inner aspect of the forward motion of entering the kingdom realm. Through meeting Christ, my conception of how this separation through sin manifested also changed. Instead of seeing God as either drawing people toward Him (or pushing them away), it is as if the energetic force field of God's holiness is such that it repels all that is not holy. It was not a question of God's picking and choosing some people over others—a painful concept that causes so many people to reject Him. Rather it is impossible for anything impure to be assimilated into His person, and *this* is why we, as humans, are separated by sin. It is like trying to mix water with oil—they simply do not blend.

Alternative spirituality teaches that it is our *forgetting* of the fact that beneath layers of conditioning and obfuscation we are inherently divine that inhibits us from knowing and experiencing God (which is understood to be more a state of being than a living person). In Christianity, we are understood to be image-bearers of God, but we can only come into relationship with Him through a process of repentance in which we fully surrender to God's sovereignty. In alternative spirituality the boundary between the human and the divine is reducible to a matter of perception, and the more enlightened one becomes through ascetic praxis, the more one's perception is purified, so one can see that there is no separation between God and humankind. No one, absolutely *no one*, talks about sin in alternative spirituality.

In terms of the heavenly host, when I had come to the monastery for the first time at Christmas, I had found certain terms in the Psalms incredibly worrying. This intense focus on the separation between humanity and the realm of darkness jarred my nondual worldview.

"Everyone's got a chance to go to heaven, right?" I asked my sister, following the recitation of a particularly violent Psalm.

"Even with the devil. Shouldn't we love the devil in order that he is healed and can then return to heaven?" I looked at her in distress.

She nodded to demonstrate understanding of my line of thought. A line of thought that she, as someone who came from the same social world as me, and who had dabbled in eastern practices, had probably had herself.

"The general understanding is that the devil and his followers, in choosing to rebel, eliminated themselves from the spiritual feast of everlasting life with the Trinity."

I could see that she was choosing her words carefully, so as not to upset me.

"However, the Fathers say that the salvation of the spirits is not our responsibility. We are to instead focus on our own repentance."

I was getting used to this teaching that we are not actually supposed to delve into the kingdom of darkness, gaining knowledge of its every aspect. It is vast and it is evil. Instead, we are commanded to be totally set apart: *"Come out from among them and be separate,"* says the Lord. *"Do not touch what is unclean, and I will receive you"* (2 Cor 6.17).

This had come up with Father Theophan and Mother Syncletica while driving to Liturgy one day during Lent. It was an unusual treat to have Father in the car with us, so everyone was asking him theological questions as we drove to the church, to make the most of his presence. Aleja and I sat side by side behind him, leaning forward so as to hear him.

"But what about praying for the spirits?" I began. "Isn't it through our prayers that the spirits will also be able to come to God?" Father Theophan shook his head.

"So, as believers we do not engage with the kingdom of darkness at all. We do not have any communication with the spirits." He translated the question for Mother Syncletica. She closed her eyes slowly and shook her head side to side, lips pursed.

"Wait, no, I'm not praying *to* the spirits, I mean praying *for* the spirits. I'm praying for their salvation!" Everyone laughed. He translated again, to make sure she understood correctly.

"Yes, but we are to have no contact, relationship, or connection with the satanic realm. We do not engage. In the Scriptures there is very little said about the kingdom of darkness. There is little information given about what takes place in the spiritual underworld. *This is for a reason.*"

Following my conversion, I was able to see that the world was divided into areas that were presided over by different powers and principalities. As a result of immersing myself in the Scriptures, I then began to understand more deeply what they referred to. Formerly part of the heavenly host, these spiritual powers had rebelled against the unseen God's command to preside over the world, which had been apportioned into different territories. Because we were created to worship God in the garden, we tend toward this activity. But instead of the more difficult route of worshiping the unseen God, we instead tend toward worship of created spiritual beings—the powers and principalities—who were put in place by God to rule over us. Because of pride, these powers and principalities took humanity's worship for themselves rather than directing it to the true source of life, God, and in so doing, created a spiritual barrier between the human heart and its true source, the Trinity. All the different gods and goddesses I had worshiped and served were these spirits.

PART TWO

Lord of Heavenly Armies

For we do not wrestle against flesh and blood, but against principalities,
against powers, against the rulers of the darkness of this age,
against spiritual hosts of wickedness in the heavenly places.
—Ephesians 6.12

The differentiation between ranks and status made sense, because my years in the healing world had shown me enough of the spirits to know that the impure energies that caused illness and suffering were not the same in quality as the resplendent gods and goddesses I worshiped. An entity, which was the word most commonly used in that world (demon was too religious), was self-evidently dark, heavy, and the cause of sickness; while a god or goddess was light, shockingly beautiful, and far greater in power. Now there was a clear explanation. The consecrated spiritual beings who serve Christ are organized and grouped into different ranks. Because the servants of the devil are former members of this heavenly host, they too were created to have different roles and qualities. Therefore, when they rebelled, they created a dark mirror of the heavenly army of God.

Speaking with Sister Damaris about peyote, I asked for her perspective on the way it worked, in order to work out the conflict between my positive experiences with the spirit and the negative reality I now knew was the truth. She said the way it mirrored the devil when he tempted Jesus in the desert—do this for me and I will do this for you—demonstrated its alignment with the kingdom of darkness. It was such a simple answer. I then shared about a medicine man I knew, who had entered into an especially stringent contract with the spirit who gave him his healing abilities. The spirit, which was identified as a saint within our world, was feared and revered in equal measure. Normally, it took many years of hardship, pilgrimage, and a punishing schedule of sacrifices across the years (each of which took months to complete) for a person to attain the level of mastery that this man had achieved. However, it had taken him just six months. But at a price.

The speed of his development was predicated on one condition: that he did not miss a single sacrifice. Unable to maintain the agreed upon schedule of traveling, hunting, and offering prescribed by the spirit with whom he had entered into this contract, he had been severely punished. Eight of his ten children had been killed. "So," he said listlessly, in a state of drunken reverie after one of our ceremonies, "now I only have two." Christ gives freely because there is no way that we can repay the gift of everlasting life. In paganism, relationships with the spirits are nurtured and sustained through giving offerings and adherence to different rituals, ceremonies, and feasts. In Christianity, the only "offering" we are required to give is to believe that Christ is the Son of God. But God does not *need* our worship. He wants it and desires to have an intimate relationship with us, but He doesn't need us. We need God. But God needs nothing.

Through this understanding, I was then able to distinguish between the different types of spirits I had encountered. Those that had a religion organized around them were some of the most powerful, their scope exceeding their initial geographical territory to span a wide spatial range. Within Tibetan Buddhism there were different Bodhisattvas, deities (some wrathful, some gentle), gurus, and masters who existed on a lower rank than the Buddhas themselves and in Hinduism, different deities, gurus, and adepts. Based on the teaching of the Bible, the concept of a human who had rejected salvation through Christ but had ascended and was now floating around in the heavenly realms supporting life on earth was not tenable. Either you were a human created in God's image, an image-bearer, who was subject to death, or you were an inhuman spirit who was immortal, because *Man is destined to die once, and after that to face judgment* (Heb 9.27).

Therefore, all the millions of different masters, gurus, and adepts encountered by occult worshipers in meditation were in fact unclean spirits disguised as humans. In the case of my practice, the main guru under whose power I had been would often appear to me while I was channeling. He was a beloved—and loving—presence. I had taken it as a given that following his "ascension" he now existed outside the laws of death and rebirth in the spiritual field, shining light down into the world and helping his channels to heal people. According to the Bible this wasn't a possibility. I had photos of him when alive, and there are accounts of his life from followers that pointed to his humanity. If this was the case, the guru whom I then met in the channel, and who was driving this energetic matrix was *not* this same human guru but was instead a very high-ranking demon impersonating him. The other option was that he never was actually a human being (as Gautama Buddha seems to have been) but appeared to people as one.[55] Once his "life" on earth ended, he continued his work controlling territories from his position in the immortal realm. Both options were simply nightmarish. The whole thing was also very confusing. Despite what had happened to me, and all that has been revealed through Christ, the memories I had of my experiences with the spirits were of how intensely blissful they were.

For most human beings, who are as hungry as I was, encountering that density of supernatural force in a spiritual entity would mean falling prey to its charms. Which is the whole point. The inhabitants of the kingdom of darkness are more powerful and more intelligent than humans. They have been studying us for many, many years. They know what makes us tick and what we yearn for above all else. They know the deepest desires of our hearts, and what we will do to fulfill those desires. At any cost. And so they play into our weaknesses, in order to entrap us and imprison us in a spiritual stranglehold that we can't escape. First, because we are completely unaware of what is happening to us spiritually as a result of projecting God's qualities onto these dark forces and assuming that they have our

---

[55] Although there might have been a Hindu prince to whom the mythology is ascribed, that human being is not the same spiritual being encountered in Buddhist worship.

best interests at heart, and second, because we are not able to break out of these contracts without the power of Christ's Resurrection helping us to do so. It is only through grace that, once enmeshed in demon worship, one is able to be released, as my experience shows.

The Force

> *Azazel taught men to make swords, and knives, and shields, and breastplates, and made known to them the metals of the earth and the art of working them, and bracelets, and ornaments, and the use of antimony, and the beautifying of the eyelids, and all kinds of costly stones, and all coloring tinctures. And there arose much godlessness, and they committed fornication, and they were led astray, and became corrupt in all their ways. Semjaza taught enchantments, and root-cuttings, Armaros the resolving of enchantments, Baraqijal taught astrology, Kokabel the constellations, Ezeqeel the knowledge of the clouds, Araqiel the signs of the earth, Shamsiel the signs of the sun, and Sariel the course of the moon. And as men perished, they cried, and their cry went up to heaven . . .*
> —The Book of Enoch 13

The Holy Spirit began to draw attention to certain memories, so that they could be reframed by what I now knew. However, it was still extremely hard for me to understand how it was that *plants* could be working against God's purposes. They were *part of nature*. God had created nature out of love, and it was, as Genesis attests, good (Gen 1.31). A particular memory from my life with the plants helped me to see how nature, having become accursed, could support the kingdom of darkness. Ayahuasca rituals often began with the application of *rapé*,[56] a potent tobacco

---

[56] *Rapé* is one of the strongest medicines in the jungle and is revered for its healing and purifying properties. In the tradition in which I studied most extensively, it was taught that the ayahuasca (a feminine spirit) was the consciousness, while *rapé* (which is

snuff used by tribes in the Amazon. The medicine was applied through the nostrils, either by another or through self-application. It was used widely throughout the medicine world, with people applying it all through the day and all through the night. Outside of the ritual, the snuff could be used to clear one's energy field, to ground oneself, or to receive messages.

In the context of a ceremony, the medicine was offered in order to—amongst many things—help the receivers purge the blockages and entities that the ayahuasca was working into within them. One would often feel intensely sick (especially in the early days) as the plant spirit burrowed into all the toxins in the body. Because the medicine caused nausea, *rapé* would then be used in order to release what was within. During the ceremony, the amount given would increase with the shaman blowing two small piles into each nostril. After the medicine had been administered, the attendees would then go and sit in their places until they purged. Tobacco is in and of itself bitter in taste, but the way the powder would hit the throat and then enter the stomach (if you swallowed—which you generally would) meant that the contents of the stomach were forced up in a particularly violent way. While this process was happening, a potent connection with the plant spirit would activate, and one might receive messages or visions. Although the attendees were keen to demonstrate their aptitude with this medicine, its effect on westerners was undoubtedly stronger than on that of our indigenous teachers. They would hoover up small handfuls of the snuff before nonchalantly jumping into the river for a swim.

The purgative effects of the medicine meant that it was used in other contexts as well. I had a love/hate relationship with *rapé*. I loved the release it gave me during the rituals—as well as the sense of power that resulted from being someone who received strong doses—but outside of ceremony it made me feel extremely sick. Yet I continually used it. It was such a

---

masculine) healed: She opened up the psyche, but he forced the entities out through purgation. How the *rapé* was made would change from region to region. Most medicine lineages would have a strong mythology around the ritualized use of tobacco that was unique to each tradition, as well as different uses for it.

central part of the Amazonian tradition I was involved in that I didn't feel like I had a choice. Everyone used it. I wondered what was wrong with me, that I reacted to it in the way that I did. A story was shared about this medicine during one of the circles I had organized when in Brazil. It was the early morning, and thirty of us sat in a large, straw-roofed *maloca*. The ritual had just ended, and it was now time for the sharing circle. It had been an exhausting night. All sat up as best they could, but heads were frequently bobbing down into sleep. Baniweye, one of the shamans, began to teach everyone about the history of the medicine. She spoke in Portuguese as Verena, her student, translated into English.

"The way that we experience the medicine now," she began, "is very different from how it was experienced in the past."

She shifted in her seat so as to better load the ceremonial pipe that she had been using throughout the night.

"They would say that when they took the medicine before, they would feel fire tearing down their throat and into their chest. They would be screaming and would jump into the river to try and take away the heat. They would be throwing up in the river, trying to vomit their heart out of their mouth to take away the burning."

It was during that particular tour that I had my worst experience with *rapé*. I had met Verena in the Amazon during an ayahuasca festival I had attended with Fernanda. Western Brazilian, but a long-time student of the tradition, she was one of the helpers guiding our group. I fell head over heels in love with her. She was deeply committed to the forest path, and she would sing haunting songs from her time with other tribes. I felt so inadequate in her presence, and so I didn't pursue anything, reasoning that this fiery Amazonian medicine goddess was not going to be interested in a pale English girl who could barely speak a word of Portuguese. We, however, formed a strong bond, and several years later, I agreed to organize part of the medicine tour she was doing with Baniweye, her indigenous teacher. Big mistake. Verena had a natural fierceness that was wild and beautiful. However, this had turned into something much more disturbing,

PART TWO   157

as a result of her increasingly intense journey into the absolute darkest depths of violent, jungle witchcraft. I had watched in distress as the light in her, to which I had initially been so drawn, was gradually stamped out by the influence of the extremely powerful spirit to which she had given absolute control of her life.

Although she was never physically violent with me, I later found out that her girlfriend, with whom I had become close, would bear the brunt of her rage. Working for Verena had left me drained beyond belief. However, the nature of the plants and the machinations of the spiritual realm to which they had given me access meant that stopping for rest was not an option. The work needed to be done. Six weeks of ceremonies and twenty-four/seven shaman care-taking. It was during the tour that I lost trust in the medicine for the first time. Ayahuasca was more to me than a spirit, or a medicine, or a healer. My entire life, my entire being, was devoted to her. She was my mother. I loved her unconditionally. It is impossible to explain how much I loved this spirit. The way she made me feel, the things she opened up inside me, the way she had taken me out of the darkness of the partying world and into this empowered, edenic, celestial reality. I was willing to do anything to serve her and help the knowledge of her healing power spread throughout the world. But then that changed.

The rituals had gotten so dark that I had begun to doubt ayahuasca's goodness. During one of the nights in the lead-up to the final night, an entity that had been extracted from an attendee during one of the in-ceremony healings (for which the person would then be asked to pay $180—whether that person had wanted the healing or not—a system I violently opposed) came to attack me while I was sleeping. In a state of sleep paralysis, I had found myself suspended in a huge valley of flames, the fire burning through me, as I, screaming, desperately tried to escape the demonic power approaching the vestibule in which I was locked. After a while of semi-conscious terror, Nick shook me awake. I was actually screaming. I had woken him up. Heart beating, I began to cry until he soothed me back to sleep. *I can't take this anymore.* I would say this a lot, most often during particularly grueling purging sessions with the *rapé*. I had been sick for five weeks with a virus that had developed into a lung infection. I would leave the *maloca* during the ceremonies to cough and cough, bringing up phlegm, before returning and drinking more medicine. It gave me the energy I needed to get through the prayers. Unable to stop the work, my body had started to cry out for help. But listening to my body, or my heart for that matter—or even my mind—was not an option. I had to keep going, virus or no virus.

The day before the final ceremony, I applied some *rapé* as I often would. Because I had been ill, my sinuses had been blocked, and so I used more than usual. This time, however, there was no resistance, meaning that the medicine hit me hard. I began to feel dizzy. Sometimes the effect—for me—of using it was that my entire body would go cold and clammy, and I would feel as if I had been administered poison. After hours of feeling awful and not being able to shake it off no matter what I did, I dug deep within myself to find the energy to do a healing and created a crystal grid in the shape of a cross. Yeshua will help me.[57] I felt like the top of my head had been wrenched open, and I couldn't bring myself back to normality. One of the spirits of the tradition was making its ownership of this unseen nexus known to the foreign entities (I was one of them), who had come into its orbit, and who were taking—as well as profiting—from its matrix of underworld power.

Opening the grid as normal, I was shocked by what I saw. It was unlike anything else I had ever seen in that psychic field. As was often the case, I was suspended in the astral-realm (this time on top of a grid in the shape of a cross), with the world beneath me and the cosmos around me. But whereas I would normally be in a state of peaceful presence, I instead saw

---

[57] Verena and I had bonded over our love for Jesus. When I met her in the jungle, I told her that she reminded me of a friend from Israel. "This is Jesus' land," she responded smiling, "I like this!" Before leaving, I had engraved a wooden crucifix from Jerusalem that my aunt, an Anglican priest, had given me for the trip, with some words we had shared, as a present for her altar.

a pillar of fire in the center of my body, extending for miles upward. The burning pillar blazed and blazed as I began to try to alleviate the problem, calling on all the gurus and guides of the lineage, and using all the tools I had developed to clean up the situation. Eventually things started to get better, and I was able to receive the flow of healing energy into my chakras. After cleansing and then energizing myself, for some time, I felt able to function again. As it was the day before the final ceremony, I had planned an intensive evening of preparatory rituals, but I instead requested of Nick, who was with me on the tour, that we eat pizza and ice cream and watch *Legally Blonde* on Netflix. I needed to check out in as many ways as I possibly could. I was completely and utterly *finished*.

Witchcraft

Regard not spells and divinations, for that is communion with Satan.
—St Ephraim the Syrian

Not at any point in my life before Christ did I employ spirits to harm others. Which is not to say that I didn't harm others—I did. But it was never my intention to do so. Likewise, for pretty much everyone else I knew. This is why we were what is termed "blind witches." We had no idea we were working for the dark side. We thought we were fighting for the light. However, witches who are aware that they are working with dark forces are still blind, because they are deceived. Witchcraft, sorcery, divination, mediumship, spiritism. The meaning of these terms is context dependent, resulting in categorizational fluidity. Although in the New Age people aspired to become "a shaman" or "a healer," generally, the process of ascribing a strictly defined title to oneself was not really the done thing. It was taught by the elders of the traditional lineages that if people really were what they said they were, it wouldn't need to be said because it would be self-evident. Your community members would be the ones to voice it. An attitude that was then upheld by the westerners who followed their teachings. You just did your work and that was that. The process of external categorization was secondary to the process of the internal experience itself.

Witchcraft, in its purest sense, is the use of manipulation and control to bring about desired ends. Commonly understood, these are ends that are harmful to others. Like most people I knew, practicing this form of magic—black magic—was completely incomprehensible to me. I never practiced it. At a certain stage in her journey, a healer I knew had been told by the witch who introduced her to the plant she worked with—though he was not himself a member of the tribe she was connected to—that it was time for her to begin working with dark spirits. She refused and contacted the tribal elders to terminate her work. The tribal elders said that she could continue regardless, and so she began to work directly under their blessing instead. However, the spirits that she, and everyone I knew, served were also dark. But this darkness was disguised as light. The lack of a clear boundary between the dark and the light meant that all the different practices—regardless of whether they manifested with (what was seen as) white, black, high, low, pure, impure, gentle, strong, healing, or harmful consequences—were considered to have the same root: spirituality.

Sorcery, as described by St Paul in the New Testament (Gal 5.20), is the concentrating of energy, either with or without the use of plants, in a ritual context for magical purposes. It is grouped with the other *works of the flesh* (Gal 5.19)—sexual immorality, impurity, sensuality, idolatry, enmity, strife, jealousy, anger, dissensions and divisions, envy, drunkenness, orgies, and associated phenomena. In terms of my life before Christ, in the context of St Paul, sorcery, rather than witchcraft, would be the more appropriate term to describe most of the ceremonial activity that was taking place (whether through plants, ritual song, or ecstatic dance). Both sorcery and witchcraft are predicated on the belief that spiritual experience takes place automatically, and that there is an impersonal cosmic source of power that can be tapped into, and "channeled," without any effort on the part of the practitioner. But when it comes to Christ, it is not like this. The Holy Spirit is a *person*. He is alive. Therefore, it is not automatic. Contact requires a mutually participatory relationship. The Lord will draw near—but only if *He* wills to do so. In the end, the definition of a practice or set of practices as being either sorcery or witchcraft is not that important. Both draw their energy from the darkness that exists outside—and, crucially, in opposition to—the holy kingdom of the living God, Jesus of Nazareth.

The Body

In order to abide in the love of God it is essential for anger and "hate" to attain their maximum intensity but to be directed against the sin that lives in me, against the evil active in me—in me, not in my brother.
—St Sophrony of Essex

Time in the monastery was divided between monastic labor, studying, services, personal prayer, and Scripture reading. Something about the way my conversion had happened, about its irrefutable nature, meant I was able to enter into a relationship of trust with Christ. And it was this that kept me connected. Things that would have otherwise hindered my surrender to Him and His Church (for example gender roles, a perceived lack of care for nature, and alignment with conservative politics) instead served as tools that pushed me toward Him. Forced to find ways to accept things that would have previously been unacceptable, the mystery of surrendering to the wisdom of God and trusting Him, even when I could see no logical reason to do so, began to lead me into a deeper state of communion.

Experiencing inner conflict when I came into contact with behaviors or beliefs that were to me clearly not Christian, I would resist the urge to judge and pathologize the situation, instead bringing my focus to Jesus and asking Him to show me the situation through His eyes. Through denying my mind's desire to be right, the possibility of growth opened up, and the discord was then able to act as a means of opening my heart, rather than closing it. As this is obviously extremely difficult, I was not always successful. On one occasion we had attended a Liturgy in which Abouna Mikhail, the priest who had baptized me, had given a sermon in which he mentioned teaching children to respect the Church through smacking them. I had toxic shock syndrome as a result of inadvertently inhaling a significant amount of the harsh chemicals that the hardy Jordanian nuns used to counteract bug infestation, and so I was not in the mood to find ways to see hurting children as being conducive to believing in God's love.

I abruptly stood up and stared at Abouna Mikhail, whose gaze had flicked over to the unexpected movement in the congregation, my arms crossed. I turned, marched down the aisle and out the chapel door. I refrained from slamming it behind me, but it was a close call. Enraged, I sat in the refectory and began to sob. Whenever I would hear something derogatory about homosexuality or women, or something that condoned harmful behavior, I would imagine myself surrounded by all my former holistic health community looking at me incredulously in horrified shock. "You think *this* is the truth?" Obviously, I was unconsciously identifying with these children, but it was more that any evidence of violence triggered thoughts of Christianity's murderous history (at that time the Christianity of the West was still much more vivid to me than that of the East) and implied an unconscious alignment with it. Did everyone sitting inside agree with this? Did the *nuns* agree with this? Surely not. But maybe. The thought horrified me.

Sister Cherubima, Sister Damaris, and Sister Eleni came to get me, comforting me and telling me that Christ was distinct from all those who believe in Him. Man is sinful, but Christ is sinless. They encouraged me to come back, and against my ego's wishes I decided to humble myself and return to take Communion. Mother Syncletica had requested that the Eucharist be brought back out for me, and I received it from Abouna

Mikhail's father, who was also a priest (I think that Abouna was keeping a distance).

As I swallowed and walked back to my place, I began to feel the same tingling warmth inside my body and began to shake, seeing a flash of the spinning crucifix from my conversion during New Year. Christ's love flowed over my body, and I knew it marked a transformation. Taking the final blessing from Abouna Mikhail at the end of the Liturgy, I received the soft, square pillow of perfumed bread and kissed his hand. However, I couldn't bring myself to look into his eyes, after what he had said. It was painful because I loved Abouna Mikhail. He had demonstrated wonderful qualities in many scenarios, especially in the tender way he had taken care of me during my Baptism. His vision of gender seemed a little skewed to me, but I loved him anyway. He poured every ounce of himself into his church, and my life had been transformed as a result of what the Holy Spirit had done to me in his services.

I left thinking about the dynamic between Christ's purity and the brokenness of His sons and daughters. We are sinners. That's the whole point. And it is for this reason that He commands us to change: *Do not be conformed to this age, but be transformed by the renewing of the mind, so that you may discern what is the will of God—what is good and acceptable and perfect* (Rom 12.2).

Cosmology of the Cross

I do not know a Greek Christ, a Russian Christ, an English Christ, an Arab Christ . . . Christ for me, is everything, the supra-cosmic Being.
—St Sophrony of Essex

From the moment I returned to the monastery, the thought of writing, both experientially and academically, repeatedly entered my mind. I messaged Father to ask him what he thought about my doing a Ph.D.

in theology. His enthusiastic response, and the way in which he began to outline how the plan could come into being, confirmed that the idea was coming from God and not from my own desires. Taking a break after sweeping the yard in the monastery garden, I decided to search for information about Native American and First Nation Christianity. I came across an article by Terry LeBlanc, detailing the ways in which the western Christian traditions that had come to America and Canada frequently struggled to understand Native responses to, and integration of, the gospel, and had imposed their worldview onto these cultures through force, as a result. Oxygen. It was everything I had been contemplating, both on my own as well as in conversation with Father.

Clicking on the link to NAIITS (formerly the North American Institute for Indigenous Theological Studies), the academic organization that LeBlanc directed, I excitedly realized the possibilities ahead of me and began to put together a doctoral research proposal on the role of holiness in Orthodox missiology.[58] Father Theophan once shared that all civilizations have aspects that harmonize with the gospel and others that don't. The ones that align illustrate the innate beauty, compassion, and goodness of God, shared through His immeasurable generosity and love. This is evident across the whole world. The aspects of a culture that contradict the gospel are a distorted vision of the original icon—of humanity, of the world—in Eden. All cultures have elements of both.

---

[59] NAIITS is a non-sectarian organization dedicated to developing and articulating indigenous perspectives on theology and practice. It seeks to facilitate the creation of a written theological foundation for envisioning new paradigms to reach Native North Americans and other indigenous peoples. NAIITS encourages the development and implementation of indigenous learning styles and worldviews through the building of a body of written work that addresses biblical, theological, and ethical issues from within Native North American and other indigenous perspectives, doing so in concert with those of other ethnicities who would speak into this context. NAIITS has five-degree programs, offering B.A., M.A., and Ph.D. qualifications. At that point I hadn't discovered St Herman of Alaska (or St Innocent Metropolitan of Moscow) but as soon as I did, I fell head over heels in love. A fire of love that rages on in my heart to this day.

Through the sanctification of the individual in communion with the Holy Spirit, what is of God's kingdom will be refined in the fire and will remain (Zec 13.9), and what is not will be thrown into the fire and burned (Jn 15.6) by the *spiritual fire* of the Holy Spirit. The crucial point being, however, that each individual must enter into this relationship willingly, consciously, *freely*. That is what was so beautiful about the Orthodox confession of faith. The formation of Christ within the believer did not require the loss of one's innate, God-given cultural imprint. Rather, it sanctified it from within, but in a way that took into account the entire ontological reality of the human being, including his or her interpersonal and cosmological relationships and language—whether corporeal, linguistic, philosophical, or phenomenological.[59]

As I read, I thought about the ways in which historical misuses of Scripture, a lack of understanding regarding the difference between *cultural* practices unique to indigenous peoples and non-Christian *spiritual* practices, and ignorance regarding the ascetic nature of the faith of the early Church, had meant that there had often been a total erasure of anything that did not align with European conceptions of Christianity.[60] However, as LeBlanc and others argued, supporting and rehabilitating—in this example—Native and First Nations peoples, was not the only goal of the interaction between these different cultures.[61] LeBlanc discussed the need to interrogate the ethno-reductionist impetus within many missionary efforts, which confuses a lack of Christology with a lack of theology, full stop. And in the case of

---

[59] An approach that, it should be noted, is also present in some other Christian traditions.

[60] One example, amongst the many shared within teachings in the medicine world, was that of the untold abuse meted out in the violent mission schools that abducted Native children from their homes and families, cut their hair, forbade them to speak their language, and indoctrinated them against their original, divinely created image. The fallout of which is still ongoing.

[61] Founder of NAIITS, Richard Twiss' *One Church Many Tribes: Following Jesus the Way God Made You* and *Rescuing the Gospel from the Cowboys: A Native American Expression of the Jesus Way* discusses these issues.

indigenous peoples who are themselves Christian, that overlooks the fact that they are often figures of Christian eldership in their own right and have wisdom to share regarding the revealed truth of Christ as a result.

When I had first returned to the Old Testament at Christmas, I had been delighted to encounter unique aspects of tribal life within the Scriptures. For the ancient Israelites, like so many of the ancient lineages I had come into contact with, mysticism was not a discrete category of experience that was either employed or rejected at will but was rather accepted as the underlying basis of reality and something that, as a result, all of creation was involved in, consciously or unconsciously.[62] Because of this, spirituality was something that was lived out, practical, and characterized by simplicity and a lack of conceptual and self-referential angst.[63] My heart flickered in recognition as I noted the way in which liturgical roles were divided between tribal members according to ancestral lineage; that the names given, like many Native American and First Nation names, were comprised of circumstantial descriptors ("Son of my Sorrow"/"Attached") so foreign to the modern ear; that the ceremonial role of the "singer" in the tribe was central; and, crucially, that sung praises detailing tribal history structured the sacramental and mystagogical life of the earliest Jews and regenerated and safeguarded their identity across temporal and spatial boundaries. I realized with rising joy that tribal consciousness hadn't been wrenched from my life but rather, for the time being anyway, existed in the context of the cosmographic milieu of the ancient Israelites.

However, aware that it was important for me to give up *everything* from my life before Christ—even if only temporarily—I prayed for the grace to let go and to *wait on the Lord* (Ps 130) for indication from Him, articulated through my elders, that it was time for me to direct my focus toward this purpose. If that moment never came, I was aware that it was something that I

---

[62] Silviu Bunta, *The Lord God of Gods: Divinity and Deification in Early Judaism* (Piscataway, NJ: Gorgias Press, 2021), 7. Contact that generated a rewilding process through which I came into contact with my own, "indigenous" identity.

[63] Bunta, *Lord God of Gods*, 5.

would have to accept. The thought sickened me. However, I needed to heal from the wounds of my past, detach from the power of the spiritual underworld, and grow in the spirit if I were to be able to serve these communities in the way that I was certain Christ wanted me to *in the fullness of time*.

Gender Trouble

> *In the beginning, there is struggle and a lot of work for those who come near to God. But after that, there is indescribable joy. It is just like building a fire: at first it's smoky and your eyes water, but later you get the desired result. Thus we ought to light the divine fire within ourselves with tears and effort.*
> —Amma Syncletica

As a feminist (and a student of literature), I had always been attuned to the role that language plays in the creation and nourishment of power dynamics. Our culture teaches that language creates meaning, but the Fathers of the Church teach that God is the *Logos*, the source of all meaning. The Bible that I used was the NKJV, which is relatively accurate and one of the most poetic, but which also came under criticism in the feminist studies that I was reading for its use of gendered language. The NKJV tends to use the male as a plural descriptor: "man" denotes both male and female. The fact that strict attention is paid to gender accuracy when the subject matter involves women's sin did not escape my notice. Earlier in the year, I had started to research the scholarship around St Paul's epistles as these, in terms of the New Testament, seemed to be the source of the most problematic passages on gender. Through examining them in more detail and reading the associated research, a more fleshed out vision of his writings began to appear. It seemed that the words of the inspired theologian and original, anointed missionary had been misused by others to disempower, rather than heal and transform, women across the history of the Church. Struggling with the idea of male headship, I had been somewhat comforted by the explanation Father Theophan had given me just after my conversion that it was a mutually submissive dynamic based on loving servanthood and Christlike self-denial (Eph 5.12).

Following an email exchange about the intensity of the intrusive thoughts I was now dealing with on a daily basis, Father Theophan had told me that he would try to come and see me in a gap between the back-to-back meetings he had scheduled. Just thirty minutes later, I heard a knock on the door of the salon (as it was called in the monastery) that was connected to the guest room in which I was staying. His head jerked up as I opened the door, and his face lit up into a huge smile, hooded brown eyes crinkling. My mother said that he looked like an autumn leaf. "Hi!" he said with energy, leaning back and fanning both his hands out in exclamation. I pulled the door open wide so that he could enter, and he walked past me into the salon. I always got the sense that Father Theophan wasn't completely aware of the space in which he was located but was rather being led from place to place. He trod lightly. He sat down on the sofa, poised in expectation, and I sat down opposite him in one of the armchairs. All the furniture was upholstered with olive green velvet, and everything smelled like a mixture of incense and fried onions. Gold ornaments covered the heavy wooden table around which everything was arranged, and a photograph of the archbishop and plastic laminated icons adorned the walls.

"Father, I just want to thank you so much for everything that is happening; I don't even know what, *how*, to say thank you enough."

"It is not me, my dear daughter, it is the Lord," he responded, his hands cupped and turned upward as he spoke. He gazed up at the ceiling, smiling and then folded his hands over his crossed legs and looked at me. I looked at his hands. They were calloused bright white across the outer knuckles from his years of prostrations.

"Thank you for everything that you are doing in service *to Him*. For me . . ."

"Oh, you are welcome, my dear daughter, you are welcome." He smiled and looked at me in expectation.

PART TWO

"Okay, so there are two main things I want to speak to you about. One is the thoughts and the other is to do with gender." He nodded; his face serious.

"Since the conversion, I am experiencing these intrusive thoughts on a level of intensity that I haven't experienced before. It has *increased*." He nodded again.

"Is this normal? Is this warfare—"

"Oh, totally" he cut in, flicking his wrist.

"Of course, of course. It's warfare to do with your conversion. It's completely normal. As time goes on, it will get less, and then it will disappear completely." Okay, phew. I felt a burden had been lifted.

"Well, the other thing is with gender. You already know my thoughts on a lot of this, so I won't repeat what we have already discussed, but I just don't understand why the Bible frames the discussion of gender in the way that it does, in terms of female *submission*—"

"Oh, but they submit to one another," he interjected.

"They submit to one another," he said again.

"For me I had the exact same questions when I began reading the Bible. I asked the Lord, I asked, 'Lord, how can you say there is no Jew or Greek, no slave nor free, no male nor female, but then have passages that say the opposite?'" He looked upward as he spoke, allowing confusion to play across his face.

"How can the Bible contradict itself? It can never, it can never."

I listened in silence. It seemed to me that the Bible was always contradicting itself . . .

"But then I understood. In our spirits we are one, but in our bodies we are two. The passages are ministering to two different things."

In my first meeting with Father Theophan in February the year before, I had asked about the feminine side of divinity, and this line of inquiry had punctuated our conversations ever since. Issues of male primacy, male headship, and the dominance of masculine language within the scriptural, canonical, ecclesial, and sacramental life of the Church had been a point of intense distress, and frequently going to my cell to cry in private, I would ask God to help me understand why people didn't care about the ramifications of this apparent elevation of the masculine over the feminine. Could they not see the "violence"? However, at the same time, during those early months, both as a result of Father Theophan's teachings and because of the Holy Spirit's work inside me, my perspective on gender had started to change. I had become more detached about it and found myself increasingly less triggered when I saw gendered power dynamics play out in different situations. I enjoyed the novelty of existing within a different paradigm—I was a worshiper of Christ; my chosen godhead was male. On these occasions, I took pleasure in *not* taking offense and instead tried to understand how Christ was using my discomfort to sanctify me.

I felt as if I were being asked to loosen my grip on the thing that had, more than anything else, defined who I was in the world. It was my precious treasure. But I understood that He wanted to deconstruct it and remodel it according to His wisdom and His will, in order that He could anoint it. My mother had told me that the miracles of Jesus feeding the thousands with just a few loaves of bread and a few fish taught us this lesson. If we trusted in Christ and gave Him the little that we had, He could break our offering, and in so doing multiply it beyond our wildest imagination. I knew that Christ wanted to do this with my desire to support women. It was just a case of handing it over . . .

I considered my sensitivity to people's hidden wounds to be a gift. However, it was one that caused me a lot of pain. Mother Syncletica had said something similar to me after I had stormed out of Abouna Mikhail's sermon. The other nuns were filing into the van as we stood together under a peach tree in the church's courtyard. Sister Eleni joined us to translate. I excitedly told them about what had happened when I had taken Communion, and what I had realized. However, this was combined with an indignant critique of Abouna Mikhail's sermon, in which I enunciated all of the consequences of discipling children incorrectly, checking each point off with the fingers of my raised hand. Five points in all.

I finished and caught my breath, looking at Mother Syncletica, to see what she would say. She looked at me and grinned, her arms set straight against her round body, each hand clenched into fists. A shiver of excitement ran through her, and she took my hand and squeezed it, her arm shaking with buzzing energy.

"I have goosebumps!" she said in Arabic, pulling me toward her to hug me. Sister Eleni translated, and we all laughed. She then began to speak quietly.

"Anastasia, it is clear that you have a heart for people and want to take care of them."

I listened intently and nodded in agreement, eager for further affirmation of my strengths and abilities.

"But because you are not fully healed, you are not really able to help anyone effectively."

Oh. Right. I knew it was true, but I felt confronted to hear it. She took my hand.

"*This* is why we throw our hearts open to Christ, why we wrench ourselves open and cry out to the Lord, 'Please Lord, have mercy on me and fill me!' This is *why* we march on, enduring the pain, enduring the cross." She stared up into my eyes.

"We march on," she concluded firmly, both hands now grasping mine in resolute fists.

"So that we may be transformed from deep within. *All of us.*"

There are more sick healers in the New Age than there are those who are healed. The false empowerment generated through its techniques creates an illusion of completion. However, it is just that—an illusion. Prior to my conversion, I remember coming across an article discussing this point late at night. Nick had gone to bed while I had stayed up late, exhausted, to eat piles of cookies and numb my brain on my laptop. The image used in the header of the article was exactly that—a woman sitting in the dark, her tired face lit blue from the glare of her laptop screen. It was uncomfortable accepting that I was doing the one thing I had always been so critical of others doing: helping others in order to avoid doing my own inner work.

I didn't see it in this order, of course, but rather that the pressure of my schedule meant that I had less time than I would like, to be able to focus on my own recovery. How convenient. Although money had played a big part in this dynamic, the issue was more deeply rooted. I had low self-esteem and generated feelings of worth by helping, rescuing, and "healing" others. A few days later, I had flown to America, and so the encounter with Christ, which exposed the extent of how broken and in need of healing I really was, began.

And the area that was most broken, apart from my relationship with myself, was that of my relationship with the masculine. It seemed to me that the Bible's teachings on gender had been influenced by the culture of its writers and translators but this wasn't something any of the nuns seemed to be too bothered about. In honor of monastic humility and being set apart from the world's argumentative ways, I kept my feelings on the topic to myself and pondered it in my heart. However, when I had put together the doctoral research proposal about indigenous modes of understanding Christ, my mind had been drawn back to the topic. Reengaged with the insanity of gender violence, its pain overshadowed me, and for four excruciatingly long days, didn't leave. For the first time since my conversion, I stopped trusting in Jesus. How could a loving God let his daughters go through what women went through?

Throughout those days, my feelings toward the Bible turned from tentative love, to outright hatred. It became an instrument of emotional torture. I sent Father Theophan long emails, regarding gender violence in the Old Testament and questioning why it is that there is no comment on the sin of the men who raped Dinah in Genesis, or why the Levite was not punished for allowing his concubine to be gang raped in Judges. In a lot of the liturgical texts we used in the services, male, rather than female saints dominated. One thing after the other began to trigger me. Every time "men" was used to describe both men and women, I winced. Every word I read in which women's sin was equated to sexuality pressed painfully onto my heart. I sat through the communal reading of the book of Ezekiel

PART TWO

and the violence meted out to the sisters for their "whoredom" with rising anger having already endured pages and pages of excruciating patrilineal genealogies earlier in the day. During the chanting of the hymns, the words offended me in a way they never had before. The heavy emphasis on the Fathers and the oppressively masculine language poured down over me, climaxing with Eve's accountability for the fall of humanity.

After two days of being dragged through this, I could barely open my mouth to speak to anyone, furious with all the nuns for what seemed like their complicity in this "violence." On the third evening, I stopped attending prayers altogether. Returning the following afternoon, having missed morning prayers, I stood in silence, tears rolling down my cheeks. Following this painful service, I bent down on the floor of my cell and began to sob. My entire body was aching, as my mind replayed the images from the liturgical text, each flash releasing a fresh wave of pain through my body. *Why Lord?* I cried into the carpet as sensations continued to break over me. Although it was agonizing, I knew I was being healed. Generational trauma and the pain, shame, rage, and guilt I carried on behalf of women were being activated by the power of Christ's extremely challenging Scriptures. Something was releasing. Hearing me crying, one of the novices came to the door and whispered, "Don't worry, be happy; everything that is making you cry is a lie." She was right. We *have* been lied to.

That evening we attended a Liturgy. Raw still, I found myself more frustrated by the exclusion of women from the clergy than before, and I spent most of the service heavy in thought. I ruminated on the pain I had experienced at the hands of men, and how badly my body had been treated. I raked through everything that had happened, angrily presenting each abuse to the Lord. As the Eucharist was brought out and people began to line up to receive Communion, I asked the Lord for the healing and *justice* I, and all women, needed. That we were *owed*. The word that alighted in my mind in response was unexpected. It came immediately. Repent. Why would *I* need to repent? *I* am the victim here. I was standing at the back of the church, enclosed in a shawl. Repent for *your* sin. Oh.

As soon as my heart opened in agreement, the words began to flow, and I offered a silent prayer of sorrow, asking for forgiveness for all my gendered sin. Immediately, the oppression lifted, and my soul was released. In peace, I received Communion, reunited with Him again.

And then I understood. The *maiming* of the feminine did not come from God. God is both masculine *and* feminine, but the world, which is the domain of the devil, has suppressed the feminine. That is why subjugation, marginalization, rape, abuse, molestation, mutilation, abortion, prostitution, trafficking, and porn exist and have the power that they have in our world. The evil one *hates* the feminine, hates the womb, hates women, full stop. In that moment I realized that the devil was the source of patriarchal oppression, *not* Jesus, and not—shockingly—the Church. Jesus came to destroy the satanic, distorted structure of oppressive patriarchal *domination*, to recover the divine, harmonious image of self-sacrificial male headship, in order to liberate *all women* through entrance into the kingdom: the only place in which feminine freedom truly exists.[64] A reality where there is no violence and no oppression. Following this intensive decompression, I felt buoyant and light. Returning to my room that evening, I found an academic article about the use of sexually violent imagery in Ezekiel that I had bookmarked for later reading. I didn't open it. Jesus is the truth. I trusted Him.

---

[64] Male headship according to the divine image is something that needs to be understood if it is to be applied effectively: understanding comes through ascetic praxis. There is freedom in the kingdom because through His self-sacrifice, Christ alone has overcome the power of demons, and beyond them, the devil himself, and beyond that, death—the tripartite source of all forms of oppression.

PART TWO

Give Blood, Receive Spirit

Whoever loves tribulation will have joy and refreshment afterwards.
—Abba Elias

The monastery continued its journey toward Pentecost and the outpouring of the Holy Spirit. Despite my desire to stay focused on my Baptism, I found myself increasingly immersed in interpersonal difficulties and stepped out of my internal listening process as a result. Father Theophan had spoken before about the fact that we should approach our relationship with Christ as we do a close friend. With our friends we tend to think about their preferences and accommodate them. So we should with God. Father spoke about the way in which we should aspire for inner quietude, because Christ is someone who likes silence. It is in silence that He speaks. As someone who is very mutable, it was very easy for me to get dislodged from my center and to be drawn into other's experiences and emotional states. The Desert Fathers teach us to retreat instead into inward stillness. Sometimes people misunderstand monasticism as being an escape from, or abandonment of, the world. In a worldly sense it is true—monastics do not live the way the world lives. They do not eat the same, sleep the same, speak the same, or think the same way (they shouldn't anyway). However, if Christians live a Scriptural life, they will do likewise, because being set apart from the world is something to which all Christians are called.[65]

What had become clear through my time in the monastery, however, was that this way of living does not require an abandonment *of* the world, but rather that the follower of Christ's activity *in* the world must extend from the nexus of a life of prayer and worship. The private prayer life must

---

[65] *"Come out from among them and be separate,"* says the Lord. *"Do not touch what is unclean, and I will receive you"* (2 Cor 6.17).

come first. The Church taught that our thirst for time alone with God must not be quenched by the distractions of life, so that an inner space opens up, which creates the right circumstances for prayer. Through regular discipline, the walls of this sanctuary are fortified, intensifying the medicinal potentiality of the liturgical and sacramental work of the Church for the healing of whatever is fragmented and in need of repair in the life of the believer, whether monastic or lay. Pentecost was approaching, and I had been wasting precious time, time that should have been used to double down on my own inner work. A chat with Mother Syncletica confirmed as much, as she explained the immense importance of the period following Baptism for the newly baptized. Time to focus. I returned to the space within, going over everything I had been learning and reflecting on everything I had been receiving, in order to bring myself into preparation for the outpouring of the Spirit.

During those hot weeks, I started to write songs of worship to the Lord. On the last days before my flight, however, a humiliating event took place that turned me inside out. I had tried to help the monastery with some organizational restructuring, something in which I had experience and at which I was skilled. However, I was told—and it was more about the public rejection than the content of the rebuttal itself—that my carefully crafted plan was "too western" and was therefore inappropriate for the spiritual context of the monastery. Based on my life experience and the beliefs that I held, this hit me hard. The way my mother had described it when I called her in tears was that I had put my "gift" on the altar, and it had been rejected. The process had disturbed me, reaching into an extremely vulnerable place beneath the defense mechanisms I had unconsciously honed over the years to maintain an appearance of inner peace and self-confidence.

People often commented on how secure I was in myself. Jesus, however, knew different. In order to fully release me from this bondage of falsity, He orchestrated a situation in which I was left feeling exposed, raw, and powerless. And it stung. Every instinct kicked in to find ways of reestablishing power and control. My mother urged me to stay with what was happening and to instead sit with the discomfort. My gift had been rejected. Would I suppress the pain and re-fortify an inner boundary that ensured I was never hurt and humiliated in the same way again? Or would I allow myself to unravel into God's hands? I chose the latter and began to pray. The prayer became a silk thread that then unspooled into a song of the excruciating but exquisite pain of being crucified for Christ.

Sharing the song with Father, he sent me a voice message, detailing the need to see these words as marking an important stage in my development: "These words are very heavenly, very, very sacred, my dear daughter." "Give blood and receive the Spirit"—this quote from Abba Longinus had been appointed as an unofficial slogan for the monastery, and I was beginning to see that Christ, in His love, was eager to make sure that every part of me had the opportunity to be touched by the fire of His Holy Spirit. Sister Cherubima and the nuns had prepared a candlelit farewell dinner for me under the stars, and over an adorable feast of pizza and cheesecake, Mother Syncletica shared a final word with me before I left. The next morning, after attending the Pentecost Liturgy, I was driven to the airport and flew home. Sister Cherubima had given me a painting of the verse: *Your name is ointment poured forth; therefore, the virgins love you. Draw me away!* (Song 1.3b–4a), with messages about bridal love from all the nuns as a parting gift. The sisters waved me off, entreating me to enjoy my "honeymoon." Time alone with Christ the Bridegroom to reflect on all that had happened. I was ready.

PART THREE

The Test

You don't become holy by fighting evil. Let evil be. Look towards Christ and that will save you. What makes a person saintly is love.
—St Porphyrius of Kavsokalyvia

Discussing what my rule would be while back in England, I had sent Father Theophan a rather ambitious plan. He explained that outside the monastery it was more difficult to maintain the same intensity of prayer than it was inside. Outside its walls the world was waiting to flood in: there was a stronger countercurrent. Although I secretly thought to myself that this wouldn't be a problem for *me* personally, I agreed, and the quantity of liturgical prayer that I was to do every day was reduced. I planned to spend the months in England completely immersing myself in the Scriptures in order to go through a deep inner purification, but I soon started to understand why he had said that I might not find it as easy to read for hours on end as I had initially imagined. However, reading the Bible was, he said, the most important thing for me to focus on. He advised me to sit in order to be as relaxed as possible and to read aloud, breathing the inspired, life-giving word of God: "As you read, ask God to bring all your bodily systems, your organs, your heart, your mental processes and your will into obedience to the Lord." As I listened to his words, a flicker of resistance flared up in relation to the word "obedience."

The Church teaches that confessing the name of Christ will cause demons to flee. However, it can also make them very angry. Because of Coronavirus, I was quarantined, and after spending the greater part of the year surrounded by community, I suddenly found myself alone in the middle of the deserted English countryside. We had spent many childhood holidays staying at the house nearby, and although it had been exorcized, the stories my cousins and parents had told me about the paranormal occurrences that had taken place there were imprinted in my mind. Going to sleep that night, I started to see demons. There was a particular spirit that would appear in my mind again and again whenever it started to get dark. I was so freaked out that I couldn't even bring myself to read Revelation because of its imagery. After restless, jetlagged nights, in which I would lie in bed for hours unable to sleep, sometimes till the sun rose, I would then wake at two in the afternoon, discombobulated and drowsy. Each morning, in the light of the day, everything would feel more normal. However, as soon as it started to get dark, the ominous feeling would return, and the psychic realm would start to buzz into activity around me.

Because I had been in retreat for three months, I had barely been online. However, I had heard about George Floyd's death and the ensuing Black Lives Matter protests from one of the nuns who read the news. Hypersensitive to *any* indication of opposition to the protests from Christians, for *any* reason, I had already been angered by comments that questioned people's intentions for joining the protests, riots or no riots. "Yes, people are angry. But the anger is justified. End of discussion," I thought. The revelations of systemic racism, police brutality, and the structure of the US prison system were not new to me, but experiencing them as a Christian—and thus directly implicated because of my adherence to a religion considered by many in the West to be white supremacist—was. I felt paralyzed by the situation and began to break my steadfast rule of doing my prayers before anything else, spending hours reading slavery accounts online and following everything that was happening in the news.

After a while, I felt like I had to stop because I was now struggling to do any of my prayers whatsoever. I knew that it was not wise to flood my system with information in this way. However, even having the thought of disengaging felt in itself violent. I spoke to Sister Veroniki, who mentioned that through detaching, Christ would be able to work better through me. Sensitized to any inkling of Christian apathy, I began to get frustrated. But humanity is mourning! We are *all* part of this. I knew I wasn't dealing with the situation well, but the force of the collective outpouring, of which rage was a large component, was overwhelming. I tried to stay connected to the nuns in America, but the more immersed I became in what was happening with the protests, the more enraged and disturbed I felt by what I perceived to be a distinct lack of care on their part. I sent Father Theophan videos of right-wing rallies and screenshots of conservative politicians' written speeches, with sections underlined in red so they couldn't be missed, in the hope that he would talk about it with the monastics. In order to establish some equanimity, I would focus on Christ's command to love without limits, and my heart would open. But then a memory of something I had read or watched would rear up, and the tremulously open gates of my heart would snap shut. Recognizing that I was grieving, I tried to loosen the paralysis and pray more, offering everything inside me to Christ. He alone had the solution.

During this period, the Lord crucified a part of my identity that I was very attached to—the activist. Having abandoned my work, my community, and my life online, I had lost all my tributaries of communication into the world. I knew verbal communication beyond the handful of people I was in touch with was out of the question. Muted, my options were significantly limited. I had no power to do anything. All I could do was pray and fast. Well, I could *try* to do those things. Praying was incredibly challenging during those two weeks and my fasting, even more so. I think the main reason people wind up practicing magic rather than the purity of spirituality is that within the Christian path you really have no means of controlling reality. You can ask the Lord to do as you wish. And then you can wait. And that's pretty much it. It is a true surrendering of the self. Magical practices, on the other hand, offer an infinite range of tricks, tools, and methods to support your attempts to manifest a certain outcome. That is what witchcraft is—manipulating and directing energy toward a particular end. By harnessing "the force" and channeling it toward your desired result, whether positive or negative, you enter into a dynamic dance of being both creator and receiver.

I thought of those I knew and loved who practiced magic and imagined them leaving it to follow Christ. The prospect of being stripped of this (albeit illusory) power would put so many off. In the world of alternative spirituality, people's entire lives—and livelihoods—were predicated on their spiritual skill set: it is both religion and vocation rolled into one. To pass the time of my quarantine, I started painting the names of those killed by police as a river of blood with the verse, *I go to prepare a place for you* (Jn 14.3). I was thoughtful about the politics of me, a white woman, creating something of this kind. Was it my place? I showed the image to Lily, the friend who was struggling with my conversion, whose response was lackluster. I guess in her mind my belief in Jesus meant that I had taken the side of the oppressor. Although Christ's name has wrongfully been used to promote colonial evil (demonism on a global scale) in so many forms, the fact that Christ alone will bring about true redemption, transformation, and liberation was one area on which I was not willing to capitulate.[66] How each culture, tribe, nation, people, group, and community experiences and integrates Christ is subject to infinite possibilities. But Christ is the truth . . . then, now, and forever.

---

[66] Although the Orthodox Church's institutional hands are not entirely clean, the majority of the large-scale atrocities that took place did so outside its bounds. I do not say this to place personal blame. That these things occurred does not in any way bear on the radiant witness of the millions of Christians within those traditions today.

PART THREE

The Prince of Peace

*For if we all took only what was necessary to satisfy our own
needs, giving the rest to those who lack, no one would be rich,
no one would be poor, and no one would be in need.*
—St Basil the Great

My cousin later told me that the land on which the houses were built was a "demonic stronghold" and that she had woken up once with two hands around her neck strangling her, in the midst of a spiritual attack. Well, at least I knew I wasn't making it up! Toward the end of my media-soaked two-week quarantine, I started to feel so deeply lost, I just kept repeating, "I don't know who I am anymore, I don't know who I am anymore." America, the monastery, and my Baptism felt so far away. I spent a final night and day in the house with my mother who had come to visit and drive me home. Walking through the fields around the house, she talked about the prayerful life that many of the women in the family had led. Her presence and words began to lift the strange and oppressive energy that had been shrouding me since I arrived, and I started to feel spacious again. Driving home I could feel myself returning to normal. *What just happened.* The fact I had dipped so low in such a short space of time freaked me out. Am I really that weak? The way that peace returned as we drove toward our house, did, however, confirm that the extreme spiritual disturbance was, partly at least, geographically tethered to the place I had been staying.

What was clear was that my susceptibility to the negative energy of the spirit world was evidence of both the fragility of my mental boundaries (common in highly sensitives), and the amount of residual dark energy within me. The dark energy of my former practices. *This* was why fasting and purification through immersion in the Scriptures was necessary. I remembered Father Theophan's repeated teaching regarding renewal through the eating of the word, and I restated my commitment to being set apart from the world as a vessel for Christ. After an online meeting with him and Mother Syncletica on my return, they agreed with my conclusion that the Lord had used the two weeks to give me a glimpse of what the enemy was capable of doing, in order to show me where I stood spiritually. It was a test of sorts to help prepare me for my work as a Christian. It seemed that I had pretty much failed the test. As it had been happening, I was aware that I wasn't coping particularly well. Instead of the global uprising pushing me to surrender more deeply to the challenging mystery of Christ and His goodness, I had instead been overrun by the world's ignorance of who Christ is and slid deeper into isolation, sadness, and darkness. In life we cannot control what will happen. We can, however, regulate our response. This was the work.

Mother Syncletica spoke about her sadness at the killing of George Floyd, and Father Theophan agreed: "I hate this so much, so, so much. It really hurts my heart, the hatred because of race, or gender, or because someone is from a different country." I felt bad about the judgment I had been casting on them. Toward the end of the conversation, Mother quietly added that we must oppose all forms of violence, and that they were, of course, not of Christ. However, she gently reminded me that division and hatred because of race, class, gender, or nationality are all different faces of the kingdom of darkness. The devil is their source, and this is why it is vital to focus one's energy on this point of origin through prayer. Active prayer, praise, and worship keep us from drowning in the issues themselves. If we drown, we inhibit Christ from working through us and we are, as a result, of no help to anyone.[67] It was an appealing—but frightening—invitation.

---

[67] Like Christianity, eastern practices focus on the transformation of the inner being to shift one's relationship to the outer reality. However, the end goal is realization that all is light—inwardly and outwardly—and that in essence there is no distinction between the light and the dark. Purification and the illumination of the soul within Christianity, on the other hand, results in realization that the world is dark. One of my favorite verses as an ex-New Ager is Jeremiah 6.14: *They heal the people's brokenness superficially saying, "Shalom, shalom," there is no shalom here.* I love this forceful declaration of the fact that our world is not at peace.

So I just . . . detach? It felt so alien. Cold. Irresponsible. Heartless. But at the same time I knew it was the only way that *I* could change. How else could I help others transform? I had to go through the process myself first. Essentially, I was being asked to put aside what I wanted for the sake of Christ: *If anyone desires to come after Me, let him deny himself, and take up his cross, and follow Me* (Mt 16.24).

Garden

Assuredly, I say to you, whoever does not receive the kingdom of God as a little child will by no means enter it.
—Mark 10.15

At my parents' house, my new life began. Summer was beginning to heat up, and the countryside was fragrant and blooming. After the intensity of the monastery's schedule and the emotional and spiritual turmoil of the two weeks that followed it, I suddenly found myself floating freely. Okay, we'll put that crash landing down to experience. The honeymoon officially begins *now*. Because of Covid and the need to protect my parents, I had a concrete reason, beyond the spiritual process that was taking place within me, to avoid reengaging with anyone from my former social world. Since the conversion my life had been streamlined to the nth degree. Apart from Carina, the friend with whom I had remained in contact during my time in the monastery, and a few occasional messages here and there, I had been pretty much off-grid. But without the physical boundary of the ocean between me and the life I had lived prior to my Baptism, everything and everyone from the past suddenly started to crowd in. I began to respond to messages gradually, aware that each opening out into the world had the capacity to flood the tender and precious inner sanctuary that had been cultivated through these months of retreat. I didn't want this inner silence to end. Before leaving America, I had asked

Father Theophan how I should go about these next months in terms of connecting to those from my life before Christ. He answered simply: "Go step by step, asking the Holy Spirit to guide you, and to make your path clear. Gently and step by step, always asking the dear Lord." Ah yes, the dear Lord. He is with me in this.

I felt like I had entered another retreat. After the stress of those first weeks of spiritual chaos, everything was flowing harmoniously. Every movement felt fresh and alive, and I felt as if I were alert to everything I was doing, tasting, and hearing. I wrote an article about the ways in which the teachings of the Bible clearly oppose racism in all forms but wondered if the points I was making were extremely basic and self-evident. I didn't know exactly what the article was *for*, but I knew that the little knowledge I had the privilege of acquiring through my studies, research, and work with marginalized groups should be channeled into something coherent. I wanted to use accounts of slavery in the article but felt the Holy Spirit tell me not to go back into reading them. I was too raw, and because I had not yet fully separated Roman Catholic and Protestant history from its Orthodox counterpart, my trust in the Church was fragile, to say the least. Although it felt like a failure of strength on my part, I knew that it was better to avoid information that would increase the sense of separation between me and the Body of Christ.

"But it's a privilege to just 'tune out' of the pain, isn't it?" I said to my mother, in response to her suggestion that I direct my attention to something else for a while. The world was telling me that the option of choosing to focus on spirituality rather than what was happening in the world was itself predicated on injustice. I reflected on this tension between the world and heaven. Spirituality is free from the divisions of the world because in Christ, all forms of division, separation, and opposition are dissolved. The kingdom transcends ethnic, racial, geographical, temporal, class, and economic boundaries because, *There is neither Jew nor Greek, there is neither slave nor free, there is neither male nor female; for you are all one in Christ Jesus* (Gal 3.28). I accepted this nudging and began to stop reading the news or engaging with

PART THREE

the media in order to detach from what was going on. I knew I needed to put this, as with everything I felt a responsibility toward, on Christ's altar.

As well as His cutting away of the emotional and intellectual attachments that had formed around my sense of responsibility to other people (read—savior complex), I felt as if the Holy Spirit were probing further, into the depths of my heart. *If this wasn't part of your identity, who would you be?* Accepting that I had to forgo everything that proved that I was socially aware, alert, *awake,* was not easy. I reflected on the role these causes played into my sense of myself in the world. Would I still be of value? It was the same feeling that had arisen when I was being purified of my gender idols. I repeatedly came up against the sense that if I stopped struggling for those affected by patriarchal violence, I would be betraying them somehow. It was very subtle, but I felt that in choosing Christ and peace, I was *abandoning* those who were suffering. I had always felt that I had a responsibility to share in people's pain and to mourn with them. Which was ironic, because transformation in the area of my femininity was what I yearned for above all else. However, Christ's restoration of this part of me to its original image meant the death of a huge part of my identity. Here, as there, I felt the same direction from the Lord—surrender to Me all that torments you, and trust in Me to use it for My glory.

After the sparseness of the desert, the fluttering green of England spread around me, inviting me into its riches. There was a small forest nearby that became the location of my morning prayers. Standing in the dappled light of the bright green mantle, I began to pray and prostate, feeling the squidge of the earth and its fleece of fallen leaves compress under the softness of my folded shawl. *So this is Christianity. Worshiping Christ under the trees.* As I prayed, I would vacillate between immersion in the words and consuming self-awareness, imagining the reactions of different men I knew watching me worship in this way. *What would they think?* I began to wake earlier again, setting my alarm for six-thirty, then six, then five-thirty. Before leaving I had asked Father Theophan if I should wake at four as they did in the monastery, but he had said five or six was better, as it meant I could avoid sleeping afterward. The fact alone that waking up at this time had become not only possible, but desirable, was as clear an indication as there could be of the radical transformation that had taken place in my life. Father Theophan himself subsisted on no more than two hours of sleep per night (if that), and the mothers would frequently cycle through two, and sometimes even three days on end, without more than one or two hours of sleep, having eaten nothing at all for the duration. They would pray all morning, work all day, and then pray all night. "Step by step, Anastasia, step by step," Mother Ivana had told me giggling, "You build up to it!"

Every morning I would walk to the woods, and if I was early enough, I would find some of the deer still sleeping. After the psychic attack of those first two weeks had abated, I was able to pray properly again, feeling my heart open and the wings of my spirit unfurl and expand. In a way it was like nothing had changed. As a pagan, I would stand in nature in prayer, experiencing and being nourished by the beauty of creation. However, I now knew that Christ was the source of nature and rather than praying to nature, I was praying to Christ. And in that everything had changed. My focus was no longer on my animality but on my humanity (and the responsibilities that come with it). Rather than attempting to merge with nature, I now went directly to the Spirit, and through this relationship then experienced the gift of joy and peace with nature. By being willing to give up nature's primary position in my heart, an idol in the purest sense of the word, the entire creature–creator–creation relationship structure had been reorganized so that it more closely resembled the original picture of Eden. A total return to the unbroken union of paradise could, of course, only take place through transfiguration of the entire being. But through a prayerful life, I could begin to walk toward it.

The nuns would often tell me stories of the ways in which the saints' purification enabled them to coexist harmoniously with the wild animals that populated the remote spaces in which they lived. The depth of their inner cleansing would lessen the fissure that exists between humanity and nature. Nature that, like humanity, had fallen as a result of Adam and Eve's rebellion and God's subsequent punishment: *Cursed is the ground for your sake . . . for out of it you were taken. For dust you are, and to dust you shall return* (Gen 3.17–19). Through the process of praying written, liturgical prayers—so alien to me previously—access into the *heart* of nature, access that was previously prohibited, was granted. But rather than using plants to control my circumstances or regulate my emotions, I was now able to live alongside them in peaceful coexistence.[68] When I was on the pilgrimage, I had come across these words of St Seraphim of Sarov, which epitomize the tender and foundational relationship between the saints and nature:

> Drink water from the spring where horses drink.
> The horse will never drink bad water.
> Lay your bed where the cat sleeps.
> Eat the fruit that has been touched by a worm.
> Boldly pick the mushroom on which the insects sit.
> Plant the tree where the mole digs.
> Build your house where the snake sits to warm itself.
> Dig your fountain where the birds hide from heat.
> Go to sleep and wake up at the same time with the birds—you will reap all of the day's golden grains.
> Eat more green—you will have strong legs and a resistant heart, like the beings of the forest.
> Swim often, and you will feel on earth like the fish in the water.
> Look at the sky as often as possible and your thoughts will become light and clear.
> Be quiet a lot, speak little, and silence will come in your heart, and your spirit will be calm and full of peace.

---

[68] In giving plants (spirits) the power to elevate our mood, we also give them the power to do the opposite: it is the unforeseen—and unseen—consequence of giving plants authority over our inner state, regardless of how subtle the effects of the plant/s. No spiritual experience outside of the kingdom of God is given freely. Everything has a price.

The Prodigal Daughter

*Rest assured and do not think too much about any
matter. Leave it to God who is in control.*
—Pope Kyrillos VI

During a particularly stressful moment during the two-week quarantine, I called my mother, asking for support. She answered the phone, raising her voice above the sound in the background.

"Darling, we are currently on our Watchmen of the Nations worldwide call, and everyone is praying for you! All over the world!"

"What on earth—why are they praying for me?" I asked.

"You know, it is really quite amazing. We were having the meeting as normal, and I just felt from the Holy Spirit that I was supposed to start sharing about what had happened to you, and while I was speaking, the leader of the organization interrupted, saying that this was a 'generation issue,' and said that everyone needed to intercede for you. And now everyone is praying for you!"

"Oh my goodness, wow, I don't know what to say. Okay! I'll let you continue. Wow, thank you, thank you!" I began to smile.

"See, darling" she said, "lots of people are behind you; you are not alone."

Logging on to my online banking when back at their house, I had the unusual experience of seeing that I had more money than expected. As I looked at my account record, I saw several different payments from people I didn't know. Then another payment labeled "Watchmen." Oh my goodness, these payments are from the Watchmen community! Several hundred pounds had been paid into my account by different people. I told my parents who started smiling, "Yes, they are giving you money to support your ministry!" I was so touched. What could I do to say thank you? I started a drawing and wrote them a letter of thanks for their kindness and generosity. My mum shared it in the group. One of the administrators

PART THREE

messaged her telling her that they had a separate group set up specifically to discuss how to send me money. I couldn't believe it. I just couldn't believe it. The kindness, the love, the faith, the generosity, the trust in God. It was so beautiful. So pure and sacrificial. It was simply miraculous. There was nothing in it for them. They didn't know me, they had never met me, they might never meet me. And it was all anonymous. All the glory was to be given to God.

Across the next few days, more and more money kept coming into my account, sometimes from individuals and sometimes from groups. I continued to create illustrations and write letters of gratitude with my mum forwarding them on to them. "The Singapore family's payment is nearly ready to go!" she told me. A couple of days later £1000 had been paid into my account from the Singapore branch of the Watchmen tree. I was gobsmacked. I sent a message of thanks to them. "Everyone wants you to know that you have family all over the world and a home wherever you need to go." As someone whose whole life with medicine had centered around being a part of different families around the world, it was so beautiful to find this same welcome, but through Jesus. My family had expanded to include all Christians.

In all my years as an abundance-preaching pagan, money had always been a struggle. Apart from the people who profiteered in a way that was self-evidently unethical or who had secret trust funds, *everyone* in my former world was strangled by financial pressure. I only realized that money seemed to work differently in the kingdom when I arrived at the monastery, and Mother Syncletica had contributed to the cost of my flights. Then a close Orthodox friend of my parents had given me the £3000 I needed to pay off a loan, so that I could make a quick exit from my former world. I didn't tell anyone about this, because I knew so many would misinterpret it as something sinister. It is testament to the purity of the donor's heart that it didn't even occur to him that this gesture could be interpreted in this way. During the meeting in which the financial discussion had taken place, he had offered the money as a loan, which I gratefully accepted. Weeks later in London, when I received it, I emailed him to discuss the repayment schedule. He emailed me back, telling me that there was no repayment, because it was "just a small gift from the Lord, who is so happy that His beloved daughter has returned to His kingdom." I was the prodigal son, welcomed home with a feast.

> So he set off and went to his father. But while he was still far off, his father saw him and was filled with compassion; he ran and put his arms around him and kissed him. Then the son said to him, "Father, I have sinned against heaven and before you; I am no longer worthy to be called your son." But the father said to his slaves, "Quickly, bring out a robe—the best one—and put it on him; put a ring on his finger and sandals on his feet. And get the fatted calf and kill it, and let us eat and celebrate; for this son of mine was dead and is alive again; he was lost and is found!" And they began to celebrate. (Lk 15.20–24)

It was a firsthand lesson in the reality of God's divine Fatherhood and the immeasurability of His mercy.

Repentance: The Joy Filled Life

Life in the world is based on force, on violence. The Christian has the opposite aim. Force does not belong to eternal life. No act imposed by force can save us.
—St Sophrony of Essex

When in America, I had sent my mother a selection of books by Mother Basilea Schlink for her birthday. I had come into contact with her writings while on the pilgrimage, when I had read her *Mary, The Mother of Jesus*, and it had brought the Theotokos to life.[69] As my back-

---

[69] Basilea Schlink, *Mary, The Mother of Jesus* (Darmstadt: Evangelical Sisterhood of Mary, 1986).

ground was in Evangelical Christianity, the Virgin Mary was not a huge feature in its Christology beyond her role as Jesus' Mother. She was rarely, if ever, included in worship. Through Orthodoxy, I had started to get to know her, but it wasn't an immediate opening. Mary Magdalene, for obvious reasons, was the Mary with whom I felt most intimate. She was passionate, down on the ground, and wounded by the world's rough use of her—yet utterly loved by Christ. But Mother Basilea's book, which I read in one sitting, fleshed out an emotionally and psychologically accessible Mary, and I fell in love. Sister Damaris had once explained how revolutionary it was that Christ chose to be born from the Virgin Mary out of wedlock in the context of ancient Jewish culture. Mother Basilea's story of the Virgin Mary's journey from the Annunciation of her role as the bearer of Christ to her witnessing of her beloved Son's death on the cross enriched my understanding of the severity of the situation the Virgin Mary found herself in and brought her to breathing, grieving life.

In those first sun-soaked days, I read Mother Basilea's book on the Holocaust, *Israel, My Chosen People,* and I felt Christ speak to me through her words.[70] Mother Basilea's teaching was focused on the Holocaust, but the principles could just as easily be applied to the Transatlantic Slave Trade (I just wished that she had written on it). Repentance for the crimes of my people, particularly in relation to the establishment of the United States and the Native American and First Nation atrocities that took place, had been something I had always known was part of my purpose on earth. The guilt consumed me. I remember asking Michael, the medicine man I worked for, what I could do to help repair the damage inflicted as a result of my ancestors' crimes. He looked at me, his brow furrowing and then looked ahead.

"My grandma used to say, 'Don't suffer again. We already suffered over it.'"

He looked at me, his shoulders rising in a barely perceptible shrug.

---

[70] Basilea Schlink, *Israel, My Chosen People: A German Confession Before God and the Jews* (Darmstadt: Evangelical Sisterhood of Mary, 1987).

"Do what you are doing. *Live.*"

The beauty of his response, the lack of bitterness, the wisdom acquired through the living—and forgiving—of so much pain and suffering was startling.

Carve Your Culture on My Heart

> *We have a choice: to follow the way of this world, of the society that surrounds us, and thereby find ourselves outside of God, or to choose the way of life. To choose God who calls us and for whom our heart is searching.*
> —St Seraphim Rose

Through the gradual process of cutting off from life online, I began to notice that the virtual reality I had entered (and become addicted to) in social media mimicked what was taking place in the unseen, with the deception of the spirits. The structure of social media in my life was like a carbon copy of the ego bolstering, sensory stimulation of the spirit world. Once the illusory power of magic had been blown away by the Holy Spirit, I was able to see my former self for who I really was—a fragile, lonely, and traumatized woman, escaping the consequences of abuse through fantasies of divine femininity, unlimited cosmic power, and supra-human existence. Again and again I experienced the same feeling as I began this new life free from the influence of the spirits and social media: I am living in the real world. This was the truth of reality. It was also scary, because the dark was palpable. I could see it clearly now. I was in the light of Christ's holiness, but outside it was darkness. Pitch black. Heavy demonic attacks had become a regular part of my life in Christ outside the monastery. Attacks that continued on, though gradually more intermittently, for months. Anyone who comes to Christ from magic will experience them.

It was the real world on several accounts. I now knew that darkness existed in the world and that it operated through the power of the devil

PART THREE 195

and his kingdom, and that the primary battle was the one that took place in the unseen.[71] I now knew that there would come a point when the world would pass away.[72] I now knew that I would die one time only, and that after this death I would be judged.[73] I now knew that no amount of yoga, meditation, raw food, fasting, fitness, or psychic empowerment could stop that from happening.[74] I now knew that as a human I was created in the image and likeness of God, and that this differentiated me from the rest of creation.[75] I now knew that I was a sinner and that prior to my conversion, this sin had marked me for death.[76] I now knew that Jesus' death on the cross had saved me.[77] Furthermore, I now knew that salvation was a constant process, as opposed to a discrete, historical event.[78]

Importantly, I now knew that all the spirits that I had previously made contact with, worshiped, and considered to be allies in my spiritual journey were in fact evil powers who had disguised their true nature as a means

---

[71] *For we do not wrestle against flesh and blood, but against principalities, against powers, against the rulers of the darkness of this age, against spiritual hosts of wickedness in the heavenly places* (Eph 6.12).

[72] *The world is passing away, along with its desires* (1 Jn 2.17).

[73] *And as it is appointed for men to die once, but after this the judgment, so Christ was offered once to bear the sins of many. To those who eagerly wait for Him He will appear a second time, apart from sin, for salvation* (Heb 9.27).

[74] *So He said to them, "Are you thus without understanding also? Do you not perceive that whatever enters a man from outside cannot defile him, because it does not enter his heart but his stomach, and is eliminated, thus purifying all foods?" And He said, "What comes out of a man, that defiles a man. For from within, out of the heart of men, proceed evil thoughts, adulteries, fornications, murders, thefts, covetousness, wickedness, deceit, lewdness, an evil eye, blasphemy, pride, foolishness. All these things come from within and defile a man"* (Mk 7.25).

[75] *So God created man in His own image; in the image of God He created him; male and female He created them* (Gen 1.27).

[76] *For the wages of sin is death, but the gift of God is eternal life in Christ Jesus our Lord* (Rom 6.23).

[77] *Who Himself bore our sins in His own body on the tree, that we, having died to sins, might live for righteousness—by those stripes you were healed* (1 Pet 2.24).

[78] *For the message of the cross is foolishness to those who are perishing, but to us who are* **being saved** [emphasis mine] *it is the power of God* (1 Cor 1.18).

of stopping me from coming to know the truth of Jesus.[79] Unaware of the absolute battle between light and dark, I had assumed my prayers, offerings, and sacrifices had been received by God. But they hadn't. I had been praying to demons, offering to demons, sacrificing to demons.[80] Demons that had real power and real presence in the physical world.[81] And although these demons had a distinct and at times physically tangible presence, their essence was devoid of life. I, like many who engaged with healing practices that had tangible results, and who did so for the benefit of the world, had been deceived that this alone guaranteed that the source from which the practices were drawing their energy, was, by extension, good.[82] But the Church warns against these practices for a reason. The references to (and commandments against) underworld spirituality in the Scriptures are not metaphorical, nor are they derived from a superstitious, prescientific age.[83]

Through these insights, I really understood how it was that the enemy approaches us and steals the blessings, opportunities, and gifts given to us by our loving Creator. I had quit my Ph.D. without a second thought, never looking back with anxiety, regret, or anything else. God had, as in so many areas of my shockingly privileged life, blessed me with the incredible opportunity to complete a fully funded Ph.D. The supervisors were amazing, and I'd had the freedom to do whatever I pleased. Even though the thesis was in conflict with the revealed truth of Christ, the nature of

---

[79] *You shall not permit a sorceress to live* (Exod 22.18).

[80] *Rather, that the things which the Gentiles sacrifice they sacrifice to demons and not to God* (1 Cor 1.20a).

[81] There are examples throughout the New Testament, but I like this one from Job particularly: *Then a spirit passed before my face; the hair on my body stood up* (Job 4.15).

[82] *But even if our gospel is veiled, it is veiled to those who are perishing, whose minds the god of this age has blinded, who do not believe, lest the light of the gospel of the glory of Christ, who is the image of God, should shine on them* (2 Cor 4.4).

[83] My further thanks to Dan Buxhoeveden for the feedback he gave me on my exploration of this topic, and for his synthesis of the Church's role in moderating spiritual activity on Earth according to God's commandments.

the project meant that I was in frequent contact with the Scriptures, so I would have had some exposure to the truth. Now aware of the fact that true darkness existed and was invested in taking me away from the light at every opportunity, the process that had taken place around the Ph.D. began to appear in a totally new light. And it wasn't good. I was suddenly aware of what I had so carelessly thrown away. This was compounded by a new understanding of all that I had wasted as an addict. Suddenly my whole life before Christ, everything I had worked for, everything I had *stood* for, all that life itself had consisted of whether socially, emotionally, intellectually, or materially, amounted to nothing. My entire life up to meeting Him was like sand in my hands, carried off by the magical winds of deception.

Honor Your Father and Mother

Be gentle to all and stern with yourself.
—Teresa of Avila

My initial plan had been to stay with my parents for a few days before renting a room from one of the neighbors nearby. However, having prayed about it together, my parents felt that they were supposed to keep me near them under the spiritual covering of the house. So I settled in, making a small altar in the living room where I would sleep. I was relieved as, having not spoken to anyone outside my family in person, it would mean avoiding polite daily conversations with the neighbors with whom I would be staying. As we didn't know when I would next be going to America, I thought that it was best to treat my time at my parents' house as a retreat, ensconced in the confines of a mini monastery. I knew I needed to maintain the rigor of monasticism. The nuns had inspired a new level of industriousness in me, and so I suggested that I should do daily "obediences" in the house as a means of contributing for all that I was receiving.

My parents are two of the most encouraging and tender-hearted people I know, so my small daily tasks would incite a level of gratitude and celebration that was entirely unjustified, but lovely all the same.

I began to see the extent of how spoiled and self-indulgent I was. Returning to my parents' home in this way gave me an opportunity to make amends. Christ's emphasis on eldership, obedience, and putting aside one's needs to serve the other had started to change me, and expose how easily irritated and impatient I was. Before Christ, there had been a fairly equal distribution in eldership between me and my parents. Of course, they were my parents, but I didn't defer to them on small matters because of this fact. Furthermore, in a more general sense, I actually considered them to be spiritually younger than me. Now, however, God's commandment to honor one's parents meant submitting to their authority in a way I never had before. They are probably the two least authoritarian people on the planet, which made doing so very easy and pleasant, but it was quite healing to step back from the position of the all-knowing therapeutic observer and to allow them to look after me and guide me. Having been so immersed in Jordanian Christian culture, I had become aware of the fact that my inner respect for elders tended to rely on whether I actually had respect for their behavior. But the monastery taught me that one is to respect and defer to elders, simply because they are older, regardless of their behavior and regardless of what you think of them.

Learning what it really means to honor one's father and mother, and to be held by them, was a beautiful and completely unexpected blessing. Allowing oneself to be a child. Boundaries, limits, and safety were a medicine after so many years living according to my own rules. Sam, the youngest of my brothers, came over with his wife, Marie, and their baby, and we talked about God, work, and the ways in which worth is defined in our society. Amongst my peer group, the fact that I was single, twenty-nine years old, and living with my parents would typically be seen as cause for a breakdown. Yet I was content. It was a joy I had never experienced in my life before. The joy of handing my future over to God to arrange as He wanted. It was ironic, because according to the world's standards, including that of many of my friends, I had exchanged a life of modern freedom—and its social, financial, and sexual proclivities—for a life of religious extremism. Yet I had never felt free like this before. It was a unique freedom born from confining my body and mind in order to liberate my spirit. The corner of the living room became my monastic cell and the task of staying strong against the temptations of the world that were flooding in became my obedience.

I received multiple invitations from friends to join them for holidays in various locations around Europe, but because the monastics occasionally went on pilgrimages, I wanted to save all my money for this, were it to occur. In any case, having been plucked out of the occult, thrown into the spiritual fire of the last six months, and then delivered safely to my parents' house, I was in no rush to go anywhere. Spiritually speaking, I was an infant and needed to be looked after. I also didn't want to subject myself to further geographical spirit attacks unless strictly necessary. There was, however, one possibility. Carina, the close friend with whom I had remained in touch during my time in the monastery, had invited me to go and stay with her in Portugal. It was a very special place, and I wanted to go. But I wasn't sure if I should. I wondered if being around my friend (whom I had met through medicine) would open me up to the spirits she was connected to and result in more warfare. I tried to discern whether or not I should go, but unable to hear what God was saying, I put it aside, hoping that the answer would come.

Newly plugged into the alternative universe of Christian YouTube, a video of a Christian preaching the gospel at an LGBTQ event came up on my feed, and I began to watch it. A shy man with a southern drawl stood at the side of the entrance of the event and softly spoke about Noah and the flood. The people attending started to surround him, shouting.

"Why's God a man? Why's God a man? Why do you think He's a man?"

"I'm just saying 'He' because that's what the Bible says. I'm not making Him a man; I'm just reading," he responded.

Hmm, maybe I could learn from him. I was still frequently wringing my hands about the use of male pronouns in the Bible. My life would be so much simpler if I thought like this. I then watched another video of a pride march in Australia, in which a street evangelist was standing at the side of the parade, with a big speaker backpack and headset mic on, preaching about the repentance of sins to the crowd. As you can imagine, this was not going down well. Hold on, this is the same video one of the nuns had handed around on her phone when I had been in America. As Jordan is a particularly conservative country, the concept of a gay pride march was completely alien to the elder generation.

"It is a march to celebrate sin?" Mother Isidora asked, peering over wire framed glasses.

As the phone passed by Mother Syncletica's side of the table, she looked around at the younger nuns with a bemused expression on her face, bright eyes twinkling. I sat at the other end of the table, my heart beating in my chest. Sister Damaris shook her head in dismay.

"In Boston, the churches are flying rainbow flags, the actual *churches*—"

"Yes," I interjected, my voice rising.

"They're advertising their allegiance with *pride* in order that people feel *welcome*, so that they can come and *meet* Christ. It's a way of *sharing* the *gospel*—"

"No," Sister Eleni cut across, dismissing my point with a sharp shake of the head.

"The pastors are actually preaching that homosexuality is okay."

I swallowed my next sentence, too angry to speak. However, I kept thinking about it long afterward, kicking myself for not talking about the parable of the good Samaritan and the fact that we should not judge someone because of their identity, but rather love them as Christ loves them. I hadn't seen the video but had heard a demented voice shouting, "Repent for your sins, repent for your sins." I mean, is this what Christians think is going to bring people to Jesus? I would bring it up as an example whenever the topic of homophobia, transphobia, or any kind of hatred toward the

PART THREE   201

LGBTQ community would come up, asking how anyone who considered himself or herself a Christian could do such a thing.

Except, to my surprise, I now understood why he was doing what he was doing. It was admittedly a very forceful way to go about it, but I respected that he was willing to speak the truth of Christ, even at the risk of being hated. Which he was. By the end the participants had all formed a huge circle around him screaming, "Out, out, out, out" in unison. There were thousands of comments on the video, many of which were from Christians who had been transformed through being born again in Christ. Others were saying that they were themselves Christian but didn't know how to feel about what the preacher was doing. One of the comments stayed in my mind afterward:

> I know it's really difficult, but I remember years ago attending a march, and there was a Christian preacher there, and although it made me really angry, I knew what he was saying was true. His words convicted me, and now I have been born again and am so grateful for what happened. So keep doing it, because even if just one seed is planted and it brings them to Christ, it will be worth it.

This event made me realize the extent to which I had changed as a person. It was surreal. What was interesting was that the process hadn't been at all intellectual. I hadn't spent hours poring over different Bible verses and their original meaning, so as to get a deeper understanding of the passages around homosexuality in order that I could make a scholarly informed decision about whether or not homosexuality actually is the sin that Christians say that it is. I hadn't even prayed about it. But the presence of the Holy Spirit inside me as a result of my Baptism had just . . . changed me. I felt like I was beginning to see issues through Christ, rather than through myself. It was like an automatic aversion or attraction that required absolutely no input from me at all. I think people assume that when Christians talk about changing their sexual orientation or becoming comfortable in a gender identity, it means they believe in suppression or violent and harmful interventions. But that is not who Jesus is. As Father Theophan had told me during one of our conversations before I converted, "Christ is not like people who say, 'This is right' or 'This is wrong' or 'Do it My way,' no. He is so gentle, so loving. He will come and talk to us in a way we understand."

Rest

Go over the Jordan and you shall find glorious rest.
—The Life of St Mary of Egypt

One of the clearest indications of the real-world power of Christ's restorative work in the body, mind, and soul of the believer came through the changes that I observed in my sleep. For almost fifteen years, I had struggled with insomnia as a result of my—highly sensitive and frequently charged as a result—nervous system activating and dispersing adrenaline through my body. Although I might have technically had a sufficient amount of sleep, the consequence of this process was waking with an unbearable sense of feeling drained, extremely anxious, and completely defeated by the day that had not yet even begun. Over the years, I learned how to channel the fractious energy into work or tasks in order to purify it; however, those days were not enjoyable. Although I'd had some experiences of it during childhood, the insomnia first really arrived when I was fifteen as a result of smoking weed. Getting high had always been something I would do to *get* to sleep, but one day, it began to have the opposite effect. I was already binge drinking at this point, but alcohol had not yet become my primary form of anesthetic. When I began to drink more habitually and heavily, I stopped smoking weed completely, finding the release I was craving in alcohol. It became my first love and my best friend. My sleep problems, however, got worse.

Throughout the drunken years that followed, my sleeping problems drove me to the point of contemplating suicide. I would drink to fall asleep but would struggle to stay asleep as a result of the alcohol, and so I would wake up feeling terrible, needing to drink more that day in order to cope. The only way I would then be able to sleep after that was if I was so wasted that I would pass out. It wasn't technically sleep, but at least I was unconscious. On and on it would go. A vicious cycle. Although this fraught relationship with rest vastly improved on getting sober, the big shift came on entering the world of plant medicine and purification. The immersion in nature and staying up through the night—sometimes for several nights in a row—in ceremony began to alter my sleeping and waking rhythms and released me from the "eight-hour" tyranny that many in the West live under as a result of the—seemingly endless—array of articles, blogs, books, and podcasts that have been produced as a result of our inability to succeed in this basic human task. The nomadic circumstances of the lives of many of the indigenous meant they had an innate knowledge of how to rest and recharge. When they were tired, they slept. When they had a moment of quiet, they stocked up, aware of the energetic exertion that each day might demand. Being with them was healing as a result. Likewise with food. They always ate everything they took, aware of its scarcity—and sanctity—in a way that overindulged westerners often weren't.[84]

My indigenous elders' way of being was much less cerebral and analytical than that of their western followers. They taught me about silence. Words were not wasted but were spoken with intention. They also taught me how to share, and that I should always give more than I received. Fire, water, earth, air, trees, animals, rivers, sun, moon, and stars. Although what

---

[84] I look back in disgust at a memory from one of my journeys with Don Mateo and the three young men with whom he traveled. Desperate for concrete evidence that I was loved by him, and that I was part of the family, I had been thrilled to see him indicate that he would pay for my food at the restaurant in which we were dining while on the road. I have a sensitive stomach and was unable to finish the huge portion of salmon and rice that he had so generously paid for. Looking around the table to see if the meal was finished, I remember his expression as his gaze alighted on the half-eaten food that I was obviously planning to throw away. He said nothing. It is a moment I have never forgotten.

I am saying is characterized as an ethno-reductionist cliché, the reality of the situation is that the majority of indigenous peoples I've had the blessing of spending time with *are* connected to creation (even if they don't necessarily relate to it religiously) in a way that was not—in my experience, anyway—as evident in the modern, western milieu from which I came. Their relationship to physiological processes and how to live as embodied humans within the natural world reflected this. Through their example and their simple, experiential wisdom, the sleep complex that had kept me bound while living in the secular world began to be broken apart. However, over those six years, it would still rear up. Especially in relation to stress. From the moment I arrived in the monastery, however, this shifted. Although life in nature had profoundly changed me, my soul remained in a state of spiritually separated anxiety, desperate to be held by her Creator. On meeting and connecting to Christ, however, this came to an immediate end. I finally found rest.

Silence

Humility collects the soul into a single point by the power of silence.
—St Isaac of Nineveh

The task at hand was to assimilate to the Body of Christ. This is, of course, a mystical process, and one that can be neither rushed, nor controlled. A huge wave of heavenly grace had cascaded over my life, and this period was the sweet aftermath in which that wave of living water gently receded back into Christ's heart. I had been cleansed and renewed and made all new. Now I had to build up my inner man and through it be integrated—it was not something I myself could do—into His Body. Orthodoxy taught full surrender to the fact that Christ is the power that enables us to be saved, but that this is a synergetic process in which the believer's participation is required. I knew that I had a responsibility to guard the flame that had been lit within me. When I had stayed at Sister Veroniki's monastery prior to my Baptism, several of the nuns kept telling me to enjoy everything that was happening and not to worry when the grace left. Inside I kept thinking, well, if the grace leaves why don't you pray more and do more of the things that fill you with grace. As an extremely strong force was needed to propel me out of the occult, I was being carried by a current that meant entering into blissful experiences was possible without that much effort. I understood that they were pointing to this potentially changing with time, but, because it was my only experience of Christ, I wondered why one would let the grace leave. Before I left, Sister Barbara, a Romanian nun who had a gorgeous, easy warmth, gave me a message to pass on to Sister Cherubima: "Remember, Christ is down in the depth of Hades with you." I spoke about sanctification and the growth of the inner man with Sister Veroniki afterward, but we did not understand each other and so went round and round speaking at cross purposes until I asked outright:

"But why not just *do* the things that fill you with grace, rather than wallowing in the depths; why not put all your *effort* into becoming holy?"

"Because it takes time, Anastasia!" She countered. Ah, time.

Over the summer the Lord allowed me to better understand just how much of a gift His grace was. So *this* is what they were talking about when they said that grace would leave. It was not actually comparable, as their monastic vows meant they had entered into a specifically deep form of asceticism. However, I started to experience first-hand this mystical process in Christianity, in which grace moves according to the will of God and God alone—it cannot be controlled solely through human effort, nor is it automatically available. Across those summer months, I would go through waves. For a period of days Christ would feel very close, my daily rule would be alive, and I would find it easy to enter into free prayer afterward. Then the days of waking early would build, and I would crash and sleep in. It was very healing. I felt like I was catching up on years of disrupted sleep and running on empty. But then a spirit of self-indulgence would take over, and a few days later I would wonder why I felt deadened. The lack of physical deprivation meant my spirit had numbed slightly, and prayer had become more rudimentary. Then I would remember that getting up early was part of my rule, so I would psych myself up to get back into the early morning flow and would return to a more spiritually awake state as a result.

It was humbling because I had assumed that I would be able to master the process quite easily, but actually there was a lot to contend with. Mastery is a pagan concept. In Christianity there is only one master—Jesus Christ. As soon as I entered into the mindset of self-determined achievement and results, I realized I was sliding into idolatry. Grace is always a gift, never a right. Of course, I wanted to do my best and work as hard as I could, but that was out of love for Him, not for the reward. It was in this that I understood what the nuns had been talking about. When the initial grace retreats, you have to maintain the same amount of effort, if not more, regardless of how little good you feel it is doing. Perseverance. The famous teaching of St Silouan is "Keep thy mind in hell, and despair not." This idea of being in hell was not yet something I was sophisticated or sensitive enough to understand. Speaking with my sister after weeks of not catching up, I noticed how the pressure within the New Age to present one's life as nothing less than amazing and perfect still influenced the way I was thinking. Asking her how she was doing, she replied in a mellow voice, "Yeah, things are good, just, you know, in hell." I loved the way the Orthodox entered into this mystical collapsing. By acknowledging the darkness, they allowed the glory of God's light to shine more brightly. Their asceticism and how hard their life was meant inviting the suffering of the world to enter their heart and crucify them.

While moving through this period of assimilation, I started to have headaches that would continue for grueling ten-day periods. No amount of medication helped. The enemy would also attack through those close to me. I knew that I needed to work on getting better at not taking things personally. Everyone—especially in the West—has an opinion on Christ

PART THREE   207

(which is usually pretty strong). Because of the nature of the gospel, they will feel entitled to inform you of it. There is a lot of cultural wounding. Many are traumatized as a result of experiences, especially to do with education, at the hands of disobedient Christians who were dishonoring Christ's name through physical, emotional, psychological, or sexual abuse (or who had not received the grace of correct theological instruction). I understood because I used to feel the same way. Although people's rejection of Christ saddened me, the rejection of me personally was something I found even harder to deal with. Which was not right, of course. I should have cared more about my Lord's being rejected, but I didn't—I cared more about my ego being bruised. Father Theophan helped me, always pointing toward forgiveness, peace, and moving on. Because, as he frequently said, *Death is swallowed up by life* (2 Cor 5.4).

Following some weeks of difficulty, I realized that I had moved away from my path. Walking to the forest one morning, I asked God to show me what was happening through His eyes and saw a quick flash of myself walking forward, only to be stopped by a briar of thorns that grew up out of the earth in front of me. Telling my mother about it afterward, she told me I needed to go back to the parable of the sower:

> Then He spoke many things to them in parables, saying: "Behold, a sower went out to sow. And as he sowed, some seed fell by the wayside; and the birds came and devoured them. Some fell on stony places, where they did not have much earth; and they immediately sprang up because they had no depth of earth. But when the sun was up, they were scorched, and because they had no root they withered away. And some fell among thorns, and the thorns sprang up and choked them. But others fell on good ground and yielded a crop: some a hundredfold, some sixty, some thirty. He who has ears to hear, let him hear!" (Mt 13.3–9)

I needed to make sure that the soil was fertile and deep, so that the seeds that had been sown could take root. Realizing that the enemy was trying to choke me renewed my resolve and pushed me into a deeper state of focus. After this period of tension came a new level of understanding, and with it, release.

Alone

I am not alone. God is here, as God is everywhere. The holy angels are there. With whom is it better to talk, with people or with angels? Most certainly with angels.
—St Herman of Alaska

Summer simmered and sweated, and Covid continued. I felt like the world was being given a crash course in monasticism, confined to the "cells" of cramped houses, toxic relationships, dysfunctional family dynamics, and unhappy marriages. Whether people wanted it or not. In the monastery we would pray for all those in violent relationships, imprisoned with their attackers, and all the children in unsafe homes, enclosed with their abusers, day in and day out. After an initial silence following George Floyd's death, I would overhear the issue being discussed in my parents' online services and would reflect on the different approaches to the discussion around systemic racism that were being taken by the ministries they were connected to. My younger sister had introduced me to the online sermons of an Orthodox monk, who spoke beautifully about the nature of nationhood, race, ethnicity, denomination, intersectionality, and the fault lines that converge to make us who we are. That information was only a tiny part of the complex matrix of components that create our individual identities, so monosyllabic and monolithic in the discourse that was taking place in the world. Listening to him speak about what was happening in such a compassionate way moved me, and I started to cry, full of gratitude that I was a believer in Christ.

Waking in the morning to be with Him gave me access to another world. My mother, who was exploring Orthodoxy, had also started to

PART THREE

wake at five-thirty or six to complete a morning prayer vigil, and so we began praying together, making an altar in the middle of the living room with candles and icons. Standing side by side in the pale gray of dawn, we began to murmur the Psalms and prostrate. Having fallen in love with Christ, I tried to make my life as pleasing to Him as possible. I aimed for silence, in order that I could better hear Him, but often realized—usually after the fact—that I was fizzing in the white noise of too much sugar, YouTube, and mindless website scrolling. It was a struggle between focusing on Christ, who was to be met in the space *between* things, and the prince of the world, who was constantly trying to *fill* those delicate spaces with distractions. In the end, it doesn't matter what it is that the devil is seducing you with, as long as he's seducing you with something, then he is in control of your mind for as long as it is not focused on God.

I started to feel that online Christian content could have this double quality. On the whole, it is a force for good, and listening to talks would focus my mind on Christ and give me an opportunity to learn something new. But then after a few days, I would just feel so frazzled by the overload of visual, auditory, and intellectual information, and it would become mere noise again. Then everything was shut down, shut off, and packed up and it was back to silence, the Psalms, and reading the Bible. Although I was playing the guitar, I hadn't written any new songs for a few months now, and the wells felt dry. Every so often I would be able to write a poem for one of the nuns (I had written some for Sister Cherubima, Sister Eleni, and Sister Damaris on their birthdays when in America, and it had become a tradition), but I had stopped drawing completely.

One new thing had, however, started—writing. Father Theophan had encouraged me to pursue doctoral research, but agreed that it would require both a lot of work and a lot of grace. I could not control the grace, but I could do the footwork, and so I began to research. I would send him my thoughts, and he would give feedback and suggestions regarding what kind of academic support would be needed for the project. However, the thought of beginning something as unavoidably intellectually immersive as doctoral work was overwhelming. I felt like I just needed to breathe into what had happened, the shockwaves of which had not yet abated. It felt as if the Holy Spirit wanted to retain this specific moment, that was to a degree suspended, protected from the influence of exterior opinions and information. I was existing in a completely pure and free space. I continued to keep the plan in mind, but I allowed myself to stay entirely focused on the mystery of what was happening inside me.

A Ph.D. is only good if it's used for the glory of God. As Mother Snycletica had said to Sister Cherubima, who was due to begin a master's degree in September, "Without the discipline of asceticism, you're left with just the intellect and as we know, the intellect on its own is worth nothing at all." Having dived as deeply into academia as I had, only to find it dry and devoid of life, I was not interested in doing another Ph.D. that would end up dragging me out of the truth of the living Spirit into the dead end of the mind. What is scary about unsanctified intellectual inquiry is that it doesn't seem like a dead end at all. But untethered from the heart (which limits through compassion), the body (which limits through the laws of nature), and the spirit (which limits through obedience to the higher will of God), it has no boundary. It can just run and run. This was not the path of the holy Fathers. Their theology was spiritually integrated. Although their intellects were engaged, these were intellects that had been radically purified. The theology was not produced at the expense of the lived experience of the Spirit.

I guess this favoring of experiential wisdom over theoretical knowledge was the thing that had drawn me to oral traditions in the first place. It was also something I would experience when attending services with the nuns in America. Some of the services were in Arabic only, and I couldn't understand a word. Although there was an online outline of the service in English that Aleja would often read in order to follow what was happening, I never did, preferring to close my eyes and be "taken by the current," as Sister Eleni put it. The fact that I didn't know what was happening on the level of mind didn't matter to me at the time, because the service as a whole was doing something to me. My respiratory system was being cleansed by the burning of incense; my body was being purged through the discipline of standing for a long period; my auditory system was being fed through the chanting; my heart was being opened by the process of worship; and my mind was being renewed through what I was seeing, whether the icons that adorned the walls, the movement of clergy as they lit the candles and tended the altar, or the images I saw when I closed my eyes. All of these mystical elements converged to nurture and revitalize my spirit.

A couple of times my mother had told me to write down what had happened to me, but I wasn't particularly enthusiastic as I wasn't a diarist by nature. However, she kept coming back to the point.

"Yeah, I'm working on the Ph.D. proposal, and it's happening—"

"No," she interjected.

"Not *that* kind of writing. Not writing from an elevated position. Write what's happened, step by step, while it's still fresh. So that you don't lose it. Because as you continue on, your perception of what is happening to you will change, and it won't be the same then; it won't be as raw."

"What, so I just write down everything that happened? This happened, then this happened. Like a sequence of events?"

"Yes, just *exactly as it happened.*" She said the last words slowly to emphasize the point.

I thought about it. I had never considered writing about my personal experience in this way before. When I was doing my Ph.D., I wanted to make it experiential, to highlight the disassociated nature of academic inquiry, but it wasn't just a story about my life and my feelings.

"But, isn't that a bit, I don't know, vain? Just to write something all about me. 'I did this, and I think this, and I like this,' you know?"

"But it's not about *you*," she responded.

"It's about what God has done *through* you; your story is a means of showing *His* miraculous power."

Oooh, okay. It sounded nice. I had never really considered myself a storyteller—that was always my older sister's area of expertise (she is an author). I used to write newsletters and articles for my website, but I had never written a narrative. In fact, I had always said I was terrible at telling stories. I didn't have that knack of taking people *on the journey*. I didn't enjoy them, the audience, not knowing what I, the storyteller, knew. I wanted them to be *at* the destination, alongside me, from the get go. I thought I would experiment, writing the chapter about my first meeting with Father Theophan. To my surprise it pretty much wrote itself, and I *loved* it. It was like experiencing the joy of what happened all over again. The writing of this then became the engine that carried the summer along.

Were it not for what was coming out when I wrote, I would have been worried about my progress over those rocky months. But the writing provided concrete evidence that positive shifts were taking place. Beyond that, the process itself had the power to transform my internal state. Once I sat down to write, however afflicted I was feeling, I would be lifted, and by the time I had finished writing, I would feel completely different from when I had started—often giddily joyful with energy from having spent so many hours in focused concentration. When I tried to write about the past and anything to do with the spirits, I would start to feel a dark and oppressive energy activate around me, but as soon as I got back onto the topic of Christ, it would just glug out onto the page in a huge dollop.[85] Very satisfying.

I emailed Father Theophan telling him that I had started to write my testimony. "I am so touched, so touched by this wonderful plan, my dear daughter. It is very wonderful, you must do this, and hopefully it can be printed and be a word for your generation." As what I was writing began to shape into something bigger than the initial testimony I had imagined

---

[85] I wasn't able to write the accounts from my pagan life until two years after I completed the first draft of the book. Even though by that point two and a half years had passed since my conversion, as soon as I started to write the names of the plant spirits and described some of the things that had happened when in their presence, my body would involuntarily recall their scent and taste, and I would often begin to feel physically nauseous, and on several occasions, start retching.

it would be, I realized that the money I had received from the Watchmen ministry was specifically to support me while I wrote the book. Creatively energized, I made a plan to also start sharing articles on my website and mailing list. However, as I stopped to pray about what I was doing, I realized that an article would lose the whole narrative that led up to the shocking (to my former world anyway) viewpoint, informing its perspective. Writing in this way would also disperse my focus. Remembering that the Watchmen money had come to me in an unarguably miraculous way brought me back to the importance of recounting what had happened. The testimony. *That* would be the foundation from which I could then expand out into further, perhaps slightly less personal, writing in the future. I set a deadline for the book to be completed and made a daily writing goal so I could reach it.

Mission

For someone to do missionary work in an Orthodox way, he has to have the Holy Spirit within him, but he must also assimilate the culture of the place where he is. Then he can make a contribution.
—St Sophrony of Essex

As the process continued, however, I was conflicted about how to approach anything to do with my experiences with indigenous cultures, painfully aware of the consequences my words could have. As Terry LeBlanc articulates, the idea of Native American and other indigenous peoples as being "godless heathens" comes from a particular reading of the Bible. This was the justification for the evil done to them. Although I wanted to surrender myself to my new life in Christ, I was disturbed by the limited nature of a lot of western Christianity's vocabulary when dealing with cultures outside its cultural framework. I was trying to show my willingness to give up everything from the past, but the idea that my words would contribute to *that* conversation was terrifying. Indigenous tribes were being wiped out through the spread of disease as a result of certain types of misguided Evangelical missionary work. But what if this story galvanized them? A supposedly Christian intervention that stood against everything Father Theophan and the holy elders represented.

The idea that what I was writing could be used to support any kind of persecution of Native, First Nation, or indigenous peoples sickened me. I wondered if I could just elide everything that had happened in relation to tribal spirituality and focus instead on other elements of the story. But if I were to glide over the glaring issue of the oppression of Native peoples who had been executed in the name of Christ, I would be a silent, "violent" white woman. I had often been the person policing everyone within our community, making sure that no advantage of the Natives was being taken, and that awareness of the sociological reality of the world we inhabited was understood in congruence with all that we were experiencing mystically. I tried to find a middle ground, ending with an unsatisfying median approach that alluded to much of what had taken place, but not in enough detail to clearly explain it. The result was an imbalanced narrative that didn't deal with the nitty gritty of the spiritual reality I had experienced, a significant part of which I was now in a constant state of warfare with. I didn't know what to do.

As this internal pressure built, I found it increasingly hard to write, until I got to a point where I stopped writing altogether. I thought about it obsessively, the looping thoughts chasing me into the night. Tormented at the thought that what I was saying could be taken in the wrong way and used against indigenous peoples, I began to have trouble sleeping. Even though *I* knew that the situation was nuanced and needed to be approached with delicacy, would everyone who read the book? Time continued to pass and I felt choked, stuck between serving my Lord with the truth of what had happened, and fulfilling my duty of care to the indigenous peoples who had given me so much. On reaching its peak, this tension came to a tearful release, by the simple realization that I had to let go of control and trust God. Following this severing, the writing process became easy, and things began to flow again.

Mental Chastity

It is not an external enemy we dread. Our foe is shut up within ourselves. An internal warfare is waged daily by us.
—St John Cassian

Being outside the monastery was a double-edged sword. On the one hand I was more free to do what I wanted (though options were more limited than normal because of Covid), but with that freedom came temptation. I knew I had to strengthen my inner man through prayer and my spiritual rule—that was clear. What was also apparent was that I needed to become stronger as an Orthodox Christian more generally. And being a Christian meant being set apart for the Lord. When in America, I had thought that the Lord was sending me home to do a final cleanup of my life—to see beloved people and say goodbye to them before returning to America again shortly after. However, the borders to the US were closed and didn't seem to be reopening. Once I began writing, this started to feel like a good thing. I knew I wanted to finish the first draft of the book before I went back to the monastery, so I could fully focus when I was there: it would be a new season. I slowly allowed more and more communication back in but took care to keep it as minimal as possible, so as not to disturb what was happening within. On the one hand, I was in control of this process and was acting as a gatekeeper trying to keep things out. However, at the same time, I was dealing with the painful reality of how few people were actually calling me. In my busy life before Christ, I had always had multiple different group chats, email threads, planning forums, and work emails on the go, and if things got quiet then that would be—to my mind—indication that I now had space to organize another ritual or retreat.

However, none of the above was part of my life anymore. During those two months I would routinely go to my phone to reach out to people from my past. I rarely had time to see them before because my schedule had always been so packed with work and traveling, but now I was free. Now could be the moment. Thoughts of contacting old friends would surface repeatedly, but every time I went to message someone, I stopped myself and observed what was happening inside me. Why did I want to start up these conversations? Again and again, I would feel the urge to connect, but would resist. The ridiculous thing was that my life was so centered on Christ, any rekindled friendships were going to have a fairly short lifespan. I had to stay focused on the Lord. He was my priority. But I just wanted to know I was wanted! Silence. I understood that the Holy Spirit was asking me to detox on a deeper level. Not just in terms of taking away relationships that were not part of His plan for my life, but by starving the craving in me that sought validation through the oxygen of friendship.

During this period, memory after memory of painful and humiliating experiences from my life as an addict surfaced. Through observing this backlog of sensory data, I really understood why the Bible teaches that magic doesn't heal. I hadn't thought about the contents of the memories for years, because my life had been so full. But now, with all those distractions brushed away by the power of God's word, I was left to deal with the reality that all this toxic waste was still inside me. Because I had experienced what I thought was transformation and empowerment, through plants and the New Age, I had assumed that my vulnerability, shame, guilt, and anger had been cleaned away. However, it was now clear that they were just buried—consciously suppressed or unconsciously repressed—within inner chambers that I simply never had time, or even, in the case of the things that were repressed, the ability to access.

The magical practices had cleared out enough within me that I *felt* that I was sufficiently prepared to begin working as a vessel to distribute the

PART THREE

fleshly wisdom of spiritism into the world. However, a total and complete healing of the past had not happened. A plaster had just been placed on a festering wound. Starved of all forms of social interaction, I also was very aware of how much history my womb was still stubbornly carrying. As a pagan, I used to lead womb-cleansing workshops and would often do rituals and procedures to remove the energetic cords from the past. Under the stark light of retreat, however, I was aware of how little those magical tricks had worked. It was an awareness that only came about as a result of contact with Christ. While I was plowing through the hyper-stimulation of the spirit world, I wasn't able to notice the full extent of the imprint my worldly life had left on me. Suddenly every look, every thought. It was all there.

Fellowship and connection would take place again at some point, but it was clear that God wanted me to be isolated and set apart for a specific reason. It was a season of deliverance that was not yet complete. When I honed in on memories from the past of sitting on my sofa and sending people texts—because my phone had gone quiet—I could see the underlying need that was being indirectly met: want me, need me, love me. The Lord wanted to kill this idol of seeking human feedback for purposes of maintaining an illusory sense of belonging. Only Christ could give me that sense of completion. If I was experiencing that outside of Christ, then it's highly likely that a created substitute (an idol) was involved. Even if that created substitute was as subtle as the belief that I had everything inside me to be whole. He was showing me that my identity *in Him* was the only validation that was needed. Getting that sense of belonging and value from other people would always lead to destruction because they were a poor substitute for Christ. As Aleja said to me one day when we were lying on our beds in the monastery (there was a thin separator between our two cells), "Just always remember that only Christ can give you life, Tali. Nothing else. No one else."

The prospect of a life lived solely for Christ was open before me. No marriage, no children, no family, no partner, no boyfriend, no nothing.

Could I actually do this? Although I was a naturally relational being, a dedicated religious life was actually something I had thought about for a while. I was, after all, exploring the possibility of becoming a Buddhist nun before meeting Christ. Following that first meeting with Father Theophan in London, I had stood in my kitchen drinking a glass of water and thinking about the powerful abbess Hildegard Von Bingen (a chapter of my Ph.D. had focused on the surprising insights that this medieval Christian mystic had articulated with regards to female physiology). I imagined myself in a habit, surrounded by other nuns. Maybe I could take care of women in *that* way. It would be Wild Woman 2.0.

However, what was different now was that this was real. When on the pilgrimage, I had messaged Father Theophan, telling him that I had realized that I needed to enter seclusion for the foreseeable future while Christ worked into the parts of me in need of healing. I knew that Christ was trying to focus my attention on something within me that needed a depth of cleansing that could not happen if I were immersed in social life. With Christ before me, I didn't want to lose precious time. Paganism, with its infinite lives and world-devouring sensuality, was never in a rush. There was always a sense that there was an inexhaustible amount of time at everyone's disposal. The way the monastics and the Christians living a life of mission went about their business, on the other hand, was the complete opposite. In the monastery, every nook and cranny of each day was crammed with the important activity of sanctification. That is why the monastery was so intense. But that is also why so many miraculous things happened there.

The Orthodox way of life is very much about squeezing every last drop out of life and not wasting anything. My sister had gotten weak with laughter telling me a story about the severity of Elder Joseph the Hesychast's asceticism, and how it impacted his spiritual children, while doing the dishes one evening after dinner. "They lived under an orange tree and," her shoulders shook as she silently laughed, "they had to eat the oranges with the peel on." The chewing of the bitter pith in order to access the juicy sweetness of the flesh beneath it, which will remain tempered by the bitterness throughout, seemed to sum up the Christian path perfectly.

During this period I became aware of a new dynamic between vanity on the one hand, which was an idol that I needed to continually place on Christ's altar in order that it could be crucified, and a kind of giddy sense of feeling beautiful as a result of what Christ saw in me, on the other. My true beauty, which was not about looks. It was a strange paradox—I began to feel more attractive in direct correlation to my separation from anyone ever seeing me. I knew that this rising sense of loveliness inside me and coursing through me was Christ's loveliness. My ego wanted to show it off, to be admired in this new-found beauty. But it wasn't mine to share. The light inside me was Christ.

Energy Harvesting

For many years exorcisms must be read for those who come from doing magic. This is what the early Church did.
—St Sophrony of Essex

I understood that the frequency of the demonic attacks that I was experiencing—often as a result of watching or reading something connected to the occult but sometimes for no apparent reason at all—directly correlated with my immersion in the realm of magic and spirit contact. Through one experience, the Lord opened my eyes to the spiritual truth of tantra and the demonism on which it feeds. Instead of starting the day with my daily rule, I instead searched the internet for information about how tantra was in fact black magic in disguise. It was a pointless exercise, as I already knew that tantra *was* magic, but I was hoping to come across some conclusive written evidence, or better yet, a testimony from a former practitioner who had converted to Christianity. As I flicked from website to website, I typed in the name of Vijay, a tantric master whom I had started to follow. He had come into my life several months after I had met Father Theophan . . . As was frequently the case with the teachers I encountered whose work I admired, we had become close, and as our student-teacher/ patient-healer relationship deepened, I told him that I wanted to do a Ph.D. on feminine body armoring and trauma. Thrilled at the possibility of his controversial work gaining the respect of the academy, we had begun to put in place plans to do work on the project together, with him advising me and teaching me along the way.

Following this period of working with him, I had started to feel such a strong pull toward him, that even after my Baptism, I would think about him and be overcome by the desire to see him. I had come to the conclusion that a spell of some kind had been put on me. When I had asked Father Theophan about it, he told me that as a result of my Baptism, all contracts, cords, and spells had been cut. However, it would take time for all parts of my psyche to be renewed and restored and for all my members to be redeemed. As I typed his name into the search engine, articles appeared about his court cases and arrest. He had been to prison for three years for assaulting clients. I couldn't believe it. I had brought so many women to his talks, and many of my clients had received sessions from him. I messaged people to warn them not to see him and took the review I had written for him offline. However, while reading, I had been overtaken by the same sense of intense drowsiness that characterized the psychic attacks I had been experiencing since my conversion. I knew that if I did my rule, I would be able to cut this demonic energy from taking hold of me any further, so I began to walk to the woods to pray the Psalms.

I stood in my usual place in the forest and began to pray the canonical hours, hoping that this would end the spiritual oppression that had descended upon me. However, it did not shift. Usually when these attacks would begin, praying would clear it, but this time nothing was happening. I tried to stay focused on the words I was reading, but the force of the energy was overwhelming. Despite persevering for almost two hours and finishing all of my prayers, it remained at the same level as when I had begun. This was new. Normally after praying it stopped. Or at least lessened. I began to pray the Jesus Prayer. I repeated the words, pleading to be released. The force was so heavy that I didn't know if it would lift, but after a while of pouring every ounce of energy I had into saying the words, first very quickly, then more slowly, it began to loosen its grip. I walked home, repeating the prayer. My entire body felt toxic.

That night my mother and I held a vigil. I did not feel good. As I closed my eyes, I began to see a pathway upward that led toward blazing light in front of which stood Christ. He was standing in front of a doorway, and the light was shining around Him, though He was in darkness. I prayed, asking for help and for forgiveness for going to this tantric healer. I asked the Lord to show me what was happening in the unseen realm during my experience with this man. I knew that as a result of his doing such intimate work on my soul, a connection had been made, which he had been able to draw on when he was meditating, whether consciously through visualization or unconsciously. Despite being in his sixties, he had an intense vitality. Vitality that was in large part a result of the power that he had accumulated through tantric energy conservation practices.

A vision began in which I could see myself in the middle of the tantric master's studio. We sat opposite each other, with our legs folded in our laps, in the classic yogi pose. A "heart opening" practice was taking place, in which Vijay was generating a shaft of energy from his heart into mine. We sat in silence, staring into each other's eyes. I watched the vision unfold, as if I were looking down into the room. Above us was a shadowy space in which there were several huge demons. Dark brown in color, they sat on different throne-like structures in a vast hall. A ritual was taking place. Thousands of tube-like lesions fell from the surface of their mottled, textured faces. They were feeding off the energy generated by the exchange of energy between me and the tantric master.

Through this I understood how tantric practitioners conserve spiritual energy and offer it as a sacrifice to the deities, gods, and goddesses (unclean spirits) that rule their tradition. The process is often unconscious, the tantric practitioners are rarely aware that they are doing this, or if they are, they just see it as a beautiful offering to the gods and goddesses they willingly serve. The reason the demons harvest energy in this way is that they are cut off from the heavenly source of life—Christ, the one true God—and so have to garner the power that they need for their activity, indirectly, by way of human sources. A process that deeply grieves the Father. Sensitivity and safeguarding for those who have been abused is extremely important. But if the healing is genuine, it will only come through the power of Christ. He alone heals, and He alone gives life because He alone *is* life.

Free

If I prayed to God that all men should approve of my conduct, I should find myself a penitent at the door of each one, but I shall rather pray that my heart may be pure towards all.
—Amma Sarah

Christ is the God of truth. I had felt the force of this purifying power during my conversion. Everything that was attached to me, feeding on me, draining me, controlling me, using me, distracting me, and smothering me was burned away. As the Lord lifted me up out of darkness, I could feel hundreds of cords (to different spirits, entities, powers) being cut and my spirit being released. It is not something that can be understood theoretically. It has to be experienced. The purification had extended into every area of my life: what I read, the music I listened to, and the people I spent time with. After a painful interaction with a close family friend with whom I had always had a very difficult relationship, I came across a website on covert abuse. As I began to read, a light switched on in my mind. Ah, so *this* is what has been going on. For *years*. I ordered several books on the topic, and as I read, I began to see the situation clearly for the first time, realizing the extent of what I had experienced when growing up alongside them. The recognition that I had been stuck in an abuse cycle suddenly exposed the other toxic situations I had been in throughout my life, as well as the role that my own narcissistic traits (wanting to be the spiritually enlightened, martyric, one-who-forgives), bad behavior, and passive-aggressive tendencies had played in them, again and again. And just my anger generally, which was something this retreat time was forcing to the surface.

Furthermore, I was a *man pleaser* (Gal 1.10): a worshiper of other people, who found her worth in others, rather than in God. Released by this new awareness, I entered into No Contact, a clinical term used to designate the painful, but necessary break from the addictive highs and lows of abusive relationship cycles. I pored over Bible verses dealing with interpersonal sin in order to understand the information in Christian terms and to make sure I was approaching the process correctly. Rejecting the world's tendency to blame and judge the other is the thing that makes Christianity unique. That is the witness of the saints. I worked through the psychological literature, translating aspects of it into biblical terms, so that it was harmonious with my prayer life, while ignoring some parts of it altogether.

Following the decision to instate a boundary and uphold it, the racing thoughts, obsessive cycles of phone checking, and the interminable angry inner monologue in which I would be violently admonishing the person—and God—for their actions past and present, a constant companion in my life, all immediately stopped. Life became very calm. Although I had several times called for a break in our relationship, it was always only for a period of months, after which things would return to dysfunction. Furthermore, I was enmeshed. But the indwelling seed of authenticity that was beginning to blossom and bring forth fruit within could not tolerate this environment of inward deception and so, through Christ's healing power, I was cut loose. I wanted to be a loving presence in this person's life, but my adoration was mixed with resentment as a result of all that had happened.

And I needed to repent for this. I didn't know how long it would last, but the inner quiet and sense of freedom that bubbled up following this decision confirmed that it was Christ's will. Now it was time for me to deal with the subterranean reservoir of anger I had been suppressing and to ask the Lord for the grace to heal and change.

Solitude

The seed, swollen with moisture, bursts asunder its covering of soil and out peers the blade of wheat, full of symbols. So faith, whose bosom is filled with goodly fruits, is a blade of praise.
—St Ephraim the Syrian

Arriving at the decision to accept Carina's invitation to a week in Portugal had not been straightforward. I had gone round in circles, unsure as to whether it was a good idea for me to go so far away from my parents' while so new in the Faith. After praying about it a lot, I finally got the sense that it was, and, with Father Theophan's blessing, made my way. Carina had recently left an intensely emotionally, psychologically— and even physically—abusive relationship with one of the shamans I had worked for and had spent the past months in Portugal recovering. I had met her a little after I met Nick, and we had been close ever since, working, living, and traveling to the Amazon together. The more I read about narcissistic abuse recovery, the more events in my life, my behavior, and my issues started to make sense. Puzzle pieces were being put into place. I arrived very raw, processing the abuse I had experienced, of which some had taken place at the hands of her highly disturbed ex.

Although Carina, like most in the New Age, wasn't fully convinced by what I was sharing, I knew we would have time to get to the bottom of what had happened in her relationship, and why she had stayed in it for as long as she did. As I reflected on my own experiences of abuse, I began to see why I repeatedly latched onto those with controlling and dominating tendencies and the grandiose aspects of my own personality (such as a need to demonstrate and assert my power), which meant that I fell into these traps again and again. Before coming to Portugal, I had contacted an Orthodox friend of my parents' who was a coach, in order to discuss this new realization. She was a devout Orthodox Christian, so I knew I could do the psychological inquiry work with her in a way that was harmonious with the deeper process of sanctification in Christ. We agreed that I would contact her when I got back from Portugal to set up a session.

Across the days of swimming in rivers, walking across sun drenched hills, picking fruit, and baking delicious tarts, we processed our experiences and talked about the medicine world. It was the first time I had spoken about any of it since my conversion. Suddenly my mind was full of everyone I had left behind and the life we used to live together. Her exit was more circumstantial than mine; she was just taking a breather to process everything that had taken place with her ex. I, on the other hand, had entered a completely new reality. I was quite frank about a lot of things, and, encouraged by the lack of opposition in her, I began to think that maybe this new understanding had in some way become self-evident and now we were both on the same page. However, her lack of vocal opposition had not been because of internal agreement. After a conversation in which she expressed her frustration at the way I was talking about my Christian outlook as if it were *the* truth, I trod a bit more carefully, making an effort to translate what I was saying into terms that were understandable within the worldview we had previously shared. I didn't want to overload her. I wanted to honor the fact that she had been so open and affirming of my new life, though it contradicted so much of what we had shared together before. As she had said before I left at the end of the week, "It's like you are a completely different person."

One of the blessings of the week in Portugal was that the Lord had completely transformed my understanding of abuse recovery. The coaching sessions I had planned for my return no longer felt necessary. Christ had healed me. It was done. In one week! Just like that. That is the power of Jesus, the spiritual surgeon. On sharing this with the Orthodox coach, she messaged me back. "I am so happy to hear this! Of course, true healing will only ever come through Christ." Two of my close friends had recently given birth, and I wanted to go and see the new baby but accepted that it would be better if I waited till I was stronger in the Faith. Although enjoyable, I knew that the experiences of friendship that I had been having over summer needed to be completely cut, so that I could move forward. This was, after all, what I had been sent home to do. I had been dragging my heels a bit because it just felt so ruthless. The time in Portugal had brought me and Carina closer together, and I loved her deeply. However, I felt that it was *because* of this, that the Lord was asking me to separate from her. I emailed the handful of people I had planned to see before returning to America, telling them I was entering another retreat (people in the medicine world understood retreating and fasting, as it is common in witchcraft).

I didn't know what would happen next and didn't want to create expectations of future plans, but the idea of telling people I wouldn't see them again, *ever*, felt a little extreme. I asked my mother what I should say. "You don't know what the future holds. You don't know what Christ's plans are for you in those people's lives, so you can just say goodbye for now," she said simply. That two of the friends with whom I had been spending time over that summer had converted to Christianity out of witchcraft showed me that Christ was able to grab people at any time and from any situation. Okay, I would say goodbye—for the foreseeable. I could feel that Christ wanted one hundred percent of my focus. The loneliness I felt seemed to engender a level of closeness with Him that dissipated when I was engaged with others. *I am the only friend you need. Now come and walk with Me.* I said goodbye to everyone, even Carina, who sent me tearful messages telling me how happy she was for me and how much she loved me. It was a very sweet gift from the Lord. And then it was done.

PART THREE

Fire

And the Angel of the Lord appeared to him in a flame of fire from the midst of a bush. So he looked, and behold, the bush was burning with fire, but the bush was not consumed.
—Exodus 3.2

Passing a farm on my way home from a late summer walk, I stopped at the open gate of one of its fields. A fire was burning in the middle of the field, vivid in the twilight. The fire swooped in the breeze, its flames rolling out to lick patches of the ground. Smoke swirled upward, the plume undulating, dancing with the wind and then rapidly disappearing. I approached the fire and stopped several feet in front of it. I relaxed as the flames began to heat the front of my body. My skin was cool in the nip of dusk, but my blood was hot from the exertion of the walk. It had been some time since I had been close to a big, open fire and I wondered how to approach it. God is a consuming fire (Deut 4.24), the primordial source. Francis of Assisi talked about "brother fire" and "sister wind," and I had been pleased to see that the saints who dipped into the depths of reality through ascetic practice arrived at the recognition that the elements were themselves alive.

The fire had brought me to life and had become, as a result, the center of my life. I longed to live amidst its flames, learning directly from the source of life. The fact that the fire was the "original book of life" was a notion that was instinctively understood in my community. During one ceremony, the topic of my Ph.D. had come up, and Don Mateo had laughingly countered that he had started his "Ph.D." with the fire fifty-four years ago, and he was still far from finishing. Why read dead books when you can read the living fire? And be read by it. The power that the fire had to respond to every individual worshiper's needs, and to administer healing through certain forms of purification, was proof to me of its sovereignty.

Cooking on it (and then feeding it the first portion of food), singing to it, purging into it, or dancing around it, the fire was always there—the center of my universe.

But the fire didn't only light up our ceremonies and answer our prayers. It could also burn. During a ceremony that had taken place on the top of a mountain, the dual nature of our pagan theology manifested its full force in a particularly potent way. Maya, who was Dutch by birth, had organized a pilgrimage around different sacred sites in the Netherlands. Our days were spent trekking across wild stretches of land, scrambling down onto deserted, barely accessible beaches, and climbing up into rocky coastal caves, in order to pay our respects at ancient burial sites and power points. Generally, this annual pilgrimage was closed to the public and was just something we did as a group of friends, but Matteo, a Colombian massage therapist and his mother, Virginia, whom we had met at a retreat, had come to join us for one of the mountain ceremonies.

Dan, a recent medicine convert, had also invited his sister Letitia and her friend Daisy, in the hope that they would move into the world of transformation through the spirits alongside him. The girls had obviously missed the memo about the soggy mountain hike and had turned up with shiny, wheeled suitcases, their pristine pink tracksuits in comic contrast to the bedraggled crew of pipe-smoking, sheepskin-decked nature fiends who greeted them. We set off early in the morning, leaving two of the older members of our group with the cars we slept in between mountain climbs. We would rejoin them the next morning. After several hours of walking in the rain, we reached the summit. Night fell very quickly. A huge rock formation created a jagged half circle at the top, and we erected the "travel tipi" in its middle. A ramshackle altar was quickly arranged and we divided the space, placing a large metal fire bowl in the middle of the tent. The fire was lit, and we all squeezed into our places, trying to find a way to fit into one row around the fire.

The shamans who were with us began to chant, progressing through stages of contact with the elemental spirits of the mountain and the spirit

PART THREE

of the mountain itself. In between these songs, the rest of the group would chant, singing into the fire. After a while the men began to trail off, having exhausted their repertoires. The women organically migrated closer to the fire, forming an inner circle. Sitting at its edge all night, my entire insides felt lit up from its intense power. Loudly drumming and rattling, we chanted to activate and support the work that the spirits were doing inside each of our souls. The fire crackled and spat, joining us in our worship. We laughed in delight. One song would trigger another, and we would sing it through repeatedly until the energy of the song was used up. After a moment of silence, a word, image, or sound would resonate within us in response to the insights we were receiving, and we would start up again, moving on to the next melody. The heat, both physical and spiritual, of these fire rituals was overwhelming, but the desire to get up and escape out into the cool, clear night for a moment, in order to release the pressure, was mitigated by the magnetic pull of the fire. I was fused to the block of wood on which I was sitting, staring into its flames. Nothing thrilled me more than experiencing the power of the spirits.

"Something's going on here," Nick said, smiling.

"Yep," Maya's boyfriend chimed in. "There's something . . . feminine happening. I just feel like . . ." He trailed off and put his head in his hands, before looking up, a smile spread across his face. His tone was reverent. "There's something happening with these women and the fire. And this cauldron."

All the men voiced their agreement. Inner experience was something that was weaved into the supplications and bartering that took place across the night and we all laughed, aware of the meta layers of meaning. A scream pierced through the laughter as Matteo hurled himself at the fire, from the back of the tent. He was writhing, and his eyes were rolling back into his head.

"What's happening? What's happening?" Letitia asked as Dan lunged after Matteo to push him away from the fire.

"Oh my God, is this normal, is this normal?" Daisy asked in distress as everyone got up from their places.

"Help me, brother, help me hold him down," Dan cried out to Nick. Dan was strong, but he was panicking. This world was still very new to him. The six men in the group all held on to Matteo as his body spasmed. He was grasping for the rattles, screeching.

"It's the singing," Virginia said. "I think the rattles were too much for him. So much rattling, it triggered something."

"But maybe that's why he came," someone countered. "Maybe this is what needed to come out of him."

Different perspectives were shared as the practicalities of the situation were attended to. The two shamans were sitting in their places unruffled. These moments of uncontrolled—and uncontrollable—full-body possession were not uncommon. Usually, the person was forced against a tree and tied up with ropes until the process ran its course. The mothers were evacuating the five sleeping children from the tent, while the men attended to Matteo. Although he was slight, Matteo was muscular and this physical strength, combined with the energy of whatever it was that was inside him, meant that he was not easy to hold in place. He was writhing on the ground, again and again shouting out in Arabic (a language that Virginia verified he didn't speak). As soon as someone loosened the grip on him, he would jump up to stand. Once standing, he careered from side to side, dragging the men with him. They all made efforts to control his movements and keep him from the fire. We tried to decipher what he was saying, and someone looked up the words on the phone as we made a plan to get the children, Virginia, and the shamans down to where the cars were parked. The sun had risen, and hikers would be soon making their way up to the top of the hill.

As was the case for most people in the medicine world, the majority of us were engaged in healing practices, and everyone began to try and calm the situation through various techniques. A friend began to administer intensive bodywork, using her clenched fist to grind the sign of the cross into Matteo's chest, dripping hot wax from a candle melted in the fire onto the red imprint, and using her nails to dig into Matteo's face in order to force the demon out through expulsion. Matteo screamed and continued to writhe as others performed energy clearings, voice therapy, and tried to negotiate with the spirit through smoke offerings. As this continued, Maya and I joined the two shamans outside the tent, in order to complete the closing rite. We moved around the rock formation in sequence, saying prayers of thanksgiving, before laying down an offering of greenery and flowers gathered on the walk that we had bunched into bouquets. Returning to the tent, Maya and I sat with the female shaman at the side of the fire and looked over at Matteo, who was still being pinned to the ground and worked on by the healers.

"*Muy sagrado!*" the female shaman said, shaking her head and pursing her lips.

"*El fuego es muy, muy sagrado.*"[86]

Reverent before the fire, Maya and I nodded in agreement that the fire was not to be messed with.

"*So* sacred," I repeated, dropping a handful of incense into the flames as an offering, as Maya and I looked at each other acknowledging its power.

"*El fuego es muy sagrado.*"

Molech

They sacrificed their sons and their daughters to the demons; they poured out innocent blood, the blood of their sons and daughters, whom they sacrificed to the idols of Canaan, and the land was polluted with blood.
—Psalm 105.37–38

Before encountering Christ, I had remained ideologically bound to the pro-choice side of the debate, despite my alarm at abortion rates,

---

[86] "The fire is very, very sacred."

disagreement with the culture around casual sex and contraception, and opposition to the rhetoric of "reproductive rights." I was a feminist—what other option was available? However, things had changed. First gradually, then quickly. It had started with recognition that the work I did with women had been minimizing the severity of their situations. During my sessions, I would reassure my clients that their abortions were not their fault, and that they did not need to feel guilt as a result. The Holy Spirit showed me that I had been wrong. Only God can release people from the consequences of their sin. The fact that I had been trying to help them heal their pain was not the problem. The problem was that the healing was fake. Because those women did not know that they had to get straight with God through repentance, they were being inhibited from accessing real salvation. I suddenly saw my arrogance and my assumption of a God-like status: come to me, I will heal you, I will release you from your suffering. The best thing I could have done for these women would have been to encourage them to sit in the presence of God and repent for killing the life inside them. Because it would be through that, and that alone, that they could find actual release.

The love I had been showing these women was not the love of God. It was coddling, people-pleasing, toxically affirming love. As the Bible was showing me, the love of God does not necessarily fit our limited human definition of love. We often think love is about making people feel good (which it can, of course). But His love far surpasses this, because His love embodies the cosmic truth of reality in its entirety. Before flying back to England from the US, I realized I needed to repent more deeply for the witchcraft I had been practicing. In vocalizing my repentance, I knew a line in the sand had been drawn. In order for the transition to be fully complete, however, something else had to be revealed. An old friend's life had been thrown into emotional chaos after the abortion of her and her husband's baby, and I reflected on why so many people I knew who practiced pagan forms of spirituality had abortions.

Earlier I had spoken with these friends about how YHWH distinguished Himself from the other gods of the ancient world (who received child

PART THREE

sacrifice as a form of worship), and as I was speaking, I realized the potency of the topic, as a result of their process around the abortion. Following my time with them, the Holy Spirit drew my attention to Molech, one of the gods to whom worshipers would sacrifice their children. Suddenly it all fell into place. Molech was the "god" of abortion. People were still offering their children to him—it was just that instead of being burnt to death, the children were instead killed through toxic chemicals and decapitation. Instead of the ceremonial drums quintessential to Molech worship (employed to drown out the sound of the children's screams), there was local anesthetic-induced silence and tears of grief shed in isolation. The fact that these babies were being offered as sacrifices unbeknownst to the mothers was not a problem for Molech. As long as he received his "offering," it didn't make a difference to him that the women (and their partners) didn't know that it was this satanic force that was propelling them to place their babies in his hands.

Stunned, I ran to my father—a pro-life campaigner who had run a charity to support women in crisis pregnancies—to tell him what the Holy Spirit had shown me. He started to recite the words of a song about all the children sacrificed to foreign gods and began to cry. I couldn't believe it. People knew about this. I started looking on the internet and found multiple different Christian websites talking about it. Following this revelation of what is happening in the spiritual realm, I felt a new level of clarity regarding the Christian attitude to being pro-life. So *this* was why there was *such* fervor about it. Despite the centrality of this issue in discussions of gender equity, my actual knowledge of the practical steps involved in abortion procedures was limited to an understanding of certain terms and stages of fetal development. I don't know if all those who are pro-choice are aware of the ins and outs of what actually takes place in abortion clinics and during terminations, but I doubt it. The fact that most people don't is a huge problem, as it can allow "being pro-choice" to exist in an intellectual, theoretical sphere that is disconnected from the blood-and-guts reality of the term. Coming across a video of a doctor speaking in Congress about what the procedure involved, I realized the extent of my ignorance and its dangerous consequences.

The doctor held up the metal clamping device that is used to decapitate a fetus and explained, step by step, the way in which the baby's limbs would be yanked out before being placed on a table for inventory, how the skull would be crushed and extracted, and how a white liquid pouring out of the womb was a good sign—it was the baby's brains. This meant conclusively that the baby was dead. The doctor spoke of how throughout his career, he and his wife had struggled to conceive with IVF. After adopting a child, his wife had become pregnant, only for their adopted child to die in a car crash. Immediately after her death he performed an abortion, was awakened to the reality of what he was doing, and instantly stopped performing late-term abortions, then abortion altogether, and was now a pro-life campaigner. As he spoke, people put their heads in their hands and wiped tears from their faces.

Possession

> *Do not place too much confidence in the higher education you received in this world. The civilization we live in is a culture of fallen humanity.*
> —St Sophrony of Essex

Following this, I realized that I had been possessed. *Ideologically possessed.*[87] My newfound life in Christ meant being catapulted into a community whose political sympathies were everything I had always

---

[87] I owe this term to Jordan Peterson, of whom there is so much to say, that I find myself unable to say anything. Except this: I saw a news headline over someone's shoulder saying that Peterson had experienced a heavenly vision convincing him of the living truth of Christ. Glory to God. May your mission be blessed.

stood against. But over the summer, I began to feel increasingly skeptical of the progressive belief systems my friends were angrily pushing, which were completely antithetical to the qualities of spontaneity, joy, creativity, individuality, freedom, and mercy that characterized the living God. No ideology could adequately encompass the truth of spiritual reality because the kingdom far exceeds the boundaries of any earthly thought system. They will come to an end. The kingdom will not. Furthermore, Christ, who is a living person and not a dead religious framework, is the antithesis of ideology. He is Spirit. He is Life.

Over the course of those months, the Christian attitude to communism finally began to make sense to me. I was reared on an academic diet of ultra-far-left critical theory, and I still looked at that worldview through rose tinted glasses. However, coming into the practical and logical spirituality of Christianity meant seeing the world of politics in a way that I hadn't during those years of ungrounded magic. I, like most liberals, had always *known* about the gulags and about the evils done in the name of communist justice, but now, as a result of reading the harrowing accounts of the Romanian, Russian, and Polish Orthodox Christians persecuted under its regimes, a veil of deception was lifted, and I was able to actually *see* the situation in its spiritual entirety, for the first time.

Realizing the extent of how these ideologies had controlled my mind was destabilizing. They had controlled me almost *more* than all the other actual gods I was worshiping. Their power had begun to peter out as I got closer to God through sobriety. But not totally. Assessing my actions between my conversion and that point, it was evident that a lot of the stress and pain I had gone through was not simply because my mind was coming into contact with different perspectives that were challenging its conception of right and wrong, good and bad, love and hate. It was also because a battle was taking place in the unseen realm. Contact with Christ meant that these powerful and very deeply rooted ideological *spirits* were forced out of me. It was an extended exorcism. And one that had taken some time to complete.

I messaged Father Theophan telling him that I had become aware of the extent to which I had been possessed by these thought systems, and that I had realized that they were, on a spiritual level, demonic powers. I felt like I had woken up from a trance. He emailed me back immediately: "This is *such* wonderful news. Yes, these ideologies can have a satanic grip on our minds to the extent that they can make us blind to see and apprehend biblical facts. Thanks be to God for His special work in your life." Biblical facts? Is the Bible factual? I hadn't really thought about it like that before. However, I could feel that I was being deprogrammed and that my mind was free in a way that it never had been before. Cleansed, I was more able to receive Christ's cosmic grace and be enlightened by His love.

Autumn arrived, coating the earth in a fiery blanket of fallen leaves, and I went to the forest less, doing the vigil in the warmth of the candlelit house. Some days my mother and I would drive to the beach in the early morning to walk and speak about God. Walking through a wooded area to get to the sea one morning, we listened to the birds starting to sing and stopped at a spiderweb, exquisite and fragile in its complexity, glistening in the dew. The sun was just rising and the morning was cool and damp. Across the summer we had spent many hours discussing and contemplating the Lord. We spoke about the process of Christ's formation within, about the Church and doctrine, about different cultural approaches to understanding the Spirit, and, most frequently, about gender within the Faith. It was testament to Christ's work in me that when discussing feminism and the sanctification of gender dynamics, there would be occasions when *I* would be the one defending aspects of the Church's relationship to, and treatment of, femininity.

Toward the beginning of October, I began to think about moving out. I didn't particularly want to leave, but as I didn't know when I would next be able to return to America because of Covid, I felt obligated to make longer term plans. I had a sense that I wasn't going to spend Christmas with my family. My parents prayed about it and felt that the next step had already been prepared and decided by God. Knowing that it was in His hands, we decided to relax and wait for the message to come. A few days later, Sister Veroniki rang to invite me to the monastery at the end of November in order that I could be with them over Christmas and beyond. I began to plan my final weeks at my parents' house and complete the book.

The Holy Spirit

Be holy, for I am holy.
—1 Peter 1.16b

Arriving at the monastery a few weeks later, the Holy Spirit began to stir something in me. For several months, following a passage I had read in one of St Sophrony's books, I had asked the Lord to "give" me the Holy Spirit, in order that I could be a vessel for His grace in the world. I had prayed in faith, yearning to experience the Holy Spirit in this way. Reading another of Mother Basilea's books, *Repentance: The Joy Filled Life*, I began to reflect on the hardness of my heart and how far away from Jesus I felt, and had felt, for some time.[88] The previous month had led me away from the Lord, and I couldn't sense Him in the way that I had before. I was numb. Please Lord, let me draw close to you. My sin was separating us. My pride, my willfulness, my superior attitude. My excuses for the frequency with which I gave into temptation. My bitterness. I thought about the person from whom I had cut contact. I needed to forgive. Truly. No more excuses and self-justification. Forgiveness will set *me* free, as well as the other person. I had to heed Christ's command. I had to love.

I lay on the floor of my cell in silence. I could feel the Holy Spirit tracing what felt like a golden thread through the flesh of my embittered

---

[88] Basilea Schlink, *Repentance: The Joy Filled Life* (Darmstadt: Kaanan Publications, 1992).

heart, slicing into it, so the idols embedded within could surface. I began to understand the nature of my own sin in a way that I never had before—how far I fell short of God's holiness. I reflected back across the months I had been in England and everything that had happened. I thought about how much time I had wasted indulging my passions (through different avenues) rather than allowing Christ to cleanse me as He wanted to. I had been so apathetic. I had wasted so much time! I had taken *so much* for granted. St Silouan talked about how one's inner state could be measured by one's disgust at one's own sin, as it is this sin that keeps us from Christ. I did not have this grace. A lot of the time I was luxuriating, even, in my own disobedience, glorying in the things that supposedly made me so unique. I messaged Father Theophan, sharing the revelation and confessing all these ugly idols. He sent me a message of joy, telling me that this kind of understanding only comes as a result of the Holy Spirit's doing a special work in the heart and concluding with the words:

> I thank God that *He* allowed me to be your servant for the sake of the kingdom—this gives a chance to observe *Him* doing *His* marvelous redemptive work in a soul that belongs to *Him*. To God be all the glory. Amen.

The Logos

When I passed by you again and looked upon you, indeed your time was the time of love; so I spread My wing over you and covered your nakedness. Yes, I swore an oath to you and entered into a covenant with you, and you became Mine.
—Ezekiel 16.8

Immersed in the thick silence of the monastery, I began to look back to the previous Nativity season in America—a different monastery,

PART THREE 239

but the same feast—and scanned over everything that had taken place across the twelve months in between. It was almost impossible to believe what had happened had happened. As I was preparing to fly to America to visit my sister and Father Theophan, I knew nothing. Christ reached down from heaven and scooped me up out of the underworld. I had no understanding of the situation I was in. The first time I met Father Theophan, I had gone out of open-hearted curiosity, respect for my parents, and a sense of adventure. But as he later told me, despite the fact that he was nearing the end of his life, he had felt strongly that Christ was asking him to take me on as a spiritual daughter. The grace began to pour. It was a process that had begun at birth but that had been hijacked. After the years immersed in the living hell of addiction, the Lord had drawn me into the light of recovery and rehabilitation. I began to enter the warmth and peace of His heart, the source of life. Venturing into nature began to slough away the toxicity and energetic debris of a hyper-intellectual, modern, urban life, completely unrooted from natural reality. After so many years in a dissociated, disembodied state, God tugged me back to the earth. The Holy Spirit began to heal me—though anonymously at that point—stabilizing the ground of my being and reorienting me toward the light.

The opposing forces were, however, strong. My need for release drove me to become impatient with this progress and, ravenous, I began to consume as many partial truths as I could get my hands on, sucking each false religion dry in the hope it would satisfy my hunger. This thirst for my Creator continued to propel me toward the light, but my blindness and the idols I nurtured meant my progress toward God was constantly interrupted by the plans of the evil one. The Lord worked with me during those years of spiritual rebellion, drawing me closer to Him, despite my sin. But for every blessing of healing Christ gave me, the enemy multiplied his attacks and I, blind, welcomed them, perceiving them to be gifts. Yearning for the peace and completion that Christ alone can offer, I opened myself up to further identity erosion and demonic doctrine, until, desperate to be free from suffering, I denied God, giving Buddha godless authority over my life.

Despite the vows I took, nothing changed. Jesus, the God of Love, remained the sovereign of my soul and several months later, He stood before me and revealed Himself to me, His open arms pulling me into the safety of His heart. My body shook as the power of His light (the source of all light) met the darkness within. Faithful to the end, He held me steady until all resistance had been loved out of me, and I was His again. I rejected, disrespected, and dishonored Him consistently for years, but He never wavered, waiting patiently for me to return to Him. In those years in witchcraft, He protected me, making sure that the people I came into contact with knew God in some way or had been born into families who had some knowledge of the true love of the Father. I abandoned Christ, but He never abandoned me.

. . . .

In blessing Adam and Eve with authority over all creation and commanding them to steward it (Gen 1.28–30), God initiated a cosmic principle that continues to this day. The spirits understand the Scriptures. As supernatural entities, they know that they can only penetrate the natural realm if allowed to do so by us. It is up to us to decide whether our pride will permit them entrance and give them authority in the world, or whether we instead choose to empty ourselves, becoming one with the cruciform Christ as He walks His blood-soaked path of self-sacrificial love, abasement, poverty, purity, and disgrace down into Hades' depths. Only by going down into hell with Him, are we able to rise up to heaven. To be resurrected, we must first be crucified. The world's salvation is predicated on our self-abnegation: we must die for the other to live. Worship flows from the sensitive hearts of the many millions, who are locked, as I was, in a prison of misdirected devotional praxis. The prayer of the Christian is that this worship be redirected to the One who alone can grant that which is being sought by those called to worship, perhaps above all else: to be again made *one*.

> I do not ask for these only, but also for those who will believe in me through their word [the disciples'], that they may all be one, just as you, Father, are in me, and I in you, that they also may be in us, so that the world may believe that you have sent me. The glory that you have given me I have given to them, that they may be one even as we are one, I in them and you in me, that they may become perfectly one, so that the world may know that you sent me and loved them even as you loved me. Father, I desire that they also, whom you have given me, may be with me where I am, to see my glory that you have given me because you loved me before the foundation of the world. O righteous Father, even though the world does not know you, I know you, and these know that you have sent me. I made known to them your name, and I will continue to make it known, that the love with which you have loved me may be in them, and I in them. (Jn 17.20–26 ESV)

We hope this book has been enjoyable and edifying for your spiritual journey toward our Lord and Savior Jesus Christ.

One hundred percent of the net proceeds of all SVS Press sales directly support the mission of St Vladimir's Orthodox Theological Seminary to train priests, lay leaders, and scholars to be active apologists of the Orthodox Christian Faith. However, the proceeds only partially cover the operational costs of St Vladimir's Seminary. To meet our annual budget, we rely on the generosity of donors who are passionate about providing theological education and spiritual formation to the next generation of ordained and lay servant leaders in the Orthodox Church.

Donations are tax-deductible and can be made at www.svots.edu/donate. We greatly appreciate your generosity.

To engage more with St Vladimir's Orthodox Theological Seminary, please visit:

www.svots.edu
online.svots.edu
www.svspress.com
www.instituteofsacredarts.com

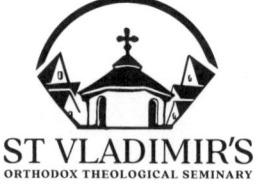